Candidates, Congress,
and the
American Democracy

Analytical Perspectives on Politics

Advisory editors:

John Aldrich, Duke University
Bruce Bueno de Mesquita, Hoover Institution and the University of Rochester
Robert Jackman, University of California, Davis
David Rohde, Michigan State University

Political science is developing rapidly and changing markedly. Keeping in touch with new ideas across the discipline is a challenge for political scientists and for their students.

To help meet this challenge, the series Analytical Perspectives on Politics presents creative and sophisticated syntheses of major areas of research in the field of political science. In each book, a high-caliber author provides a clear and discriminating description of the current state of the art and a strong-minded prescription and structure for future work in the field.

These distinctive books will provide a compact review for political scientists, a helpful introduction for graduate students, and central reading for advanced undergraduate courses.

Robert W. Jackman, *Power without Force: The Political Capacity of Nation-States*

Linda L. Fowler, *Candidates, Congress, and the American Democracy*

Candidates, Congress, and the American Democracy

Linda L. Fowler

Ann Arbor

THE UNIVERSITY OF MICHIGAN PRESS

Copyright © by the University of Michigan 1993
All rights reserved
Published in the United States of America by
The University of Michigan Press
Manufactured in the United States of America

1996   1995   1994   1993   4   3   2   1

A CIP catalogue record for this book is available from the British Library.

Library of Congress Cataloging-in-Publication Data

Fowler, Linda L., 1945–
    Candidates, Congress, and the American democracy / Linda L.
Fowler.
        p.   cm. — (Analytical perspectives on politics)
    Includes bibliographical references and index.
    ISBN 0-472-09473-4 (alk. paper). — ISBN 0-472-06473-8 (pbk. :
alk. paper)
    1. Political participation—United States.   2. Political culture—
United States.   3. Politics, Practical—United States.
    4. Electioneering—United States.   I. Title.   II. Series.
JK1764.F68   1993
323'.042'0973—dc20   93-31966
                                                                    CIP

Grateful acknowledgment to M. E. Sharpe for permission to reprint
figure 3.1 from David T. Canon's article "The Emergence of the
Republican Party in the South, 1964–1988," in *The Atmospheric
Congress*, ed. Allen D. Hertzke and Ronald M. Peters, Jr.,
Armonk, N.Y., 1992.

Preface

A decade ago, Donald Matthews (1983) began his exhaustive review of the legislative recruitment literature on a gloomy note. Scholars, he charged, had tended to assume that who lawmakers were and how they got to the legislature were important without subjecting that assumption to rigorous testing. They had developed a wealth of descriptive material about the backgrounds and career patterns of legislators but in his view had failed to show how recruitment "matters" (1983, 18). Matthews argued that the fault in the literature was a scholarly tendency to view recruitment as an independent input into the legislative system. Instead, he contended, it should be treated as an intervening process linking political elites and institutions. Matthews concluded his essay with the recommendation that future research focus on how the "selective recruitment and derecruitment of individuals [who 'fit'] the legislature reinforce the status quo" (1983, 43).

Having read and reread Matthews's article many times, I have never ceased to be troubled by it. I have been troubled because I agree with many of Matthews's conclusions and share his concern that so vast and rich a literature should be found wanting in such fundamental ways. But I have also been troubled because I believe the failings of the literature go well beyond the problems Matthews diagnosed.

The primary weakness of the field, in my view, has been its narrow focus on the connection between recruitment and legislative procedures and outputs. Recruitment "matters" because it is integral to a range of fundamental behaviors and beliefs in the American democracy. Yet the emphasis on linkages between member characteristics and institutional decisions has crowded out the investigation of candidacy as an influence in other political domains. Consequently, much of the best work on candidate recruitment has been achieved not as part of a deliberate research strategy but as a by-product of other types of studies in American politics.

Research on recruitment has also suffered, in my opinion, from a somewhat arbitrary distinction between individual actions and predetermined structures. Scholars have either studied individual calculations or prevailing norms and rules but have seldom integrated the two. Moreover, in recent years, they have been preoccupied almost exclusively with the former. Perhaps that is what Matthews meant to change when he urged scholars to examine recruitment as an intervening process. But I do not think conceptualizing recruitment as "intervention" really solves the problem, because this approach implies some process that influences both politicians and contexts but is somehow separate from them. Far more appropriate, I think, is an attempt to see recruitment as a mutually reinforcing interaction of private motivations and public contexts. After all, candidates are goal-maximizing individuals as well as products of a particular time and place; they pursue their personal ambitions in a socially and institutionally determined setting.

However, one consequence of thinking about recruitment in this simultaneous fashion is to forgo the neat boxes and simple causal models that are characteristic of the literature. As I will argue throughout this book, candidates hold an ambiguous position in American politics: in some relationships they appear to influence outcomes directly, while in other situations their behavior appears to depend on particular actors or events. At still other times, candidates appear to function as both cause and effect—as endogenous and exogenous variables in the political equation.

Although the literature is full of examples of such ambivalence, they are often overlooked—or at least ignored—because of a persistent scholarly preoccupation with careerism among incumbent officeholders. Because such politicians are already in office, researchers have less need for a theory of candidacy that addresses both the individual and the systemic aspects of candidate emergence. Instead, they can focus on lawmakers' progressive ambition and their strategies to move up the ladder from one office to another. Several consequences inevitably follow from this concentration on incumbents. The first is a failure to define the boundaries of recruitment from the onset of ambition to the culmination of a political career. The second is an inability to identify the pool of prospective candidates and to differentiate the ones who eventually run for office from among the ranks of eligibles. The third is the failure to adequately map the interaction of political actors, contexts, and events in winnowing out the few declared candidates from the numerous might-have-beens. As a result, the true influence of candidacy in framing the public's choice from among competing elites is typically beyond the scope of scholarly inquiry.

An impressive array of new research on congressional politics has raised several interesting puzzles that throw many of these issues into relief. An outpouring of books and articles on the decline of congressional elections as national referenda has sparked considerable speculation about the relative importance of incumbents and challengers in explaining recent trends of diminished competition, increased localism, and divided government. Similarly, an emerging literature on representation for women and minorities has raised questions about the adaptability of Congress to social and political change. Finally, a developing debate about the nature of decision making inside the House and Senate has opened discussion about the extent to which new members are responsible for institutional reform. Thus, it is timely to undertake a comprehensive examination of how candidate recruitment figures in each of these fields of inquiry.

This task is complicated (and perhaps made necessary) by the diversity of approaches to recruitment. Congressional candidates and their behavior figure in many different subfields of American politics—parties and interest groups, legislative and executive institutions, mass participation and voting behavior, women's and various ethnic studies, and state and local government. They have been examined not just as political actors but from such varied disciplinary perspectives as sociology, psychology, and economics. They have been used both to illuminate sweeping historical trends and to anchor microtheories of rational decision making. Such eclecticism has led to a literature that contains work of considerable individual merit but does not add up to a coherent body of knowledge.

My intent here is not a summary or overview of what has been written but an interpretation of where candidates fit into the general debate about elections, representation, and institutional change. Where appropriate, I have focused on the continuities between past and present research and have endeavored to illuminate the assumptions and conceptual biases that shape contemporary scholars' understanding of legislative recruitment in the United States. Most important, I have tried to identify fruitful areas for further work.

As my thinking about candidate recruitment has evolved, I have been fortunate to have the support and counsel of several colleagues. Richard Fenno has continued to be a valued mentor and source of encouragement as I have grappled with the issues surrounding candidates and their decisions to run for office. Sandy Maisel has been both collaborator and critic in helping me sort out the complexities of candidate decision making. He, along with Ruth Jones and Walt Stone, will recognize some of the ideas put forward here as arising from our joint efforts to develop a study of state legislators and their entry into the House of Representatives. I owe all these scholars a considerable intellectual debt. The same must be said about the participants at the conference on elective politicians at the Kennedy School in 1989. The papers presented at that meeting by Susan Carroll, Fernando Guerra, John Hibbing, Timothy Prinz, Edward Lascher, and Peverill Squire have provided useful references and provocative leads.

My greatest thanks go to Colin Day, Director of the University of Michigan Press, who provided the impetus for this project and the continuous encouragement necessary for its completion. Most important, he put my first draft in the hands of two superb reviewers, whose insight and criticism proved invaluable. Although I cannot acknowledge them by name, I hope they will understand how much I appreciated their thoughtful attention and will overlook whatever sins I failed to correct. I also appreciated help from Drew Smith in checking citations.

Finally, I have to take responsibility for the fact that my husband and son, having lived through a second book on candidates, will never run for public office.

Contents

CHAPTER 1

Introduction

> . . . the door of this part of the federal government is open to merit
> of every description.
>
> —James Madison, *Federalist #52*

The Candidate's Tale

In November 1986, voters in Mississippi's Second Congressional District narrowly elected Democrat Mike Espy as their U.S. Representative. The first black member of Congress from the state since Reconstruction and one of only six successful challengers in the general election, Espy reversed a century of white supremacy in the Mississippi Delta and bucked the tide of incumbency in the nation. He followed up his remarkable victory two years later with a smashing win over his Republican opponent in which he polled 65 percent of the vote and gained the support of over one-third of the white electorate. In 1990 he was reelected with 85 percent of the vote.[1]

There was nothing inevitable about the rise of this young lawyer from Yazoo and the political transformation he epitomized. The Second Congressional District was not automatically a black or Democratic constituency, although it had been redrawn twice under court order to enhance African-American representation in the Mississippi delegation. But under the first districting plan in 1982, a black state legislator, Robert Clark, lost a close election in what was then an open seat, while under the second plan in 1984, with the presence of African-American residents increased to 58 percent, he was narrowly defeated once more. Some observers thought that Clark could have won his first race if the 1984 district boundaries had been in effect earlier (Barone and Ujifusa 1987, 655). He was seriously underfinanced in both campaigns, however, and he had to contend with the inherent marginality of the district, which caused it to divide evenly

---

1. For more detailed accounts of Mike Espy's political career, see Swain 1993, chapter 4.

along party lines in presidential elections. Espy believed that the district was problematic for a black politician because of the relatively low turnout rates of the African-American constituents who lived within its boundaries and because he thought the census data had overestimated the number of black residents (Swain 1993, 77).[2] Despite the intent of the court to enhance African-American representation from Mississippi in Congress, then, the racial and party cleavages within the district appeared so intractable to political observers that no legislator, black or white, Democrat or Republican, seemed likely to secure it for very long (Barone and Ujifusa 1985, 742).

Espy's candidacy transformed the district's tendency toward racial competition and political marginality in a remarkably short time. Although he capitalized on the black majority established by court order, Espy's personal appeal and tactical skill were the decisive factors in converting the district into a safe Democratic seat.[3] He nationalized the campaign by attracting hundreds of thousands of dollars in political action committee (PAC) contributions, which enabled him to spend slightly more than his incumbent opponent in 1986 and to outspend his challenger in 1988 by four to one. Espy also drew on his contacts within the Democratic Party and his oratorical skill within the black community to mobilize a vigorous grass roots operation. As the *Almanac of American Politics* noted, "Espy ran a superior campaign, with a targeted voter registration and turnout drive more sophisticated than any Mississippi had seen" (Barone and Ujifusa 1989, 667). At the same time, Espy tapped the populist streak that still persists in the rural South by linking his incumbent opponent to the highly unpopular agricultural policies of the Reagan Administration.

Once elected, Espy reached beyond his African-American constituents, forging a political alliance with fellow Mississippian Jamie Whitten, the conservative chairman of the House Appropriations Committee, to bring additional federal aid to the Delta region. He developed ties to such organizations as the National Rifle Association, for which he appeared in advertisements, and he also cultivated local soybean and catfish farmers by helping them develop new markets. His voting record, according to Swain (1993, 86), has been considerably less liberal than other black members of Congress, although it is less conservative than most other southern Democrats. With this judicious

---

2. This perception was shared by African-American state lawmakers, who subsequently pushed hard during the 1992 reapportionment to increase the percentage of African-American citizens to 65 percent to ensure that it would not revert to the control of a white politician.

3. Indeed, Parker (1991) treats him as an anomaly.

blend of constituency service and policy positions, Espy claimed the Second Congressional District as his own. In doing so, he finalized the end of the segregationist era and thwarted the Republicans' efforts to enlarge their base in this deepest part of the deep South. Mike Espy's feat is an exceptional personal achievement and a remarkable historical event, but it also is a striking illustration of how candidates figure in the broad sweep of American politics. At one level, Espy's success is a clear example of the centrality of individual candidates—their personal attributes and political skills—in deciding the outcomes of particular congressional races. At another level, his candidacy reveals the constant tension in House and Senate elections between the power of incumbency and the pull of local and national conditions. At still another level, Espy's emergence as a major player in Mississippi politics served both as a catalyst for change inside the Second District and as a reflection of new political realities in the South. And finally, Espy's presence in the House contributed to the ongoing process of redefining the party coalitions and their role in the governance of the nation.

Let us first consider how individual candidates shape congressional election outcomes. Espy's decision to run for Congress in 1986 demonstrates how politicians' perceptions of political opportunity can foster competition, even against a two-term incumbent. Despite the failures of the previous African-American nominee to gain office and the presence of a well-connected white opponent in the 1986 primary who had won the backing of other black leaders in the district, Espy saw a chance to go to Congress and he seized it. He showed formidable coalition-building skills as well, by mobilizing black voters to an unprecedented extent and by attracting financial support from outside the district. And once in office, he was able to reach out to opposing groups in a classic example of the power of incumbents to disarm prospective opposition. In short, Espy's personal qualities as a politician enabled him to reconfigure the majority inside the Second District.

However, Espy's successful pursuit of a House seat challenges conventional wisdom about congressional candidates on several grounds. For one thing, Espy was not a "quality" candidate according to the most widely accepted definition, because he had not previously held elective office.[4] (His position as assistant attorney general was appointive.) For another, he raised a great deal of money from PACs and outspent his incumbent opponent, despite his status as a chal-

---

4. Jacobson and Kernell (1981) first adopted this definition of a quality candidate, and it has enjoyed wide currency ever since.

lenger.[5] Furthermore, he benefited from a surge in voter turnout and a vigorous party effort in an off-year election. All this atypical behavior then culminated in that rare political event in the 1980s—the defeat of a two-term incumbent.

Presumably, none of these things should have happened, and it is therefore tempting to dismiss Espy's election as an exceptional case, the sort of outlier, to use statistical jargon, that makes the study of politics so fascinating. But recent analyses of House races by some of the most respected observers of the congressional scene suggest that House elections are generally more unpredictable than in the past. The previous electoral margin in a House race, for example, has historically been an excellent indicator of subsequent elections but is far less significant today than it used to be (Jacobson 1989 and 1990b; Ansolabehere, Brady, and Fiorina 1988). This pattern arises because the variance in vote swings from one election to the other has increased: not only are seemingly safe and entrenched incumbents more likely to lose their seats than in the past, but once vulnerable freshmen are more likely to hang onto seats they obtained in close elections.

Similarly, the frequency of divided elections in which House or Senate candidates of the same party fare differently from each other and from their party's presidential nominee has increased dramatically (Jacobson 1990b; Fiorina 1991). Senate races, in particular, vary widely within the same state over time and across states in the same election year (Westlye 1992). Frequently, a landslide victory for a senator of one party is often followed by an equally lopsided win for a senator of the opposite party in the next election cycle (Westlye 1992, 29).

There are competing explanations for such trends in congressional election outcomes. Some scholars tout the emergence of tough competitors as the critical variable in a race, and as we shall see in chapter 4, persuasive evidence links the growing irregularity in House and Senate races to the supply of viable candidates. According to this line of reasoning, when competition fails, it is because the structures for motivating and identifying ambitious politicians are deficient. Yet other scholars regard incumbent behavior, rather than challenger quality, as the decisive factor in electoral competitiveness. In their view, savvy, hardworking incumbents avoid tough races as long as they do

---

5. In recent years, the percent of PAC money contributed to challengers has precipitously declined to less than 5 percent (Ornstein, Mann, and Malbin 1992, 101). Indeed, challenger spending has remained virtually flat during the past decade, when spending by incumbents and candidates in open seats has increased dramatically (Abramowitz 1991).

their jobs; it is only when they get careless about their voting records or lazy about going home that they need worry about the opposition. The problem is that neither approach is completely satisfactory in accounting for variability in congressional election outcomes. In some districts, incumbents win despite the presence of highly motivated and ambitious congressional wannabes; and they occasionally lose despite all outward signs of security. In other districts, incumbents maintain their seats despite scandal, criminal conviction, or manifestations of senility; and they occasionally lose for seemingly minor infractions of decorum. In short, sometimes challenger quality exerts an independent effect on election outcomes, and sometimes it appears to be determined by the incumbent's own actions. For scholars, this interactive situation requires the answers to two very different questions: first, why do candidates with a particular blend of winning attributes emerge at some times and places while they are absent from others; and second, what conditions are necessary and sufficient to bring the tough competitors—the Mike Espys of the world—into the electoral arena?

Espy's emergence as a successful candidate also dramatizes a fascinating and increasingly complex debate among congressional observers about the relative influence of local contexts and national events in shaping the partisan distribution of the House of Representatives. On one hand, the "strategic politicians" hypothesis put forward by Jacobson and Kernell (1981) credits calculation by candidates and political elites with producing the partisan swings in House election results that correspond to variations in the economy and the president's popularity. On the other hand, the sustained Democratic control of the House in the face of a resurgent Republican party signals the increasing segmentation of the electoral process and the triumph of personalized and localized politics over national concerns (Jacobson 1990b, chap. 7; Ehrenhalt 1991; Fiorina 1991). At issue, then, is the capacity of House elections to fulfill their function as referenda on the performance of the national government and the persistence of divided control of the legislative and executive branches. The series of elections in Mississippi's Second Congressional District reflect both phenomena.

In 1984, there were clear signs that national tides prevented state legislator Clark from mobilizing resources in a Republican year to capitalize on the Second District's newly redrawn boundaries. In 1986, there was equally strong evidence that national Democrats and their affiliated PACs mobilized behind Espy to provide the resources he needed to unseat an incumbent. Then in 1988, Espy engineered a "sophomore surge" in his election margin in a district that narrowly supported Republican presidential nominee George Bush. Was the seemingly strategic behavior in the first two election cycles a reflection of the relative advantage of the two parties in those election years? Or did political elites simply respond to perceived differences in the strength of two very different nominees? Was the subsequent size of Espy's reelection margin the result of incumbency and Espy's personal appeal as a politician, or did it reflect the failure of the GOP to recruit and fund a strong challenger? At present, plausible arguments and convincing evidence can be mustered in support of each of these interpretations.

In a similar vein, Espy profited from the strategic calculations of potential rivals. State legislator Clark and several other black politicians endorsed the white candidate in the primary because they thought an African-American could not win with fewer than 65 percent black voters in the district (Swain 1993, 81). Their decisions to step aside enabled Espy to run head-to-head against his politically well-connected opponent in the Democratic primary without worrying about splitting the African-American vote. Moreover, after Espy captured the nomination with a seventy-nine-vote margin of victory, key party leaders threw their support to him (Swain 1993), and Democrats from outside the district, including then House Speaker Jim Wright, gave him access to ample PAC contributions. Even President Reagan cooperated by proposing agricultural legislation that aroused the ire of local farmers.

Over the long run, successful candidates such as Espy become part of the broad sweep of American party tides. For many years, political analysts predicted a partisan realignment within the electorate that would create a new and lasting Republican majority. Much of its force was to be generated in the South, where racial and ideological cleavages had given every Republican presidential candidate but Ford commanding majorities. Now, two decades after the supposed critical election heralding the new era took place, many scholars have become convinced that either the conditions no longer exist within the electorate to create a realignment toward any party (Beck 1984 and 1989; Ladd 1991) or the theory of realignment postulated a regularity in American party systems that never existed in fact (Silbey 1991; Shafer 1991).

However, critical to this debate is the role of political elites in redefining cleavages and framing issues in ways that are meaningful to voters. Realignments need political entrepreneurs to help them along, but in many parts of the country, particularly the South, the Republicans have been unable to recruit competitive candidates to run with their popular presidential nominees. Mike Espy's relatively weak opponent in 1988, when he was a marginally elected freshman serving a previously Republican district, and his even weaker opposition in 1990 are therefore symptomatic of a major obstacle to realignment. To borrow Jacobson's (1990b) and Maisel's (1991) Berra-esque phrase, "You can't beat somebody with nobody."

At the same time, Espy's candidacy has to be viewed as something more than an unprecedented individual effort or the fortuitous joining of personal ambition with favorable national tides, for his election to the House was inseparable from the social and political transformation that swept the South during the past two decades. Espy was eligible to think about running for Congress because of enormous changes in the status of African-Americans set in motion by the civil rights movement. He was therefore able to gain the traits common to successful candidates, but not commonly found among Mississippi's black citizens during the segregationist era: prosperous family background, college degree, legal profession. Furthermore, as an assistant attorney general, he acquired the kind of officeholding experience that had previously been reserved for whites and that represented a departure from the church-based leadership of an older generation of African-American politicians.

Having attained these marks of credibility, Espy was further aided by developments in the district brought about by the enactment of the Voting Rights Act and subsequent efforts of civil rights activists to mobilize African-American citizens. By the late 1980s, for example, turnout rates for blacks had increased substantially in Mississippi, although they were still ten points below the participation rates for whites. (U.S. Bureau of the Census 1989, 36). Moreover, Espy's coalition-building task was made easier by the actions of the court and the two narrow losses of the previous African-American candidate. Espy had the political savvy to mold these conditions to his own ends, but he did not create them and he could not have succeeded in their absence. In short, Mike Espy provides a vivid example of how a congressional candidacy is affected by the existing social order, the institutional context, and the political climate operating in a particular place and time.

The tale of Mike Espy's political rise holds another lesson, for he is part of a trend toward greater homogeneity within the Democratic Party which has had significant consequences for the internal organization of the House. After two decades of chronic disunity, the Democratic coalition showed a remarkable upturn in party discipline in the mid-1980s. The hegemony of the old Conservative Coalition was broken, and both parties presented a more overtly partisan face to the public—both in terms of roll call voting and of greater visibility for the leadership. Many factors have contributed to the increasingly partisan character of the House, such as chronic budget deficits, conflicts with the executive, and escalating interest group pressures, but Congress would not necessarily have dealt with these challenges through its party system if changes in the membership—notably the liberalization of Southern Democrats—had not cleared the way for more cohesive decision making inside the party caucuses (Rohde 1991). Thus, the election of moderates like Mike Espy from formerly conservative strongholds in places like Mississippi has had profound implications for how Congress goes about its business as a governing institution.

In more general terms, however, Espy's successful bid for a House seat raises questions about how scholars think about candidacy. Quite simply, one could not have predicted his emergence as a candidate using the existing theory of political ambition, and one could not have explained his success in terms of the conventional wisdom about the progression of political careers. The widely accepted approach to congressional office seeking is ambition theory, which is based on Joseph Schlesinger's classic work (1966) and subsequently formalized and refined by Gordon Black (1972), David Rohde (1979), and others.[6] These scholars have assumed that all politicians are ambitious for higher office if they could obtain such positions without cost. The individual taste for public office, then, is a given that responds to available opportunities and the expected value of winning or losing. Politicians, being rational decision makers, do not hanker after offices they cannot hope to attain, and they minimize their uncertainty and maximize their chances of success by following clear-cut and predictable patterns of advancement. Thus, a corollary assumption in ambition theory is the existence of a stable, hierarchical structure of officeholding opportunities so that politicians can calculate the costs and benefits of attaining their desired positions.

These two assumptions give ambition theory a static quality that is its major weakness in explaining candidacies such as Espy's. By assuming the prior existence of the desire for office, it fails to consider how individuals acquire ambition and how they establish their eligibility as prospective office seekers. In the case of a black man in

---

6. See also Brace (1984); Abramson, Aldrich, and Rohde (1987); and Banks and Kiewiet (1989).

Mississippi, even in the 1980s, the onset and development of political ambition is not something to be taken for granted. But the larger problem has to do with anticipating changes in the size and composition of the candidate pool. For example, in recent years, many districts appear to have lost the capacity to generate candidates in one of the majority parties, a phenomenon that has produced a remarkable increase in the number of uncontested House seats. Conversely, many different groups that previously had not produced serious contestants for congressional races—women, African-Americans, Hispanics, Asian-Americans, Southern Republicans—have recently become much more visible and more successful in House and Senate campaigns.

In this respect, the theory's presumption of predictable opportunity structures limits its ability to account for socioeconomic and structural change. Although Schlesinger (1966, 104) found well-articulated ladders in only eleven states, neither he nor those who have followed him ever defined the conditions that render career paths less predictable or transform them altogether. In the case of Mississippi, for example, federal intervention, through legislation and subsequent court decisions, radically altered the conditions for elibility among potential candidates. But it also restructured the boundaries of legislative constituencies, eliminating at-large representation and creating African-American majority districts that transformed the state's ladders of political advancement. At the same time, partisan realignment among white voters enabled ambitious politicians to seek office through both political parties, thus shifting electoral competition from the Democratic primary to the general election. These developments not only created a favorable environment for Mike Espy but established circumstances that made party competition, not simply race, a major factor in the election. The cumulative effect of so many radical changes on the eventual emergence of a new legislator in Mississippi's Second Congressional District could be explained neither through conventional cost-benefit calculations nor through reference to established opportunity structures.

Few candidacies have the drama of Espy's, but they all serve the similar purpose of promoting electoral competition and policy change in the U.S. Congress. Candidates define the alternatives posed in an election; they mobilize the resources of a campaign; and in doing so, they contribute to changes in the demographic and partisan makeup of the Congress. The successful ones help determine the government's legislative agenda and eventually decide what actions it will take. Ultimately, individual candidacies add up to a particular distribution of partisans inside Congress and therefore affect the institution's over-all patterns of decision making. Viewed in this light, the newly elected class of 1992, with its record-breaking 110 new members, its increased presence of women and ethnic minorities, and its reformist agenda, is simply a dramatic example of the transforming power of candidacy in American politics.

But candidates do not arise in a political vacuum, and their highly personal decisions to enter the electoral arena are extremely sensitive to the external stimuli generated by political actors, events, and contexts. As these conditions change, the individuals who think about running change, too, and so does their readiness to provide the voters with the right to choose. Eventually, private motivations and calculations intersect with the larger political environment, which facilitates certain types of ambitions and hinders others. Bearing the stamp of these constraints, often quite unconsciously, candidates become emblematic, in effect, of the social and institutional arrangements dominant in the political system. Viewed in this way, candidates sometimes appear to be the driving force behind the performance of Congress as a representative and lawmaking institution, and they oftentimes seem more reflective of the complex network of electoral and structural forces that define each era of American politics. Because of this duality, their status in the congressional literature is often problematic.

The candidate's tale in Mississippi, then, exemplifies the highly individualized electoral politics so characteristic of the American democracy. It not only highlights the theoretical and empirical issues surrounding the emergence of candidates but also underscores the many ambiguities regarding the role of political entrepreneurs in shaping the nation's legislature. It is a compelling illustration of why candidate recruitment has moved to the forefront of the research agenda on Congress and why a critical assessment of what scholars have uncovered and where they are headed is so timely.

The Ambiguous Status of Congressional Candidates

Given the myriad ways that congressional candidates could influence American politics, it would be natural to assume that scholars would be actively pressing a scholarly agenda to consider where they come from and how they get to Congress. Until recently, however, this was not the case. Instead, what Donald Matthews uncovered in his exhaustive review of the literature on legislative recruitment published in

1983 was a subfield of the discipline marked by blind alleys, unexamined premises, and missed opportunities. Scholars had developed a wealth of descriptive material about the backgrounds and career patterns of elected representatives, he argued, but they had not shown how legislators' motives, attributes, and means of attaining office were linked to legislative outcomes. In sum, Matthews asserted, the biggest shortcoming of the literature was its failure to show "how recruitment matters" (1983, 18). Like the obligatory chapters in comparative politics texts on "The Land and the People," he concluded, it was not to be "taken very seriously by the authors or readers" (1983, 17).

A decade later, recruitment indisputably matters—not just to legislative politics but to a range of concerns within the field of American politics. Candidate recruitment has been implicated, of course, in the noticeable decline in electoral competition, in the substantial increase in the advantage of incumbency, and in the marked insulation of House races from national tides, all of which combined to produce a prolonged condition of divided party control of the federal government. More broadly, candidate emergence has figured in the legislature's capacity to adapt to such sweeping changes as the mobilization of women, the enfranchisement of ethnic minorities, and the partisan transformation of the South. More broadly still, it appears to have some bearing on the patterns of institutional change that have made parties and party leaders more dominant in congressional decision making. Ultimately, the behavior of congressional candidates offers a possible key to the longstanding debate over partisan realignment in the United States.

The convergence of congressional candidacy with so many different trends should not be surprising. The nation's culture of individualism and its weak party system have always placed a heavy burden on entrepreneurs for organizing political competition in the United States; and with the weakening of partisan ties among contemporary voters, the personal qualities and skills of candidates have become increasingly powerful determinants of election outcomes. This phenomenon is generally accepted, though not necessarily applauded, by academics and practitioners alike. What many political observers have failed to grasp, however, is how pervasively candidate-centered politics has affected areas that are at some remove from the hurly-burly of congressional campaigns. Thus, the work of many scholars with quite different specialties leads to a similar inference: that many features of the contemporary political scene bear the stamp of congressional candidacy.

The cumulation of evidence pointing in this direction is not the result of any conscious research strategy. Nor does it derive from a consensus in the discipline about the importance of congressional candidates as subjects for investigation. Indeed, it is doubtful that many of the scholars whose work reinforces the importance of congressional recruitment in American politics would see themselves as working in the field or would define themselves as students of either candidacy or Congress. Some would probably be appalled that their research bears any connection to an old-fashioned term like recruitment or that they have inadvertently ventured into what has to be one of the more conceptually disordered domains in political science. The primary purpose of this book, then, is to show how recruitment matters to a variety of debates in the discipline and to demonstrate how many different scholarly paths lead to the same fundamental question about who ends up on the congressional ballot.

Although congressional candidates may crop up in many interesting and debatable puzzles in American politics, their role is not very clear. Scholars often place them at the scene of the crime, so to speak, but cannot necessarily identify them with a smoking gun. Sometimes candidates appear in the literature as causal actors, and sometimes they surface as mere indicators of broad social and political trends. In social science jargon, candidates are both dependent and independent variables in the political system.

This ambiguity about where candidates fit is, in my view, the primary reason our discipline has often regarded the subject of congressional recruitment with more than a little frustration. And it follows, I think, that we will not progress very far in resolving the issues pertaining to electoral competition, representation, and partisan and institutional change noted above until we can clarify our thinking about which way the causal arrows fly. A major objective of this book, therefore, is to identify the areas in American politics where candidates appear to be central—to be explicit about relationships among actors, institutions, and events that are seldom examined critically.

However, defining the place of congressional candidacy in the American polity is only half the game. Equally important is attempting to explain why some candidates emerge and are successful, while others remain on the sidelines. Since the publication of Matthews's (1983) critique, a number of studies have been published that begin to address the questions who runs and why. Thus, the second order of business for this book is to inventory what is currently known about the emergence of congressional candidates, to highlight the inconsistencies and unresolved issues that lurk in this burgeoning literature, and to identify promising areas for further research.

This is a more complex enterprise than simply reporting what is new or gaining acceptance for a particular research agenda. The field of legislative recruitment has periodically been canvassed by several generations of scholars, and it has been found wanting just as regularly. Therefore, any attempt to chart where the literature is now and where it ought to go has to contend with its perceived weaknesses.

Those who have read Matthews's (1983) encyclopedic essay on legislative recruitment or Prinz's more recent (1989) review of elective careers must be impressed by the breadth of inquiry on the subject of candidates and their pursuit of legislative office. Yet paradoxically, this same body of work has prompted many respected political analysts to describe congressional recruitment as a neglected subfield of the discipline.

Matthews first set the critical tone in the 1950s when he urged the investigation of career patterns leading to Congress to determine whether they differed by region and by party. "Questions such as these," he commented, "have yet to be explored systematically" (Matthews 1954, 59). This view was subsequently reiterated more emphatically by Wahlke and Eulau, who observed,

> In general it seems fair to say that legislative studies to date reveal statistically significant differences among legislatures with respect to the kinds of social background and experience of persons recruited to them. But they offer little firm knowledge about the relationship of those differences to either the functions and output of legislative systems or to the behavior of members as legislators. (1959, 240)

Somewhat later, Czudnowski (1975) expanded on a similar theme in describing the field as undeveloped in an article for the *Handbook of Political Science*. Noting that recruitment is seldom a research topic in its own right, he contended that hypotheses and inferences about recruitment often are "subsidiary lines of analysis in elite studies," and he contended that although "these different modes of inquiry are evidence of a growing interest [in] the multiple ramifications of recruitment; they are also indicators of an incipient stage in the development of this field of inquiry, of the search for a paradigm, of competing models, and of methodological agnosticism" (Czudnowski 1975, 160). Furthermore, Czudnowski (1975, 229) concluded that the whole research enterprise surrounding elite recruitment suffered from the absence of a theory that could adequately distinguish between those political activists who will run for office and those who will not. Several years later, he continued to depict recruitment as a subject still in its infancy, seeking to discover the "building blocks and road signs" necessary to construct a theory of recruitment (Czudnowski 1982, 4).

Scholars in the 1980s continued the same refrain. Writing in the context of American politics rather than elite theory, Douglas Arnold (1982, 97) identified candidate recruitment as one of the "undertilled fields" of the discipline. He was particularly critical of the disproportionate amount of research lavished on citizens' voting behavior when so little information was available on how the particular pairs of candidates from which voters could choose ended up on the ballot. Lipset, too, noted in his essay on the changing role of candidates in American elections (1983) that much of the evidence about the transformation of congressional candidates was largely anecdotal. "Clearly," he concluded, "we need much more information than we now have on the backgrounds and values of our legislators and their challengers, and on the ways in which they accommodated to running for office" (1983, 103). Maisel (1982) also ended his study of contestants in the 1978 House primaries on a by now familiar note: "The agenda for the years ahead is to examine nonrecruitment, to see why prominent individuals do not seek elective office, and then to determine how the system can be changed to attract those individuals as candidates" (1982, 136). Finally, in a survey of the literature on political careers, Prinz concluded that "with a few notable exceptions . . . , the field has not progressed very far since Matthews sounded the call [in 1954]" (1989, 2). Prinz asserted that the initial decision to run for office, in particular, "has been little studied" and argued for the development of the existing work on opportunity structures so that scholars can begin to "generalize in a systematic fashion about the ways in which [they] affect the political career" (1989, 54).

To a large extent, these criticisms stem from a general disinclination among political scientists, noted by Richard Fenno (1986, 4), to observe politicians directly and to pay attention to their goals and ambitions and to the contexts in which they act. But so many harsh judgments directed at a particular subfield raise a nagging question with serious implications for any inquiry into the subject: why does a vast and rich literature that contains a goodly number of the classic works of contemporary political science inspire perennial disparagement?

In my view, the trouble lies in the failure of scholars to think about candidacy as both a cause and an effect in political life. Candidacy is a mediating phenomenon in American politics—connected to the mass public and to governmental institutions but somewhat removed from each. As self-motivated entrepreneurs, candidates provide citizens with the choices and alternatives necessary to the functioning of a democratic system. At the same time, they reflect the existing social and political order.

Scholars, however, have tended to think about candidates from either one of these perspectives or the other but seldom to consider their intersection. The result is an inability to define when recruitment begins and ends or to control for the systemic factors that winnow out the actual candidates from the eligible might-have-beens. Thus, we find many different meanings attached to the term *recruitment*, including disagreements about whether it should more properly be called *emergence*, instead. We also find confusion about which variables are endogenous to the process of recruitment and which are exogenous. And we find widely divergent models for what constitutes a good explanation of office-seeking behavior.

Some scholars have worked within sociological or psychological paradigms in which candidacy is the product of environmental influences that are largely beyond the control and comprehension of the individual participants. Others start from process-oriented or rational choice perspectives in which the would-be candidate is a strategic actor operating within a flexible and fluid set of rules and coalitions. Such diverse approaches have led to studies of considerable individual merit, but they fail to add up to a coherent body of knowledge. More important, their fundamental incompatibility has impeded systematic analysis of the pool of eligible candidates and the interactive effects among political actors, contexts, and events that shape the decision to run for office. What is needed, then, is a way of thinking conceptually and empirically about recruitment that builds on both traditions. That is the third, albeit least fully formed, mission of this book.

An Overview

Individual candidates have always been central to electoral politics in the United States, but in recent years they have moved to center stage. As a result, who wins elections and ends up governing the nation increasingly depends on who decides to run.[7] Although many people could become candidates in any given year, few actually do. Some opt

---

7. A similar phenomenon in presidential elections has been recently canvassed in Wattenberg (1991b).

out for strategic reasons because they believe they cannot win; some reject a race because they reckon the costs are too high; and many potentially competitive candidates never seriously consider a House or Senate race at all because they have found more satisfying outlets for their political ambitions. Still others actively seek congressional nominations but are eliminated, through either the inadequacy of their own efforts or simple bad luck. The few who obtain a place on the ballot in November are sometimes political neophytes, although they have more often progressed through a long and sometimes arduous process of gaining political credentials, honing campaign skills, and building support among party and community activists. All these men and women—the eligible contestants, the would-be candidates, and the actual nominees—have been the subjects of political recruitment.

It is a process that the participants only partially perceive. Surrounding them are social and political institutions that structure how they see themselves and their world. Intervening in their pursuit of personal objectives are other actors with their own goals and perceptions about who should become congressional candidates. To understand recruitment, then, is to examine the capacity of individuals to act out their personal ambitions under conditions that they cannot control and about which they have imperfect information. The decision to run for Congress is therefore unavoidably complex, not only for prospective contestants and their potential supporters but also for political scientists.

Making sense of this diffuse and sometimes inaccessible process is vital to the study of Congress as an institution and more generally to the development of the field of American politics. Candidate recruitment provides a critical link between the governed and the governors in contemporary democracies, and its effect is felt both at home and in Washington. The renewed interest within the discipline about who members are and how they got there is thus an affirmation of the enduring significance of elites in the nation's political life.

Yet the past experience of scholars working in the field invites caution about how much can be accomplished beyond mere description of the contemporary recruitment scene. By following the intellectual history of the literature and exploring its unexamined assumptions and biases, scholars can perhaps avoid the pitfalls that have hindered their predecessors. And by evaluating the present state of knowledge about candidate emergence, students of Congress can estimate the payoffs of their own research agendas. My intent in writing this book, then, is to remind scholars of the enduring importance of congressional recruitment in American politics, to demonstrate its relevance to several interesting puzzles that currently engage scholars, and to critically assess the current state of the literature with the aim of developing a different theoretical and empirical approach.

In the next chapter, I trace the origins and development of candidate-centered politics in the American political tradition, from the writings of Madison, Tocqueville, and Bryce to those of Schumpeter, Dahl and Schlesinger. I show how politicians' motivations in pursuing congressional careers have shaped the institutional structures of the Congress and affected the contemporary phenomenon of partisan dealignment and realignment. In chapter 3, I consider the various theoretical paradigms that have been used to explain the emergence of candidacy and suggest where they might be joined to provide a more general conceptualization of candidate emergence. In chapter 4, I examine the role of candidates in shaping electoral competition and argue that the resolution of the debates over incumbents, quality challengers, and their impact on divided government depend on fundamental issues surrounding recruitment. In chapter 5, I examine the many ways in which congressional recruitment has affected the capacity of Congress to adapt to social and economic changes among women, ethnic minorities, and Southern voters. In chapter 6, I take up the nascent debate over the nature of organizational change in Congress and whether or not it depends on membership turnover. Within this context, I also consider how candidate recruitment might be relevant to current efforts to reform Congress through term limits and rules changes. Finally, in chapter 7, I offer some observations on the implications of these arguments for the future study of candidates and elites in American politics.

CHAPTER 2

Candidacy and the American Political Tradition

Perhaps no form of government needs great leaders so much as
democracy does.

—James Bryce, *The American Democracy*

In mass democracies, candidates are indispensible links between citizens and their government. By organizing competition for power, they ensure that regimes operate with popular support. By articulating a platform, they provide outlets for dissent. By identifying unmet needs, they prod political institutions to innovate. It is hard to imagine a regime that is both legitimate and dynamic that does not have a healthy supply of candidates.

What is true for democracies in general is especially true for the United States. Candidates have always been central to electoral politics in America, and this aspect of our political life is an important feature distinguishing it from other democracies. Indeed, given the perennial weakness of American parties, it is difficult to imagine our electoral campaigns as anything other than the personalized rituals that such slogans as "I Like Ike" typically invoke. An individualistic approach to electioneering fits the American ethos, and it is now deeply ingrained in the political mores of the nation.

Not surprisingly, successful candidates carry this same individualism into our governmental institutions, including the U.S. Congress. The legislative branch bears the stamp of its various members so strongly that scholars regularly characterize it as the reflection of the personal goals and strategies of the men and women who serve in it.[1] Congressional history, in fact, reveals several distinct eras that correspond to a particular mix of career patterns among the members.

For all these reasons, therefore, political scientists have long

---

1. See for example, Mayhew's (1974a) classic essay on how electoral incentives shape the institutional design of Congress, Fenno's (1973) consideration of the committee system as a reflection of member goals, and Fiorina's (1977) linkage of bureaucratic growth with the desire among legislators to court the electorate with casework and pork barrel projects.

been drawn to the recruitment of candidates, a process broadly defined as covering their *socialization* into public life, their *certification* as eligible members of the governing elite, and their *nomination* and their eventual *selection* for elective office, to understand legislative politics (Prewitt 1970; Seligman 1971). Despite the significant amount of scrutiny leveled at candidates for Congress, however, their status in the American tradition remains perplexing.

Since the founding of the republic, Americans have mistrusted political ambition. Yet they built it into the constitutional system of checks and balances and later depended on it to compensate for weak parties. A similar duality marks the organizational development of Congress. In many respects, professionally minded legislators molded the institution to suit their desire for electoral security and personal power, but at the same time, their career ambitions were shaped and constrained by pressures from the external political environment. Democratic theorists, too, have added their own ambiguities to the role of candidates in American politics. On the one hand, they have viewed candidates as the competitive force behind democratic governance; on the other hand, they have regarded candidates as symbols of consensus or dissensus among political elites.

In this chapter, I explore the many meanings attached to candidacy in the American political tradition. I first consider the attitudes of the framers toward candidacy and how their inattention to structures of recruitment laid the groundwork for failures of congressional performance in the nineteenth century. I next examine the rise of careerism among legislators and Congress's institutional adaptation to member expectations. I then turn to the views of contemporary political theorists and their interpretations of candidacy generally as a force in the American political landscape. Lastly, I reflect on the relationship between congressional candidacy and other types of office seeking in the United States. In sum, a variety of contradictory ideas about political ambition and entrepreneurship are deeply imbedded in the intellectual history of American institutions. Congressional candidates, because they are positioned at the nexus of local and national politics, provide a particularly good vantage point to examine these conflicts.

Candidates and the Republican Tradition

One of the most spirited debates at the founding of the American republic was whether or not the new nation would be governed by a political class. The Federalists expected the reins of power to be held by the propertied elites and intended the new government to promote economic development by restoring fiscal responsibility in the nation's capital and promoting commerce at home and abroad. Such activities required the election of men with political experience and broad understanding of public affairs. By contrast, the Anti-Federalists advocated a government much more limited in scope and closely tied to the will of local citizens. Their vision rested on the notion of citizen legislators who returned to ordinary life after brief service to their country and who brought no special requirements to office other than a love of liberty and empathy for the people in their constituencies. Thus, from the very beginning there has been conflict about the characteristics of federal representatives that the framers never formally resolved in the constitution.

Instead, they set themselves the task of constraining the power of fallible elected officials by striving to create a "government of laws, not of men." Their constitutional system repudiated the classical quest for just rulers and was constructed to prevent the enactment of bad policies by creating multiple centers of power through federalism and the system of checks and balances. Indeed, one of the most famous passages of the *Federalist* papers asserts that each branch of government would have the "constitutional means and personal motives to resist encroachments of the others . . . so that ambition [would be made to] counteract ambition" (*The Federalist* No. 51, 337).

Although Madison and his colleagues were political realists with few illusions about human nature, they nevertheless believed that skillful and wise leadership was essential for the survival of the new republic. Madison clearly hoped that the government would rest in the hands of elected officials "who possess most wisdom to discern, and most virtue to pursue, the common good of the society" (*The Federalist* No. 57, 370). If he and Hamilton were a bit vague about how the wise and virtuous might be induced to enter public life, both men recognized the power of incentives to shape the flow of ambition toward the federal government. Hamilton, for example, argued at the constitutional convention that men of talent would shun a weak federal government if they had no opportunity to exercise power and influence. However, their desire to have men of affairs in Congress is most evident in *The Federalist* No. 53, in which they counter the arguments of the Anti-Federalists, who insisted on legislative terms of a year or less, mandatory rotation in office, and other schemes intended to democratize the membership of the Congress.

On the one hand, Madison and Hamilton agreed with critics of the Constitution that frequent election was necessary to keep lawmakers responsive to the public will. On the other hand, they argued the need for a cadre of legislators in Congress who would have long experience with legislative business acquired through prior service in state assemblies and through frequent reelection. These "members of long standing," they noted, "will be thoroughly *masters of the public business,* and perhaps not unwilling to avail themselves of those advantages" (*The Federalist* No. 53, 352, emphasis added).

The "masters of the public business" were important to the framers' theory of republican government because they would bring expertise to domestic and foreign affairs. Through ample experience in public service, they would acquire the understanding of other states and regions needed to balance the interests of a large and complex nation. Furthermore, Madison and Hamilton saw seasoned lawmakers in the legislature as a protection against faction and demogoguery, because such men would be less susceptible to the passions of the moment. They concluded: "the greater the proportion of new members, the more apt will they be to fall into the snares that may be laid for them" (*The Federalist* No. 53, 352).

Despite Madison and Hamilton's desire to have master lawmakers in control of Congress, they gave little attention to the problem of enlisting them to public service. Beyond a few assertions that members of Congress would likely be drawn from the state legislatures and provisions written into the constitution setting the minimum age for senators and representatives and requiring them to be residents of their states, Madison and his colleagues in Philadelphia seem to have given little thought to the recruitment of future leaders. Their dislike of political parties and their fear that too much ambition would lead to "a rottenness of conduct" (Jefferson, quoted in Auden 1962, 304) focused their attention on controlling the behavior of those holding office rather than creating incentives for them to stand for election.

The consequences of neglecting legislative recruitment quickly became apparent in the early Congresses, which were populated with lawmakers who came reluctantly to Washington and who organized themselves into "boarding house coalitions" along state and regional lines (Young 1966). These lawmakers were raucus and unruly participants in the legislative process who lacked a sense of common purpose and who "adopted the disparaging attitudes of outsiders toward the capital" (Young 1966, 50). Intensely factionalized around particular causes or leaders, they were often dominated by powerful personalities in the Cabinet, such as Hamilton, or, in Jefferson's day, the president himself. The volatile membership and fluid organization accurately reflected the mistrust most Americans felt toward the authority of the central government, but the consequent lack of an experienced and cohesive cadre of lawmakers often left Congress paralyzed, even to the extent of permitting the British to burn the capital during the War of 1812. As Young (1966, 108–9) noted, the anti-power motives that legislators brought to Capitol Hill fostered conflict, a strict constitutionalism, and an excessive sensitivity to constituency concerns that made it nearly impossible to govern.

What institutional growth and development did take place during this early period has been traced at least in part to the changing attitudes among incoming members, although popular antipathy to a political class continued. Swift (1989) demonstrated that changes in committees, parties, and rules in the Senate from 1789 to 1840 were partially attributable to a transformation in the "institutional vision" of the members—that is to say, how they saw the chamber's role in the federal government. Furthermore, she concluded that the rise of an aggressive and proactive leadership provided the impetus to take advantage of the transformed attitudes toward legislative authority. Nevertheless, it appears from Swift's analysis that the political environment in the country remained hostile to a stronger and more professional Congress, and amateurism remained the dominant norm for legislative service, even in the supposedly august Senate.

In subsequent eras, the absence of mechanisms to develop a legislative elite was a feature of the American system foreign observers often criticized. The noted French writer, Alexis de Tocqueville, for example, remarked on the dearth of talented men serving in the Congress when he traveled in the United States in the 1830s. Mediocre leadership, Tocqueville argued, was an inevitable consequence of the condition of equality in a democratic society in which "life is generally spent in eagerly coveting small objects" (1945, 2:258). According to Tocqueville (1945, 2:105), when human beings believe that their advancement comes only from their own efforts, they lose sight of the past and forget about the judgment of future generations. Moreover, they become reluctant to serve the general good because they fail to see how the destiny of the state is connected to their own well-being (Tocqueville 1945, 2:111). For these reasons, the most capable individuals in democratic societies would be unlikely to dedicate their energies to the public welfare.

Tocqueville concluded:

I believe that ambitious men in democracies are less engrossed than any others with the interests and judgments of posterity: the present moment alone absorbs them. They are apt to complete a number of undertakings with rapidity than to raise lasting monuments of their achievements, and they care much more for success, than for fame. (1945, 2:261)

Lord Bryce voiced similar concerns in his lengthy treatise on American government published near the end of the nineteenth century. Bryce observed that politics had fallen "into the hands of mean men . . . [who] used government for private gain or menacing the power of wealth" ([1916] 1961, 120). American concerns with preventing the abuse of power, he argued, had blinded them to the dangers of petty corruption and incompetence, which were as destructive to democracy as monarchic or aristocratic monopolies of authority. He concluded, "Of the deficiencies summarized in this chapter, those which might seem to go deepest have least to do with constitutional arrangements . . . [and result from] the prominence of inferior men in politics and the absence of distinguished figures" ([1916] 1961, 119).

Bryce made these observations in the aftermath of the Gilded Age, a period notorious for scandal and legislative excess in American history and equally remarkable for the new demands on the Congress spawned by the end of Reconstruction and the rise of corporate capitalism. Although historian Margaret Thompson (1985) has demonstrated that commentators of the day exaggerated the influence of special interests on Congress, she made a convincing case that lawmakers of the period, lacking either the incentive, the expertise or the institutional support to formulate a coherent legislative response, were often overwhelmed by petitioners of all sorts (1985, chap. 1). Lobbying, she argued, was a predictable strategy for citizens to use because the amatuerish legislature was incapable of acting on its own. And interest groups, with their scandalous activities, thus became the scapegoats for the failures of members of Congress to get their institutional house in order.

In sum, for much of its history, the American polity has struggled with its ambivalent attitudes toward the recruitment of federal lawmakers. The desire for statesmen in office, was offset by a strong suspicion that even the wise and virtuous could not be trusted, and this mismatch of expectations ironically made Congress particularly susceptible to the personal ambitions and agendas of its members. The institution has struggled ever since to find an appropriate balance between its needs for "masters of the public business" and popular antipathy to the emergence of a political class.

Recruitment, Careerism, and Institutional Change

The contemporary Congress, as we know it, has evolved into a highly stable legislature with well-defined norms and rules, predictable patterns of advancement and, until 1992, low turnover. Among its most distinctive features today are its highly decentralized committee system, episodically weak party leadership, and extraordinary openness to constituency pressure. But Congress was not always like this, and its evolution into a *professional, institutionalized* body was neither preordained by the constitution nor driven by the imperatives of a modern, industrial society. From what one can observe of legislatures in other democratic societies, or even within our own states, things could easily have turned out differently. The questions naturally arise, then, why did a careerist orientation take root in Congress at the turn of the century, and what caused it?

Most scholars ground their explanations of increasing professionalism in the transformation of member goals and expectations (cf. Swenson 1982). When politicians found the rewards of congressional offices increasing and developed the capacity to both secure reelection at home and perpetuate power in the Capitol, they argued, then legislators were more likely to view their job as a long-term investment. All these stimulants to careerism—motive, means, and opportunity— supposedly came together between 1890 and 1910, setting the stage for the rise of professional legislators and perpetuating them ever since.

This view of careerism places a heavy premium on recruitment as the cause of legislative professionalism because it treats organizational structures as the consequence of the ambition for personal power and autonomy among successive generations of representatives and senators.[2] Considerable empirical support for this interpretation arises from the pattern of legislative careers inside Congress, but in the end, it is not a completely satisfactory explanation.

Throughout the nineteenth century, Congress was largely a part-time institution whose membership was in a perpetual state of flux. It steadily absorbed new members as additional states were admitted to

---

2. A professional legislature is typically defined as one in which members serve full time, are reasonably well paid, are supported by professional staff, and serve relatively lengthy terms. Polsby (1968, 145) defines an "institutionalized" legislature as one with three major characteristics: (1) it is relatively well bounded and differentiated from its environment, (2) it is complex and internally differentiated, and (3) it uses universalistic rather than particularistic criteria or discretion for conducting internal business.

the union. It routinely denied seats to members whose elections were contested and granted positions instead to candidates put forward by the majority party. It often lost legislators to other governmental offices before their terms had expired, and it frequently witnessed the departure of senators and representatives who rotated in and out of office according to the dictates of state and local party leaders. The combination of expansion, voluntary retirement, and party rotation ensured that the percentage of first-term legislators averaged about 60 percent.

Within this overall pattern of high turnover some differences distinguished the careers of pre–Civil War legislators from those who served in the latter part of the nineteenth century. For example, their frequent rotation out of office was not enforced by disciplined party organizations, as in later Congresses; rather, it reflected a weak attachment to the federal government and a distaste for life in Washington. Moreover, their careers inside the institution were far less structured by parties, committees, and parliamentary rules, all of which changed dramatically in the postwar era. Finally, although members in both periods spent a disproportionate amount of their time on private bills and were highly influenced by sectional concerns, their issue agendas in later Congresses were broader and more structured around partisanship (cf. Brady 1973).

Turnover began to decrease after Reconstruction, so that average tenure grew to roughly three to four terms by the turn of the century and the frequency of members with long service increased appreciably (Witmer 1964; Polsby 1968; Price 1971; Bullock 1972; Fiorina, Rohde, and Wissel 1975). The data show the biggest gains occuring between 1888 and 1910. With the development of a stable membership, both chambers developed norms of reciprocity and courtesy (Price 1971) and regularized procedures of advancement, particularly the seniority rule (Polsby 1968; Polsby, Gallaher, and Rundquist 1969). At the same time, the system of party leadership underwent a radical transformation (Polsby 1968; Price 1971; Swenson 1982). The House speaker lost his capacity to reward and punish party loyalty in the revolt against Cannon in 1911, and both parties formalized the award of chairs according to length of service. Equally important, leadership positions inside the party no longer went to relative newcomers or alternated among rival factions but instead were conferred on individuals who had spent many years of continuous service in Congress and had worked their way up the party hierarchy.

These sweeping changes produced an institution in which power was both fragmented and personalized. No other legislative body in the country, or in the world for that matter, dispersed legislative responsibility so broadly or permitted individuals to create influence on the basis of their own expertise and persuasiveness. Moreover, these unusual arrangements took place without an appreciable change in the social composition of the membership. Despite the democratization of the parties and the extension of the franchise, changes that in Europe caused the diversification of legislative bodies and encouraged the growth of party-based government, there was little alteration in the social makeup of the House and Senate.[3] Instead, Congress followed a different developmental path and drew its legislators from the same socioeconomic strata in the modern era as it had in the eighteenth century (Bogue et al. 1976). However, the politcal elite somehow ceased to view public office as a part-time pursuit and developed into a body of professional, career-minded politicians (Bogue et al. 1976, 300).

Several different alterations in the political environment could account for these patterns because they created greater incentives for the pursuit of congressional careers. First, the introduction of the direct primary system and the advent of the Australian ballot diminished party control over the electoral system and made it easier for individual lawmakers to seek office on their own (Kernell 1977). Second, the realigning election of 1896 created safe Republican seats in the Northeast and safe Democratic seats in the South, which made it easier for incumbents to secure reelection (Price 1975). Third, the increased power of the federal government in domestic and foreign affairs made service in Congress more attractive than service in state government (Price 1971). Fourth, the lack of economic opportunity in the war-ravaged South and the desire among southerners to halt federal meddling in the region's affairs drew ambitious politicians to Washington to establish lengthy careers (Fiorina, Rohde, and Wissel 1975).

Each of these trends facilitated legislators' long-term aspirations for careers in Congress. The disappearance of the party system of rotation, for example, accounted for about 22 percent of the reduced turnover between 1880 and 1890, while decreased competition accounted for nearly 45 percent of the drop between 1890 and 1900 (Kernell 1977). But the major factor in every decade from the 1850s to 1900 was ambition—the desire to seek reelection (Kernell 1977, 690). Once members connected their futures to the institution, it was

---

3. Even the advent of direct election to the Senate after 1911 did little to change the makeup of its membership.

inevitable that they would adopt rules and procedures to enhance their chances of reelection and their opportunities to exercise power once in office.

However, no one has developed a satisfactory model to explain the nature of the distinctive changes that produced the modern Congress (Cooper and Brady 1981). Polsby's (1968) theory, which he labeled "institutionalization," was the most ambitious approach and treated the developments in Congress as an inevitable movement toward the specialization, differentiation, and universalism characteristic of any mature social organization. The structural-functionalist flavor of Polsby's argument implied that Congress evolved in particular ways as a response to external changes in the political system. But there was nothing in the concept that pointed to the particular mix of rules and authority that eventually emerged, and even the most cursory reading of congressional history suggests that Congress did not follow a steady organizational continuum after professionalism set in. For example, between 1910 and 1946, the House, at least, experimented with several different methods for allocating power—such as the party caucus in the Wilson era—and deferred to greater or lesser degrees to the leadership of the party and the president. More telling perhaps, Polsby's concept of institutionalization did not lend itself to prediction about what future developmental course Congress might follow.[4] Thus, although the trend toward careerism was unmistakeable, its impact on the Congress was hardly linear: a change in the pattern of turnover did not necessarily bring about a commensurate change in institutional structures.

In the absence on any compelling theory of legislative professionalism, scholars turned again toward ambition and recruitment to explain the sudden increase in incumbents' reelection margins and the disappearance of marginal districts in the 1960s and 1970s. Both Mayhew (1974a) and Fiorina (1977) strongly argued that the reelection imperative had become so powerful by this time that members of Congress skewed the entire institution to serve their political needs. Both authors contended that the growth of staff, the increasing time and resources devoted to the constituency, and the emphasis on particularized benefits and pork barrel projects were designed to enhance incumbent popularity in the district.

Mayhew elaborated his argument by pointing out how the committee system and the lack of party discipline enabled members to claim credit for legislation and to take symbolic positions that were

---

4. See Cooper and Brady (1981) for a detailed critique of the limitations of institutionalization as an explanatory concept.

popular but lacked policy impact. In short, he contended that members of Congress turned their institution into a highly efficient and specialized "reelection machine" (1974a, 81). Fiorina saw incumbents' reelection imperative in even starker structural terms, for he asserted that members erected an elaborate bureaucracy and regulatory apparatus to create casework opportunities for themselves. As hapless citizens became more and more enmeshed in red tape, he argued, they turned with increasing frequency to their representatives and senators who happily interceded on their behalf with government bureaucrats and thereby earned reelection from grateful voters.

At least two empirical studies, one by Born (1979) and another by Collie (1981), indicated the presence of generational effects in incumbent reelection success, suggesting that a new type of lawmaker did appear at about this time. Loomis's case study of the Watergate Class of 1974 seemed to confirm their conclusions. But Jacobson (1987a) disputed the idea that electoral competition in the 1970s had diminished; he contended that high margins of safety were less protection against future incumbent defeats than in previous eras. Similarly, Hibbing's recent longitudinal analysis of House members' careers inside the institution indicated that legislators elected after 1964 were not necessarily more ambitious for reelection or for institutional power than their predecessors. I will turn to Hibbing's provocative study in greater detail in chapter 6, but for now, I will simply note two of his findings: first, that incumbents of all age cohorts increased their electoral security during the 1960s and 1970s and, second, that junior House members were somewhat more legislatively aggressive during the 1970s but have become less visible in the past decade.

In sum, four distinct eras mark the evolution of professionalism in Congress: 1789 to the Civil War, the 1860s to World War I, the 1920s to the mid-1960s, and 1965 to the present. Each era varies according to members' length of service, to levels of leadership and partisanship, to the complexity of the legislative agenda, and to the availability of institutional resources. Recruitment—notably the change in member goals—clearly played a large part in the adoption of professionalism and its subsequent evolution, but the career aspirations of ever more ambitious legislators do not tell the whole story. Scholars have not fully recognized the institutional and political contexts that constrained lawmakers' ability to define their institution in purely individualistic terms.

The first problem in placing the explanatory burden for legislative professionalism on legislators' goals arises from the logic of institutional power, and it crops up in several different guises. Dodd, for example, pointed out that the influence of individual members depends upon the influence of the institution as a whole, which in turn depends upon its internal unity and discipline (Dodd 1985 and 1986; Dodd and Schott 1979). If individual power undermines the coherence of Congress, it ultimately leaves the Congress vulnerable to the disintegrating pressures of constituents and interest groups and invites encroachments from the president and the bureaucracy.

Dodd began his argument with a premise based on recruitment that "members of Congress enter politics in a quest for personal power . . . [and] this motive places every member in a personal conflict with every other member" (1985, 490–91). He saw the decentralization of authority in Congress as a cooperative solution to the problem of conflicting individual goals and demonstrated how a variety of rules, norms, and structures associated with committee government served to accommodate the maximum number of members. However, the drive for personal power inevitably created weaknesses in the institution that diminished its capacity to act, to set fiscal priorities, to take responsibility for decisions, to oversee the bureaucracy, and finally to anticipate policy change (1985, 495–500). Once this happened, Dodd reasoned, Congress lost respect and legitimacy in the eyes of the public, it eventually turned to presidential leadership to meet its responsibilities and then it reacted to the constraining influence of executive dominance. The constant tension, then, between the drive for personal power and the imperative to preserve institutional power produced a cyclical pattern of institutional change.

Dodd demonstrated that some periods of congressional history have been marked by reform efforts to disperse control of the legislative process, while others have been characterized by increasing moves to centralize authority in the hands of party leaders. As long as the desire for power is the primary objective of federal legislators, Dodd asserted, the cycle will continue. In his view, then, the motivations of people who run for the House and Senate and their objectives once in office are key factors in the development of rules and structures governing careers inside the professionalized Congress. But the decisive factor in how far members can push their own career agendas is the dynamic balance of power between Congress and various external actors.

A related line of inquiry emerges from the work of Arnold (1990). Arnold demonstrated that for reelection-minded legislators, autonomy was not necessarily a desirable feature of the Congress. Given issues with particular types of characteristics—what he termed *traceability*—legislators willingly acceded to the discipline of rules and party leaders to screen themselves from constituent retribution at the polls. In Arnold's view, therefore, career-minded legislators may be as anxious for the political cover of institutional structures as they are for the freedom to engage in logrolling and pork barrelling. If he is correct, then we cannot trace the distinctive characteristics of the professionalized Congress solely to members' career drives for autonomy and personal power. As Matthews has observed, legislative institutions may have more autonomy from their members than scholars have typically supposed (1983, 43).

The other obstacle to drawing a direct connection between personal ambition and institutional professionalism lies in a curious empirical coincidence. What is striking in thinking about the various eras of congressional careers is their correspondence to distinctive patterns in the American party system. According to Joel Silbey (1991), party history can be classified into four periods, each marked by particular patterns of voter turnout and partisan preferences across time and across offices: the prealignment era from 1789 to 1838, the alignment-realignment era from 1838 to 1893, the realignment-dealignment era from 1893 to 1948–52, and the postalignment era from 1948–52 to the present (1991, 17).

Whether or not one agrees with Silbey's use of these eras to challenge the theory of critical elections, the cutpoints he chose anticipate changes in congressional career patterns by ten to fifteen years. In other words, roughly a decade after the country experienced a major shift in its party system, the Congress experienced an alteration in its patterns of turnover. Whether or not the transformation of parties has a lag effect with respect to congressional careers is unclear, but it is nevertheless interesting. Because congressional candidates are deeply imbedded in the party system, however it might be configured, their fortunes are tied to whatever party recruitment practices predominate. Thus, the winners invariably transmit features of this external system to the internal structures of the House and Senate.

In sum, professionalism is a longstanding feature of life in the U.S. Congress—a fact that serves many of the personal interests of the members quite well. But rather than credit its existence solely to the career ambitions of lawmakers, it is appropriate to consider how external actors and constraints have contributed to the Congress's unique pattern of institutional development.

Candidates and Democratic Theory

In the twentieth century, candidate recruitment has occupied a central, but not always explicit, place in theories of democratic governance in the United States. Extending beyond concerns about the caliber and ambition of legislators, it became central to models of electoral competition, to debates regarding the distribution of power and influence in the society, and to judgments about the capacity of the regime for political change. But here, too, the influence of candidacy can be either explicit or implied, direct or indirect.

Writing fifty years ago, Joseph Schumpeter (1942) made candidates the indispensible agents of popularly elected government. Schumpter defined democracy as the competitive struggle for free votes in free elections, and he saw political entrepreneurs as the driving force behind that competition. In the process of bidding for ballots, candidates organized resources and packaged issues for party campaigns. Power, not profit, was the motivating force behind their actions; and policy, not product, was their means of satisfying citizen demand. Voters played a reactive role in this exchange, according to Schumpeter, by accepting or rejecting the planks and principles offered to them. But candidates "wielded the initiative" by determining the alternatives from which citizens might choose (1942, 282). In Schumpeter's political marketplace, just as in his commercial one, ambition, innovation, and sales ability would be the hallmarks of successful competition.

Joseph Schlesinger put forward a similarly strong case for the competitive force of candidates in democracies in the mid-1960s. Schlesinger (1966) recognized that the entrepreneurial function of candidates was connected to their private motivations. In his view, the voters' sanction of removal was an empty threat unless incumbents had ambitions to remain in public office and challengers had a powerful urge to displace them. "The desire for election, and more important, reelection," he wrote, "becomes the electorate's restraint upon its public officials" (1966, 4). Voters depended on candidates, then, not just for presenting policy alternatives but for their very prerogative of choice.

In addition to their entrepreneurial role, candidates also have been regarded as reflections of the distribution of political power in society. Harold Lasswell assumed that politics determined the allocation of influence (1951, 295) and concluded that the political elite consisted of "those who get the most (quoted in Eulau 1976, 11). The composition of the elite therefore revealed what values were dominant in society and how broadly they were shared.

Lasswell believed that political power could never be exercised equally, so he argued that democracies needed to pay special attention to devising systems of broad access to the governing elite. Ideally, this elite would be "society-wide," drawn from the community at large rather than a few social strata, although Lasswell appears to have harbored few illusions that the American democracy was fulfilling this criterion (1948, 109). Nevertheless, one can infer from his writings that a reasonably democratic regime required a large and diverse group of eligible leaders. The number and type of prospective candidates would therefore indicate how widely power was allocated in a particular society.

Candidates serve the additional function of promoting and protecting democratic norms. The triumph of fascism in the 1930s and the spread of authoritarian regimes in the postwar era provided such compelling evidence of the fragility of popular government that many democratic theorists turned to political elites as the guarantors of democratic rule.[5] Early surveys of public opinion further called the capacity for self-government among ordinary citizens into question and indicated that many voters did not fully subscribe to basic constitutional principles (Berelson, Lazerfeld, and McPhee 1954; McCloskey 1964). By default, then, the maintenance of the democratic order seemed to fall to the small, politically active leadership that managed the nation's political affairs. It was therefore imperative to understand whom elites recruited to the governing class and how they transmitted values to its new members.

In his classic critique of Madisonian democracy, Robert Dahl (1956) gave further weight to the role of political elites in perpetuating popular government. Dahl argued that majority rule was "mostly a myth" and that policies tended to be "products of 'minorities rule'" (1956, 133). More important than constitutional provisions, Dahl argued, was the underlying consensus in society about its rules and objectives (1956, 83). He concluded:

> what we ordinarily describe as democratic "politics" is merely the chaff . . . . Prior to politics, beneath it, enveloping it, restricting it, conditioning it, is the underlying consensus on policy that usually exists in the society among *a predominant portion of the politically active members*. Without such a consensus no democratic system would long survive the endless irritations and frustrations of elections and party competition. (1956, 132, emphasis added)

In the hybrid democracy Dahl described as polyarchy, consensus was maintained partly by social training and partly by allowing nu-

---

5. See Eldersveld 1989, ix–xviii and Aberbach, Putnam, and Rockman 1981, chap. 1 for summaries of this literature.

merous elites to compete. This system operated most satisfactorily, he thought, when constitutional rules did not unduly affect the participation of any particular groups. In the end, Dahl was compelled to judge the performance of democratic polyarchies by the access they granted to the political arena. As the personification of this accessibility, candidates could be said to provide a measure of the distribution of power in Dahl's political scheme, just as in Lasswell's.

Candidate recruitment has implications for the theory of partisan realignment as well. For many years political scientists have attributed the periodic sea changes that sweep the American system to shifts in the partisan attitudes of voters and the mobilization of new sectors within the electorate (Key 1955; Burnham 1970; Andersen 1979). Although this was the pattern in the New Deal realignment of the 1930s, it did not fit very well with earlier transformations that took place in the 1850s and 1890s, because major policy changes and new governing coalitions occurred in those eras without substantial alterations in voting behavior (Clubb, Flanigan, and Zingale 1980). Moreover, recent events suggest that realignment, whatever its merits for explaining political eras of the past, bears little resemblance to the partisan changes that have taken place since the late 1960s. Therefore, the very concept of realignment as a theory of partisan change has been called into question.

Joel Silbey (1991) has suggested that only one period in American party history actually bears the characteristics of a classic realignment, and that was the period from 1838 to 1898. In other eras, the conditions of stable partisan majorities in the electorate, coherent governing majorities in the federal government, and periodic shifts marked by high turnout and intense party competition were either absent or only partially realized. In the years leading up to the critical election of the New Deal, for example, the capacity of parties to organize political competition had already been seriously eroded by reformers, so that the events so often regarded as archetypal of realignment politics turned out to be something much less. Our own era, Silbey argued, far from being in the midst of an imperfect realignment, is much more similar to the volatile and atomistic politics of the late eighteenth and early nineteenth centuries than to the pattern of the New Deal.

If Silbey's interpretation of American party history is correct, then there is little reason to expect the long-awaited realignment to appear in this or any subsequent political generation. But it would still be necessary to explain why the pattern set in 1932 ended with the steady erosion of party attachments in the electorate and the appearance of divided government. And if Silbey's analysis turns out to be off the mark, then it becomes necessary to explain why the party realignment so many political observers saw gathering steam with the 1968 election was derailed.

Several scholars have pinned the demise of realignment on the voters, who have "dealigned" from either political party (cf. Beck 1984). The growth of self-declared independents, the decline of strong partisans, and the widespread practice of split-ticket voting all signaled an electorate that was disinclined to organize its political thinking around party labels. These attitudes, when coupled with popular ambivalence about the proper role of government and a political environment that was both technologically and organizationally less amenable to party dominance of electoral competition, would ensure that when the public demanded change, it would not necessarily confer a new or stable mandate on the out-party (c.f. Ladd 1991).

Missing from these explanations of the state of the contemporary parties is the role of candidates in framing new issues. If political elites fail to provide meaningful alternatives to the status quo or to structure cleavages in an intelligible and coherent fashion, then the public can hardly be faulted for aborting the periodic adjustment in the party system that political scientists have predicted with such certainty. One of the important outstanding issues in the realignment debate, then, is to explain why candidates today have been less successful than their predecessors in converting political shocks and new cleavages into stable governing coalitions. One possibility is suggested by the work of David Brady (1988), and the other is developed in an article by Byron Shafer (1991).

Brady's work (1988) suggested that major shifts in voter attitudes and in popular support of the two parties is neither a necessary nor a sufficient condition for realignment to take placc. Instead, he focused on the competitiveness of House districts and the increases in member turnover as the defining characteristics of critical elections. When the number of constituencies with close races is large, he demonstrated, a relatively small shift in votes can produce the committee turnover and cohesive party majorities in Congress necessary to bring about the policy innovation associated with realignments. In Brady's view, realignments will occur if and only if the parties recruit strong candidates to run against each other in a large percentage of House races.[6] If this is the case, then instances of long-term shifts in the relative influence of the parties would be elite-driven rather than mass-driven phenomena. Indeed, the long-predicted Republican realignment has

---

6. A similar pattern seems to hold for a more gradual development of regional party strength described by Key as secular realignments (1959), such as that taking place in the South today.

not taken place in the 1980s, despite substantial GOP gains among voters, because a high incidence of uncontested seats and uncompetitive Republican challengers has prevented the party from capitalizing on its strength at the top of the ticket, particularly in the South (Brady 1988, 177; Brady and Grofman 1991).

Shafer has laid the blame for the demise of realignment as an empirical phenomenon to the emergence of cross-cutting majorities on social welfare issues, cultural values, and national defense among the voters. Shafer grounded his argument in the appearance of blue collar conservatives, who remained liberal about government spending and management of the economy while espousing conservative views on life-style issues and nationalism, and the emergence of middle-class liberals, who were hostile to government activism in the economic sector but took progressive views on social issues and accommodationist views on foreign policy. These voters projected their inconsistent preferences onto various institutions of the government—choosing Republican presidents to satisfy nationalist and socially conservative sentiments and selecting Democratic members of Congress to take care of their material demands on the government. In this respect, Shafer's argument is similar to one made by Gary Jacobson (1990b), which I will explore in greater depth in chapter 4. But what is distinctive about it is his contention that political elites—activists in the parties and interest groups—keep the system in its current state of disequilibrium.

One does not have to be a Downsian to believe that reasonable politicians would try to find ways to create a more coherent majority to improve their chances of winning and holding office. Among contemporary activists, however, ideology is by far a more compelling incentive for political participation than winning elections, Shafer argued. Consequently, they not only refuse to modify their own positions but reject candidates who attempt to redefine issues along more consensual lines. In sum, the intermediaries who link the public and the government have obstructed the normal process of reconstituting a new political order. Inside each of the party coalitions, they have institutionalized a particular set of beliefs—support for social welfare, foreign policy accommodation, and progressive cultural values among the Democrats and just the opposite for the Republicans—even though such an alignment does not correspond to the belief system of large numbers of voters. Shafer concluded:

> at the elite (but not at the mass) level, new issues divisions were effectively "grafted onto" [rather than "laid across"] the old. . . .

The activist base of each political party had become effectively committed—energetically, consciously, even desperately committed—to precisely those positions on which their party would necessarily *lose* one or another major public office. (1991, 61)

From both these arguments—Brady's and Shafer's—candidates become the vital link in facilitating or hindering realignment. In Brady's model of realignment, candidates reflect or create the competitiveness of the two parties. Hence, any party that has an inadequate supply of high quality candidates in a significant number of districts will be unable to bring about the marginal shifts in election outcomes sufficient to produce a governing majority inside Congress. According to Campbell (1990) and Canon (1990b), this is precisely what has happened among Republicans to impede realignment in the South. In Shafer's model, however, the emphasis is on the winnowing processes activists employ to recruit like-minded candidates and to ensure that they remain faithful to the cross-cutting cleavages that produce incoherent majorities. In neither formulation are candidates causal agents by changing voter preferences or defining the salient dimensions of mass attitudes. But they do provide the necessary interface between citizens and governmental institutions that enables emergent public opinion to crystallize behind a new policy agenda.

On several grounds, then, politics in the United States depends on candidates to provide leadership, to foster vigorous competition, to ensure that a wide range of interests in society has access to political power, to uphold the principles of popular sovereignty and individual rights, and to give expression to citizen demands for policy change. By assuming these functions, the men and women who run for Congress illuminate aspects of democracy that extend far beyond their own institution.

Congressional Candidates as Central Actors

The U.S. Congress has the unique responsibility in American politics of representing local constituencies in the federal government. Prospective candidates have to appeal to a relatively narrow electorate while harboring an inclination to pursue a national agenda far from home. With a foot in two very distinct environments, they are responsive, as well as vulnerable, to a wide range of political stimuli. The local roots of federal lawmakers and their national prominence therefore make them particularly good subjects for examining the ambiguous status of candidates in American politics. Standing as they do at the nexus of local and national politics, congressional candidates can tell us something about both worlds.

Given its location in the federal system, it is hardly surprising that the Congress is both the pinnacle for many legislative careers and the proving ground for men and women aspiring to even higher office. State lawmakers, for example, often move on to the House of Representatives, and some eventually wind up in the Senate; but far more retain their connection to state legislative politics. Furthermore, many seek statewide office, such as governor or attorney general, while others return to county and municipal government or leave politics all together. Therefore, in examining politicians' pursuit of congressional careers, one inevitably confronts the incentive structures that lead to other types of political office-seeking behavior.

Similarly, House members frequently seek seats in the Senate, where they are then in a position to bid for the presidency. Within the 101st Congress, for example, thirty-eight senators had previouly served as representatives, and of the ten presidents in office since World War II, all but four—Eisenhower, Carter, Reagan, and now Clinton—have served in the House. But members of Congress also leave Capitol Hill to run for governor or to assume mayoral positions. Despite all this moving about, the average tenure of representatives has remained relatively constant between 5 and 6 terms in the postwar period, although the mean jumped to an unprecedented 6.2 terms in the 102d Congress (Ornstein, Mann, and Malbin 1992, 19–20). Senators, whose tenure averaged nearly 2 full terms from 1965 to 1975, had somewhat shorter careers than their House colleagues during the 1980s, and today they average 11.1 years of service (Ornstein, Mann, and Malbin 1992, 21). Clearly, recruitment to Congress is an ongoing process as members decide whether to stay in one chamber or seize other opportunities.[7] Such calculations tell us a great deal about the institution and its relationship to other types of public office.

Although Congress is attractive to career-minded politicians of many different stripes, at the same time it is permeable enough to admit political amateurs to its ranks. In recent years, for example, there has been an influx of House members and senators who lack prior experience in public office. Indeed, in some Congresses amateurs make up as much as 40 percent of the new members (Canon

---

7. John Hibbing argues that progressive ambition among politicians is not simply a move from a lower office to a higher one but also includes the search for institutional positions of leadership. In his view, careers are best understood in terms of "position-seeking," and internal opportunity structures are therefore as important as external ones in predicting career patterns. See Hibbing 1989, 28–29.

1989b). The presence of alternative patterns of entry to the federal legislature thus suggests that the stimuli and experiences motivating people to run for Congress can be quite diverse.

Given the variety of legislative institutions found in the fifty states, there is ample opportunity to investigate how congressional ambition develops in diverse political contexts. Differences abound across states and regions in the amount of authority granted legislative bodies, in their organizational complexity, in the level of professionalization of their memberships and staffs, in their responsibility for budgets and bureaucracies, and in the strength of their party organizations. These conditions make it systematically possible to control for many of the environmental influences that have a potential impact on individuals' interest and success in obtaining a seat in Congress.

Congressional recruitment further provides an arena for studying the networks of activists that connect states and districts to the nation's capital. Successful campaigns for the House and Senate are federal efforts in the sense that they require the cooperation of local and national parties and the interaction of these organizations with PACs and interest group activists throughout the political system. At the same time, individuals in the constituency remain an important source of money and volunteer support. As congressional candidates evaluate these various sectors of activism and negotiate with prospective supporters, they offer scholars the opportunity to observe a broad spectrum of elite behavior at multiple levels of government.

For many reasons, then, the nation's legislature offers a promising setting for exploring a wide variety of research questions concerning candidates and their emergence in American politics. The House and Senate draw their members from diverse political and institutional backgrounds, they offer a considerable range of outlets for political ambition, and they encompass a broad set of actors and stimuli in the decision to run. If we want to understand the many facets of candidacy in the American tradition, it is hard to imagine a better laboratory for studying recruitment than the U.S. Congress.

CHAPTER 3

Theories of Candidacy

> . . . politicians are both goal-seeking and situation-interpreting individuals.
>
> —Richard F. Fenno, Jr.

If congressional candidates stand at the confluence of the broad political trends noted in the previous chapter, it remains to be seen how they act as causal agents in the American polity. In some respects, candidates seem to drive the electoral and institutional changes that have occurred in Congress over many generations; in other respects, they seem to act strategically in seizing opportunities available within the political system. In still other respects, candidates seem unwitting players in a process they only dimly perceive. Nowhere is their ambiguous status—agent, opportunist, or pawn—more evident than in the theoretical literature on recruitment.

There has never been a single theory of candidacy but a set of theories all bent on explaining different aspects of the selection of public officials. Roughly speaking, the earliest conceptualization of candidacy was sociological in orientation, and its primary purpose was tracing the origin of political elites and the values they imposed on the rest of society. Somewhat later came the psychological approach to office seeking, with its concern for how the unconscious drives and motivations of political leaders affected their behavior in office. The next development was process oriented, and its preoccupation was competition among groups for political power, with particular emphasis on parties as agents of leadership development. The subsequent phase was goal directed, and its primary objective was explaining the strategic calculations of individual candidates. The most recent development is rule based, and its intent is to demonstrate how rational decision making about ambition is constrained by political institutions.

Each tradition has looked at the consequences of candidacy quite differently; each has addressed the problem of defining the pool of eligibles in its own way; and each has treated the interactive effects among candidates, elites, events, and structures with varying degrees of emphasis. However, what has been missing from the theoretical work on candidacy is an integration of microlevel behavior and macrolevel phenomena. Congressional candidates are not only ambitious individuals operating in a particular political environment but also products of the existing social and institutional order, yet scholars have tended to address either one side or the other—either the individual candidacies or the social and institutional constraints—but seldom to mesh the two. As Prewitt (1970) noted, scholars have attempted to deduce the nature of structural influences by examining the individuals who get elected, or they have drawn conclusions about candidates from studying political rules and organizations. His conclusion, still valid today, is that "political recruitment theory often suffers from being either too institutional or too individual. . . . [Both are useful], but singly they lead to misplaced inference" (1970, 15).

More important, theorizing about candidacy has most often and most effectively addressed political careers—the advancement from one office to another. These are theories of *progressive ambition* that take the desire and eligibility for public office as givens. They concentrate on how individual politicians assess and manipulate the strategic aspects of winning and losing various types of positions, but they have little to say about where candidates come from and what factors, besides those associated with victory, affect potential office seekers' motivations and prospects.

What should a more comprehensive theory of candidacy look like? First, it should identify the eligible contestants within the population at large and explain why those prospective candidates who eventually run are different from those who do not. Second, it should account for the interactions among candidates and political elites as they occur within varying local and national contexts. Third, it should be dynamic to allow for changing expectations and circumstances that move politicians in and out of the candidate pool. The task of the theorist, then, is to reconcile the goal-seeking behavior of prospective candidates with the relevant socioeconomic and institutional constraints that govern their emergence and determine their success.

Existing theories have seldom reached so broadly across the spectrum of factors influencing candidacy; nevertheless, we can learn a great deal from examining the various scholarly traditions that have developed to explain legislative recruitment. Each theoretical paradigm has adopted a particular definition of recruitment, which in turn has dictated the choice of dependent and independent variables; each has set particular boundaries that define the onset, prosecution, and termination of candidacy; and each has made different judgments about which rules, actors, and events are relevant to office seeking. Table 3.1 is a summary of the different approaches.

In revisiting these various conceptualizations of candidacy, two things must be kept in mind. First, the study of recruitment turned to the analysis of political careers quite early because of problems of data and measurement. Although scholars continued to define recruitment as the socialization and apprenticeship leading to public office, they became interested primarily in the end result—the electoral success of declared candidates and the upward mobility of incumbents. Second, little of the literature grew out of an explicit concern with Congress as an institution or the unique place of its members in a federal system of coequal, governmental branches. Despite these limitations, we can still derive some important lessons about the causal implications of candidates in American politics by considering their place in the large body of research on legislatures of many different types, which is in turn subsumed in an even larger literature on political elites.

The Sociological Tradition

The study of political recruitment originated with the great European sociologists of the early twentieth century—Weber, Michels, Mosca, and Pareto. Their interest in the hierarchical ordering of society led them to consider how elites came to positions of power and how they created institutions to perpetuate their privileged position. Weber (1965) explored the development of politics as a vocation to identify the specialized attitudes and skills that distinguished members of the political elite from the administrative class. Michels (1962) and Mosca (1939) demonstrated how democratic governments would eventually succumb to oligarchical tendencies within mass political parties. And Pareto (1935) examined how the circulation of elites affected a society's ability to resist or assimilate change.

These men thought it inevitable that the few would reign over the many, and so the concept of political class—its origins, its training, and its capacity to enlist new members—was central to their writings. In this sense, their view of recruitment is close to the meaning of the word's Latin root, "to grow or replenish," because it entails the maintenance and restoration of the leadership echelon through generational replacement and the accommodation of emerging rivals.

Several features are important to this early sociological paradigm of recruitment. In the first place, it offered a *deterministic, macrolevel*

TABLE 3.1. A Summary of Theoretical Paradigms of Candidacy

Paradigm	Terminology	Dependent Variable	Boundaries: Eligibility/Time	Interactive Effects
Sociological	Recruitment	Values of governing class	Dominant elite/early training	Minimal-social determinism
Psychological	Recruitment	Leadership behavior	Ego driven/early experience	Family/culture impact on personality
Process	Recruitment	Stages of competitive process	Organized groups and parties/apprenticeship	Rules/structures constrain group strategies
Rational actor	Ambition	Decision to run	Self-identified/winning credentials/political career	Subjective probability estimates
Rational/institutional	Ambition	Decision to run	Self-identified/local contexts/political career	Rules/structures constrain individual strategies

theory of elite behavior. Wealth and social status decided who was eligible to pursue political power, and within the elite strata, competition for power was regulated by a complex web of interpersonal relationships and norms. The relative homogeneity of the elite ensured that prospective office seekers would hold similar motives and pursue similar objectives once selected. Thus, political ambition was acquired quite unconsciously through socialization, and political positions were conferred on those best able to serve the interests of the elite. Individual motivations and strategies counted for relatively little against the overwhelming weight of social and economic structures within the polity.

Similarly, the boundaries of the political elite were strictly defined according to the class structure. Those inside the charmed circle were eligible; those outside were not, except in times of social upheaval. Within the privileged group, advancement was indirectly governed through social training and role assignment, which engaged the entire ruling class. Specialized agencies, such as parties, were instruments rather than autonomous agencies in this ongoing process of certification and selection. One consequence of this view of recruitment is that it had no identifiable beginning or end, although it tended to focus on the early aspects of political careers. Moreover, within the clearly marked province of the elite, it was impossible to tell which individuals would eventually emerge as leaders. Given the commonality of interests that bound the ruling class, such predictions did not necessarily matter.

The social determinism underlying this tradition of elite recruitment offered little scope for thinking about the interactive aspects of recruitment. With the exception of Pareto, who examined the displacement of one ruling elite by another, these writers led one to examine the social characteristics of political recruits as clues to their behavior rather than the political conditions and tactics that enabled them to assume positions of power.

In the behavioral revolution that took place after World War II, the sociological approach to recruitment was adopted by many political scientists. Under the influence of structural-functionalism and revisionist thinking about the existence of a political class, scholars in the 1950s and 1960s added several interesting twists to the European paradigm they adopted, but in essentials, most remained remarkably close to the original.

Like their predecessors, the structural-functionalists saw politics in macrolevel terms as the product of the dominant social norms and organizations within a particular system. Recruitment, in their view, served the critical function of "system maintenance" by ensuring institutional continuity while at the same time providing for adaption to ongoing changes in the society. According to Almond, "by [taking up] where the general political socialization leaves off . . . it inducts members of society into the specialized roles of the political system, trains them in the appropriate skills, provides them with political cognitive maps, values, expectations, and affects" (quoted in Czudnowski 1975, 160).

In the more egalitarian climate of the postwar era, political recruitment was viewed less as a vehicle for perpetuating a privileged elite than for sustaining the continuity of constitutional regimes. Its function was to ensure that individuals in the society learned how to govern, so that chaos and authoritarianism would be kept at bay. Nevertheless, the social status of elected officials retained its dominance as an explanatory variable because it was regarded as a powerful predictor of role orientation.

From this theoretical perspective grew the extensive descriptive literature on the social background, education and officeholding experience among candidates and elected officials (Matthews 1954 and 1960; Davidson 1969; Seligman 1961 and 1971; Prewitt 1970, chap. 2; Fishel 1973, chap. 2; Bogue et al. 1976; Aberbach, Putnam, and Rockman 1981). Political scientists who investigated the social characteristics and role orientations of lawmakers tried to establish empirical connections between such variables and performance in office, but this effort proved inconclusive (Matthews 1983, 25). Furthermore, they never endeavored to ascertain how social characters affected the decision to run or how they influenced the selection of winners (Canon 1992). In short, the sociological perspective yielded a wealth of descriptive data but little in the way of an explanation of legislators' strategic calculations, winnowing activities among elites, or legislative institutions.

Furthermore, the concept of recruitment as perpetuation of the ruling elite did not fit very well with the pluralistic social structure and decentralized party system in the United States. Several theorists challenged the existence of a self-perpetuating political class because they believed that elites could neither sustain nor legitimize their position in the transformed social and economic environment of the postwar era (cf. Keller 1963). Such trends as the emergence of the liberal welfare state, the expansion of the middle class, and the rise of a populist culture all undercut the idea of a self-conscious political class able to forge political institutions to maintain itself. At the same time, the development of technology and mass communications challenged the assumption that elites could control events or solve problems sufficiently to justify their unassailable status in the eyes of the masses.[1] These intellectual currents encouraged American political scientists to adopt a broader notion of social roles in the theory of legislative recruitment.

With the publication in 1962 of *The Legislative System*, a study of legislators in four states, the sociological paradigm lost much of its deterministic outlook. Wahlke, Eulau, and their colleagues put forward a definition of role theory that incorporated behavioral, institutional, and functional approaches. These scholars argued that a politician's skill and prior record were instrumental in shaping his or her advancement up the political ladder, and they further contended that political structures shaped the career patterns of elected officials. Although granting that prospective office seekers had an advantage in or were impeded by their initial social position, Wahlke et al. (1962, 71) asserted that political institutions, more than social status or tactical skill, accounted for the emergence of successful legislators. The constraints imposed by such factors as primaries, party organizations, voting procedures, and the like were sufficiently powerful, they believed, that even the most driven or socially favored candidates could not prevail when institutional structures were balanced against them.

In attempting to incorporate individual attributes and political institutions into an explanation of legislative recruitment, Wahlke and his colleagues resorted to a distinction between political recruitment and political careers. They defined the former as the process that determined the social characteristics of elites, and they characterized the latter as the summation of the individual's political experiences. More precisely, they defined a political career as "a developmental pattern in the life histories of politicians moving into positions made available by the framework of institutions" (1962, 71). Comprising this career development sequence were the following stages: (1) socialization, in which the prospective office seeker developed political interest and ambitions; (2) accumulation of experience, in which politicians acquired contacts and occupied party and other positions; and (3) expectation, in which they made determinations concerning reelection and aspiration for higher office.

This formulation represented an attempt to treat candidate emergence as both a macrolevel and microlevel phenomenon. On the one hand, it retained socially determined aspects of the early recruitment theorists while explicitly incorporating the institutional structures that

---

1. Shils (1982) provided a pithy statement of these arguments.

were only implied in earlier writings. On the other hand, it focused on individual attributes and expectations as factors shaping career paths. The authors concluded,

> a political career is not simply determined by the politician's skill in occupying available offices. . . . it may be facilitated or impeded by the politician's initial position in the social structure. . . . it may be furthered or limited by the ways in which the political system itself is structured. From the patterns of political careers in a given system, therefore, we can indirectly learn something about the recruitment process for various institutionalized groups, and the patterns of role potential among them. (1962, 71)

However, the distinction between political recruitment and career, had the effect of shifting the analysis of candidate emergence to individuals rather than social or political systems, because that was what Wahlke and his associates could observe. By asserting that an explanation of political recruitment could only be inferred from individual attitudes and behavior, they separated social structures from political ambition and its advancement and set the study of candidacy firmly on the side of methodological individualism. Furthermore, in treating recruitment as a largely unobservable social process preceding a politician's career, they neatly sidestepped the question of eligiblity. They took the pool of prospective candidates as a given and therefore avoided having to explain why certain types of individuals were more likely to enter the electoral arena than others. Thus, their assumption that the developmental sequence of careers would reveal the underlying mechanisms of recruitment encouraged them to concentrate on incumbent officeholders rather than potential office seekers, just as more conventional practitioners of the sociological approach had done.

The approach of Wahlke et al. entailed a more interactive theory of candidacy, because it attempted to show how patterns and expectations of advancement shaped lawmakers' role orientation once in office. These scholars tended to view politicians' relationships with party and community activists as intervening variables in the formation of roles, however, and in the end devoted little attention to the strategic aspects of the decision to run. Since their focus was on the predictive value of the attitudes acquired during the developmental sequence of a political career, they consequently paid scant attention to how political elites influenced the initial supply of candidates or used the winnowing process to further their own political ends.

Despite its strong connections to the sociological model of elite recruitment, then, *The Legislative System* is best understood as a major departure from this tradition. Wahlke et al.'s concept of role theory extended far beyond the realm of social class. Furthermore, the authors' emphasis on political structures and organizations, their interest in well-defined career paths, and above all their discussion of party and community activists in shaping politicians' expectations were a clear break with the structural-functionalist approaches to elite recruitment. Wahlke et al. never explicitly stated that these factors are exogenous to the social system, but they nonetheless treated politics as an independent influence on leadership selection. In the final analysis, their distinction between recruitment and careers decoupled the analysis of office-seeking behavior from its origins in the class structure— a development that paved the way for more process-oriented studies of recruitment.

The Psychological Tradition

The psychological approach to recruitment examined the motivations behind political behavior and attempted to demonstrate how particular actions flow from certain personality traits. It grounded ambition for public office in the unconscious desires and needs of individuals and thus provided a basis for assessing whether political actors are likely to act as democrats or as tyrants. Although centuries of writers have debated the relative importance of leadership in shaping the course of history,[2] the catastrophic impact of charismatic leaders in the twentieth century provided compelling evidence that a leader's psychological profile held enormous consequences for democratic governance. Against the backdrop of terror and mayhem so prevalent in the modern era, it was therefore crucial to understand why leaders sought public life and what manner of aggression or fantasy they might act out once in office.

Harold Lasswell pioneered the application of psychology to the problems of leadership recruitment and remains the most influential figure in the field even today. A Freudian by training, Lasswell (1948) depicted political leaders as deviant personalities who had imper-

---

2. The two sides of this debate are best captured in the work of Thomas Carlysle, who viewed history as the "biography of great men," and Sidney Hook, who contended that strong leaders were merely the product of their times.

fectly resolved their conflicts with parental authority. Many people, Lasswell argued, project repressed antagonism toward their fathers onto public objects, such as the king or the state, a tendency that explained why politics is so often marked by violence and hatred. But in his view, what separated the political man from the average citizen was the rationalization of displaced anger in terms of "public interests" ([1930] 1960, chap. 65). The leader's frustration was thus transformed into a sense of grievance about the treatment of a particular class, the workings of particular institutions, or the fate of the nation.

In later works, Lasswell continued to view political outcomes as the result of individual predispositions, but he recognized that such inclinations arose from a variety of environmental factors extending beyond the family and encompassing the values and structures of the community at large. He summarized the relationship in a simple formula,

$$E \rightarrow P \rightarrow R,$$

in which E stood for the environment of the political actor, P represented the predispositions of the political actor, and R was the political response of that actor (Lasswell and Kaplan 1950).

Lasswell's argument that political action flowed from the psychological drives of individuals raised particularly troublesome questions for democratic societies. How were they to provide themselves with leaders who would respect and protect democratic values and institutions, given political man's potential for pathological behavior? Lasswell's answer was to structure society to encourage the development of democratic personalities. "The democrat," he wrote, "identifies himself with mankind as a whole and with all subordinate groups whose demands are in harmony with the larger loyalty" (1948, 108). Citizens would have to rear, recognize and support such personalities if they wanted to sustain a state based on democratic principles. And only in polities with widely diffused power and influence in which the political elite was "society-wide" would such personalities develop and thrive (Lasswell 1948, 109).

More contemporary analyses of recruitment continued in the direction established by Lasswell. Their normative concern regarding politicians' psychological fitness to serve a democratic society and their emphasis on the individual ego meant that the dependent variable in studies of leadership recruitment would be elected officials' behavior once they were in power. In particular, analysts were interested in the values politicians pursued in public life as well as their style of decision making. What ends did they seek? Were they authoritarian or consensual in carrying out their objectives?

The Lasswellian tradition was appealing to contemporary students of politics because they saw office seeking as a stressful activity and public service as an occupation fraught with uncertainty and isolation. As Shils noted in an essay on the McCarthy hearings in the U.S. Senate, the acrimony and mistrust lawmakers expressed grew out of their frustrations from "too many demands and the disquiet of displeasing someone" (1950–51, 573). Those who willingly subject themselves to this sort of life, it followed, must have deviant ego needs at least to some degree. In this respect, the decision to seek a particular office and the ability to get elected were subordinate issues compared to the causal link between motivations and political acts.

The adoption of Lasswell's perspective ensured that any psychological theory of political recruitment would be a *microlevel construct*. Despite the recognition that environmental influences shaped personal predispositions toward power seeking, leadership behavior was seen as arising from the ego. However, this focus on the individual was at odds with the lengthy and heated debate among psychologists about the relationship between personality and situation (see Greenstein 1975, 18–30). Some theorists, for example, argued that individual predispositions were artificial constructs that could be neither observed nor measured and hence were irrelevant to the explanation of behavior. Others contended that personalities reflected the cultural milieu or social setting in which an individual develops. Finally, some writers challenged the very idea that individuals shaped events, asserting instead that personalities were simply a reflection of the times or found expression because of particular configurations of social, economic, and political events.

The theoretical disagreement over the origins and power of political personality is further confused by a lack of convincing empirical connections between psychological predispositions and lawmakers' behavior. For personality to be a relevant variable, the politician must be in a position to influence political events (cf. Mongard 1974; Hermann 1986). But legislatures, by their very nature, are institutions that constrain the individual—through the formal equality among members, the need to arrive at collective decisions, and the existence of parliamentary rules and procedures. If legislatures are not conducive to the pursuit of Lasswellian predispositions, then how much can a psychological theory of recruitment explain about congressional candidates?

Unhappily from the theorist's point of view, although not necessarily for the public, legislators in the United States exhibited few of the pathologies attributed to them by Lasswell and his successors. Although Italian legislators scored high on measures of authoritarianism and dogmatism (DiRenzo 1967a), American state legislators had psychological profiles that did not differ significantly from the general population on most dimensions. Indeed, they were less prone to authoritarianism than individuals in private life (McConaughy 1950; Browning and Jacob 1964), and they proved to have motivations that were very similar to those found among business executives (Hodgson, Levinson, and Zaleznik 1965, cited in Greenstein 1975). Furthermore, in a comparison of legislators and adminstrative officials conducted among elites in five western democracies, including the United States, legislators emerged as having much stronger orientations toward democratic norms than nonelected government officials (Aberbach, Putnam, and Rockman 1981).

If power needs failed to predict legislators' political attitudes and actions, they have fared no better in distinguishing candidates from the politically active segment of the population. In the absence of a clear model linking situational variables—family, culture, social and political structure—to predispositions for office seeking, it has proved impossible to predict in advance who would compete in elections and who would remain on the sidelines. Some scholars have tried to correct for this problem by linking the drive for public office to the organization of political opportunities. Browning (1968), for example, distinguished between the socialization processes that produce self-starters and those that lead to party-recruited candidates for local office. He argued that certain experiences and circumstances develop individuals with stronger power drives who are then more likely to initiate their own candidacies. DiRenzo (1967b) also provided evidence that linked the psychological orientation toward power to the level and function of political office, and he concluded that differences in recruitment methods and structures might attract individuals with very different motivations and personalities.

But even when ambitious individuals had revealed themselves by winning public office, the predictive power of psychological variables turned out to be limited. Not only did psychological indicators prove unreliable in differentiating public officials from private individuals, they exhibited strong variation within the ranks of incumbent politicians themselves. In several studies, lawmakers appeared to satisfy a diverse set of psychological drives through legislative office. Barber's (1965) innovative analysis of legislators in the Connecticut Assembly, for example, revealed four distinct power needs among the members.

The Reluctants, the Advertisers, and the Spectators all pursued very different personal and political objectives, and only the Lawmakers emerged as having a genuine bent for legislative leadership and bargaining. Barber's typology thus undermined the very notion of a political, or legislative, personality.

Still other scholars have contended that variations in self-esteem and the complexity of self-concept predict differences in legislators' propensities toward constituency responsiveness and ideological rigidity (Ziller et al. 1977). Finally, Payne et al. (1984) argued that politicians respond to a variety of political incentives—programmatic, status, obligation, and so forth—that engender various types of emotional satisfaction. From extensive interviews with politicians in a variety of positions, Payne and colleagues concluded that one incentive tends to be dominant for each individual lawmaker, although they were unable to explain the origin of such incentives or their differential effect on politicians. As a result, they could not assert whether or not the incentives they identified were necessary or sufficient for office seeking to take place.

Taken as a whole, this entire branch of the recruitment literature seems ad hoc because the concepts and measures are vaguely defined and imprecisely measured. More than anything, it adds fuel to the ongoing debate among psychologists about what is personality and what is environment. Furthermore, the psychological paradigm does not predict when competing personality types will defer to political rivals. Presumably, some personality types are more successful at translating their personal drives into results, but existing theory does not effectively differentiate between motives and tactics. Consequently, the most successful applications of Lasswellian theory seem to be found in the biographies of individual politicians. The Georges' (1956) account of Woodrow Wilson is the standard for this genre, although several fascinating and provocative treatments of legislative personalities exist in the literature as well (cf. Johnson 1977; Kearns 1976; Glad 1986). Here, the psychological orientations toward power became evident once lawmakers attained leadership positions, and they related to leaders' styles of coalition building. However, such research did not typically address the prior motivations that led legislative leaders initially to seek congressional office.

From the perspective of 1992, a serious flaw in the psychological paradigm is its neglect of the emotional costs of public life. Because psychological theorists have been so intent on looking for abnormal personalities and on explaining the behavioral consequences of political ambition, they have rarely thought about the conditions that inhibit the desire for elective office. Office seeking does not simply fulfill politicians' ego needs; rather, it imposes significant costs in terms of the loss of privacy and family relationships. Moreover, qualitative research by Ehrenhalt (1991) and Fowler and McClure (1989) suggest that the life of the professional politician varies in its attractiveness even to ambitious individuals.

The recent wave of retirements from the House, for example, raises questions about individuals' continued willingness to put up with the rigors of congressional office depending on their age, their party status, and the competitiveness of their electoral situation (Moore and Hibbing 1992). Certainly, many of the departing incumbents who complained about the price of political service were encouraged to leave by unfavorable political conditions, such as disadvantagous reapportionment plans in their states or the taint of scandal from the check-writing fiasco in the House bank (Hibbing, Forthcoming). Some undoubtedly were tired of the conflict bred by divided party control of the federal government, and a handful left to take advantage of a loophole in the campaign finance laws that enabled them to pocket any unspent balance. But incumbents have encountered such adversities before and hung on to their careers: what was different for at least a few lawmakers that year, such as Senator Tim Wirth, was a loss of appetite for the fight.

Overall, the psychological paradigm fostered a wealth of descriptive data about the mindset of practicing politicians, but it has neither accounted for the origins of these predispositions nor convincingly shown that they exist only in the political arena and nowhere else. The Lasswellian tradition, with its emphasis on the displacement of ego needs onto public objects, posits a personality type that does not fit with what is known of legislators and legislative institutions. Finally, it has not established a causal link between psychological variables and actual behavior.

The Process Tradition

The processs paradigm treats candidacy as one phase in a series of stages leading to electoral competition and eventually to governmental decisions. Process-oriented theorists were not indifferent to social and psychological influences, but they were more interested in how rival individuals competed for political power through constant adaptation to and manipulation of the rules of the game. Accustomed to viewing politics as the result of pluralist bargaining and accommodation among organized groups, they naturally extended this same perspective to the study of candidate emergence. Dwaine Marvick, one of the early researchers in this tradition, summed up the predominant approach to candidacy as, "the study of politics with a special eye to how the participants got there, where they came from and by what paths, and hence what ideas and skills and contacts they acquired or discarded along the way" (1976, 30).

The clearest statement of the process theory of candidacy is found in Prewitt's (1970) study of city council members in the San Francisco area. Prewitt drew an analogy between the process of leadership selection and a Chinese Box puzzle in which a few governors were gradually and continuously winnowed from the general citizenry. In Prewitt's scheme successively smaller boxes, representing segments of the population, nested inside each other with the smallest and innermost box containing elected officials. Each stage, in his formulation, had its own distinctive dynamic and its own theoretical construct that traced how the many eventually were narrowed down to a few (1970, 7–10). First, the pool of eligible individuals was created through processes of social stratification to create a dominant group in accordance with *socially based leadership theory*. These citizens then were exposed to networks of political activists and salient events, some joining the ranks of activists themselves in a process encompassed by *theories of socialization and mobilization*. From among the activists, a few were apprenticed and groomed to be candidates for public office, as predicted by *recruitment theory*. Finally, a few officeholders were chosen in accordance with *electoral theory*.

The major area of research on candidacy for process scholars was the middle box: recruitment. This focus derived from the conclusions of Wahlke and his colleagues (1962) noted earlier that processes of stratification and socialization could only be inferred from observations of the social characteristics of those already in the leadership echelon. Recruitment, on the other hand, was more open to the scrutiny of researchers because it focused on those already in the political realm and the observable channels they pursued to elective office. In Prewitt's scheme, recruitment theory attempted to explain "how the politically ambitious focus on political offices and how political institutions fill the many posts that keep institutions operating" (1970, 11). It was essentially a theory of careers, much like Wahlke and Eulau's, in its embrace of both individual variables (such as social background and experiences, personal affiliations, political positions, and career expectations) and institutional parameters. These latter included legal arrangements, such as the requirement for nonpartisan election, and screening agencies, such as interest groups, incumbents, and parties.

However, like most process-based models of politics, Prewitt's formulation was more of a diagram than an explanatory theory. He was vague about precisely what went on in the boxes and how the procedural flow from one box to the other actually took place. Furthermore, he was unclear about how he derived the criteria for defining the patterns associated with each box and which conditions were necesssary and/or sufficient for the particular stage to take place. Most important, he asserted that each box was governed by its own theory but failed to specify how the separate theories related to each other. In sum, Prewitt's analysis provided a rich overview of the many different kinds of behavior that surround candidacy, but it was more effective as a classification scheme than as a theory.

The most influential attempt at constructing a theory of individual political careers was Joseph Schlesinger's (1966) comprehensive analysis of the opportunity structures leading to statewide and federal office. Schlesinger started with the premise that elections could serve as controls on the behavior of public officials if and only if politicians had a strong motivation to seek and retain elective office. Ambition, then, was the key to governmental accountability, and all else depended on the polity's ability to inspire and channel it. Schlesinger further assumed that political ambition would not develop and flourish unless there were feasible outlets for its expression. From these two premises, it followed that the structure of political opportunity held the key to candidacy.

Schlesinger's most important contribution was his explicit incorporation of institutional and contextual variables into a theory of candidacy. He wrote, "We can develop a theory of ambition only if we adopt reasonable assumptions about when such ambitions occur. The most reasonable assumption is that ambition for office, like most other ambitions, develops with a specific situation, that it is a response to the possibilities which lie before the politician" (1966, 8). Schlesinger then demonstrated that the number of opportunities to run for office and the structure of party competition influenced the level of aspiration among officeholders. This in turn led to identifiable patterns for statewide officeholders, although not in the majority of states or for the House of Representatives.[3]

This emphasis on individual ambition later made Schlesinger the patron saint of the rational choice theorists, because he saw personal goals as a major key to understanding political outcomes. Instead of focusing on the social bases of recruitment or the role of elites in

---

3. Although Schlesinger's work has had a profound influence on congressional scholars, he did not apply his arguments or empirical analysis to the House.

apprenticing and grooming promising newcomers, as earlier recruitment theorists had done, he concentrated on the constraints of candidacy imposed by a state's opportunity structure. Moreover, he distinguished among *discrete, static,* and *progressive ambitions* to define
different types of political career paths.[4] Despite the purposive behavior inherent in Schlesinger's model, however, I think he properly
belongs in the category of process-oriented scholars because the dependent variable in his analysis is not the individual's decision to run
but the presence or absence of processes and structures that permit
ambition to follow its course.

Schlesinger's primary concern was the existence of stable ladders
of advancement so that prospective candidates could make reasonable
estimates about their chances for success. The very notion of opportunity structures is, in fact, predicated on the assumption that the
polity has defined a process for aspiring politicians to pursue and
that success is conferred on those who follow the prescribed route.
The candidates do not establish the ladders themselves, nor did
Schlesinger suggest that they can alter them. Instead, he hypothesized
that opportunity structures are determined by the institutional and
political environment within the states—the number of base offices,
the strength of the party organizations, and so forth. Most important,
Schlesinger confined his empirical analysis to demonstrating that such
structures exist; he did not go the next step to show how they affect
the candidate pool within states or how they influence politicians'
decisions whether or not to run. In my view, what would move
Schlesinger fully into the rational choice camp would be an examination of opportunity structures as strategic variables—how their stability, complexity, or predictability influenced the supply of candidates
and the decision not to seek office.

Like earlier theorists, however, Schlesinger assumed the existence of an eligible population of politically ambitious people. Thus,
he could not account for the candidacies of the states in his study that
lacked opportunity structures. In these respects, then, his theory is not
a theory of ambition at all but a theory of political careers. Furthermore, although Schlesinger recognized three types of ambition, he
was not able to predict what types of individuals (or states) would

---

4. By discrete ambition, Schlesinger (1966) meant politicians who briefly held a
single office before returning to private life. By static ambition, he meant politicians who
held the same office, but only that office, for a period of time. By progressive ambition, he
meant politicians who sought ever higher levels of office. Thus, a state legislator who was
elected to Congress and served the remainder of his or her political career there would have
manifested both progressive and static ambition.

manifest these different orientations toward public office or to explain why such varying career patterns arose. In the end, the individual preferences for political office, while essential to the logic of Schlesinger's model of office seeking, were nevertheless outside its operation.

Following in Schlesinger's footsteps, Mezey (1970) endeavored to map the career ladders of House members. He demonstrated that states with strong party organizations tended to produce more experienced candidates, a pattern that both Haeberle (1985) and Kunkel (1988) confirmed in subsequent analyses. Furthermore, Mayhew (1986) demonstrated that the level of party competition in a state was related to the incidence of primary contests for House seats, and Schlesinger (1985) showed how the rise of the GOP in the South raised competition for Senate seats and reduced the incidence of uncontested House races.

In sum, Schlesinger's attempt to explain individual careers led him straight to political institutions. His blending of the two facets of recruitment was a major breakthrough and remains the most ambitious and successful effort at modeling the interaction of microlevel and macrolevel aspects of candidacy even today. Schlesinger's findings were also relevant to the other strand of recruitment theory Prewitt identified—the institutions and organized agencies that channelled eligible participants into apprenticeships and eventually into electoral competition.

It was inevitable that the observation of political parties would be central to the study of recruitment because of the legal necessity of acquiring a party label for candidates to get on the ballot. Schlesinger's demonstration that party systems mattered therefore fit nicely with another strand of the process-oriented literature—the overall concern with political parties, particularly the general failure of responsible party government in the fragmented American system.

Although scholars writing in this tradition drew heavily from Wahlke et al. (1962), they were also influenced by V. O. Key's classic works on political parties (1949 and 1958). Having defined the nomination of candidates as a prime function of parties (1958, 345), Key and many others were troubled by what they saw as a lack of involvement in recruitment. He observed, "To assert that party leadership develops candidates is more an attribution of a duty noted in the textbooks than a description of real activity" (1956, 271). Thus, a central concern in this literature was the extent to which candidate recruitment and nomination contributed to the decentralized decision making inside Congress and the lack of responsible party government in the American polity.

Several scholars examined how party leaders carried out their textbook task of enlisting and grooming candidates (Seligman 1961; Sorauf 1963; Snowiss 1966; Huckshorn and Spencer 1971; Seligman et al. 1974), and their work confirmed Key's gloomy conclusions. Congressional candidacy was particularly at odds with the presumption that parties should develop candidates because congressional districts typically involved multiple counties or cut across county lines and because congressional offices brought little in the way of patronage into local party headquarters. House candidates consequently were often orphans inside the party organization when it came time to distribute campaign resources, and once in office they could afford to remain apart from party politics because no one county chair could determine their political futures.

In a study of candidate recruitment in the Chicago area, Snowiss (1966) provided a detailed picture of how differences in party recruitment at the local level translated into distinctive patterns of partisanship on Capitol Hill. Lawmakers who worked their way up through the ranks of the famous Daly machine to eventually gain a safe seat in Chicago's inner city proved themselves to be loyal Democrats in Washington with a decided propensity for pragmatic compromise and pork barrel policies. In contrast, lawmakers who gained nominations in the more fluid party environment of the Chicago suburbs tended to be political entrepreneurs and proved themselves more independent and more issue oriented once in office.

However, as scholars delved more deeply into the interaction between individual candidacies and party elites, they concluded that the institutional and organizational side of recruitment was less significant in explaining congressional candidacies than the attitudes of office seekers. Surveys of candidates by Kingdon (1968), Leuthold (1968), Sullivan and O'Connor (1972), and Fishel (1973) all demonstrated that individual motivations and expectations were critical in differentiating winners and losers. This disjuncture between the survey data on the one hand and Schlesinger's aggregate results on the other had important consequences for the theory of candidacy. It turned scholars' attention to individual calculation and focused their attention exclusively on the unfolding of political careers. Ironically, Schlesinger, the institutionalist, came to be seen as the father of rational choice theories of candidacy, and the stage was set for the purposive actor—the self-starter, the freebooting entrepreneur, the strategic politician—so familiar to congressional scholars today. This autonomous individual is now at the core of theoretical and empirical work on candidacy, which appropriately bears the name of ambition theory.

The Rational Actor Tradition

The rational actor tradition of candidacy treats decisions about running for office as a relatively straightforward calculation of costs and benefits discounted by the perceived probability of winning (Black 1972; Levine and Hyde 1977; Rohde 1979; Brace 1984; Abramson, Aldrich, and Rohde 1987; Banks and Kiewiet 1989). The equation below gives the key elements:

$$U(O) = p(B) - (1-p)C$$

This simple expected utility model predicts that an individual will run if $U(O)$ is positive, which occurs when the estimated probability of success (p) is high, when the perceived benefits of the office (B) are great, and/or when the costs of losing (C) are low. Alternatively, one can argue that a positive outcome occurs when candidates are tolerant of risk and do not require a "fair" lottery to induce them to run (Fowler 1979). Either way, the logic of the decision is the same.

The methodological individualism underlying this approach makes sense because so many congressional candidates are self-starting entrepreneurs. But the rational actor theory of candidacy has several limitations, some of which are endemic to rational choice theory and some of which are the result of the particular questions theorists have asked.

Like all purposive theories of behavior, the rational actor paradigm of candidacy treats individual preferences as a taste whose origins are not relevant. As long as prospective candidates can rank order their desires for various public offices vis-à-vis the status quo, the analyst is free to concentrate on the selection of *means* to maximize the most preferred goal. Consequently, if the individual runs, one simply infers that $p(B)$ turned out to be greater than $(1-p)C$. This means that a rational actor theory of candidacy can have no provision for explaining where the initial desire for public office came from or why the calculation turned out positively for one individual and negatively for another.

Some of the best empirical work on candidacy that uses the cost-benefit framework profitably exploits this theoretical weakness in examining the progressive ambition of particular groups of officeholders. Both Rohde (1979) and Brace (1984) started with a pool of similarly situated individuals—House members—and assumed that they all have a desire to win election as senators or governors if they could do so without cost. Abramson, Aldrich, and Rohde (1987) adopted a similar stance in examining the aspirations of senators for the presidency. By holding ambition constant, these scholars were free to hypothsize about a variety of independent variables that affected the p term and distinguished actual candidates from potential aspirants. Thus, they could predict the likelihood that a House member or senator would attempt to move up the ladder, given certain conditions. The results of these studies demonstrated that within a particular opportunity structure—House to Senate or Senate to presidency—progressive ambition was highly variable and dependent on the presence of an incumbent; such personal factors as seniority, age, party label, propensities for risk-taking, prior electoral margins, and political liabilities from past actions; or such constituency factors as district size, competitiveness, and reapportionment. However, because ambition was controlled in these studies there is no way of telling the relative weight of each factor in comparison to the influence of the opportunity structure itself.

If the rational actor theory of candidacy helps to explain particular cases of office seeking, it is less applicable to the emergence of political amateurs. Canon (1990a) has argued that amateurs are drawn to public office with very different objectives and political characteristics in mind. Some are "ambitious" amateurs, some "policy" amateurs, and others "hopeless" amateurs, differences not readily predicted by existing theory. Canon contended that the calculations amateurs make are fundamentally different from those incumbent officeholders make because giving up one office for another is not comparable to the decision to move from the private sector into public life. For these reasons, Canon concluded that the rational actor model is not a theory of candidacy but a theory of "progressive ambition."[5]

Canon's concerns gained credence from his demonstration that a sizeable percentage of inexperienced candidates win seats in Congress: over 25 percent in the House and 20 percent in the Senate (1990a, 2). But Canon's analysis foundered, too, on the meaning of ambition because his attempt to explain the differences between ama-

---

5. In purely formal terms, Canon's criticism is not valid because the rational actor model does not make interpersonal comparisons among candidates but simply requires that they evaluate the value of a particular office vis-à-vis the status quo. It is in devising measures of the costs and benefits of running that scholars applying the rational actor model encounter the problem Canon raises.

tuers and experienced candidates for the House and Senate produced two curious anomalies. First, some candidates who lacked prior officeholding credentials turned out to be quite successful at the polls and therefore were hardly distinguishable from their more experienced peers. These Canon labeled as "ambitious amateurs" on the basis of their having run for Congress before or having gained at least 40 percent of the vote. But their very existence and the fact that Canon was compelled to define them in such an ad hoc fashion is a telling example of why theorists need to pay more attention to the origins of ambition in congressional elections.

Second, Canon observed that amateurs tended to be more successful during periods of political change marked by presidential landslides (1990a, 67). Under such favorable conditions, progressive ambition, not amateurism, is supposed to flourish, as seasoned politicians take advantage of the boost in the p term. Yet Canon was not able to account for the unexpected frequency of amateur victories within the framework of ambition theory. Instead, he speculated that in one-party areas, the minority has such a small pool of talent from which to draw that amateurs can obtain nominations without having to compete with more experienced candidates. In making this argument, however, Canon altered the thrust of ambition theory from individual calculation to political structures. Thus, he posed a tough question for rational choice theorists about where congressional ambition comes from and why districts produce different mixes of amateur and experienced competitors in House races.

Rational choice scholars have compounded the problems inherent in treating ambition as a given because they have been inattentive to parameters other than p in the cost-benefit model. The size of the B term, for example, is a key component of these models, but theorists have not controlled for the factors that might cause it to vary. The same criticism applies to variation in the C term.

Recently, Lascher (1989) attacked this particular deficiency of the rational actor tradition in explaining political careers.[6] Drawing on theories from industrial psychology, Lascher argued that job satisfaction is an important component of the decision to seek reelection or to move on to other types of office and that gratification from elective office does not simply arise from people's heads or hearts. In examining the attitudes and career paths of California supervisors, he uncov-

---

6. Lascher (1989) has measured variation in the B term for California supervisors through survey responses. He finds that job satisfaction is a key component in supervisors' continuance in public office.

ered a number of contextual influences that affected how these legislators evaluated their positions. His (1989, 27) finding that supervisors with the highest job satisfaction were the most likely to evidence progressive ambition independent of the opportunity structure in the community led him to conclude that political scientists need to think more systematically about the variables that affect perceptions about the rewards of particular public offices.

An additional shortcoming of the way rational choice theories have been applied to candidacy has been the absence of provisions controlling for the intervention of other actors or events. A variety of theoretical tools within the family of rational actor models—game theory, decision analysis, even linear programing—could be applied to the interactive behavior that shapes the decision to run, but with the exception of an article by Banks and Kieweit (1989), discussed in the next section of this chapter, no one has undertaken such modes of analysis by excluding the strategic calculations of other players in the decision to run, theorists have relegated them by default to the p term, whose value is solely a function of the perceptions of the prospective candidate. In other words, p is a *subjective probablity estimate,* not a sample parameter of the true distribution of events.

The problem with excluding interaction effects in the cost-benefit model stems from the fact that would-be candidates are not autonomous decision makers. Contexts and rules determine who can think about public office and how many potential competitors will be interested in the same positions. These objective conditions, rather than the subjective estimates, dominate the size and composition of the candidate pool, which in turn have a profound impact on the perceived costs, benefits, and probabilities associated with a particular race. In sum, Richard Fenno's dictum that politicians are "both goal-seeking and situation-interpreting individuals" (1986, 4) is especially apt when applied to candidacy. It is therefore necessary that a theory of candidate decision making systematically account for situational influences.

The theorists' task is hindered because the interaction among prospective candidates and political elites has proved extremely difficult to specify. As the process-oriented scholars have demonstrated, not only do activists directly influence candidates' decisions to run, but they affect who is in a position to make that calculation. Moreover, political elites are themselves affected by the pool of available talent; they may clear the way for someone whom they think is going to be successful without their help or back a loser who is the only available alternative. In this respect, political elites are both exogenous and endogenous to the winnowing process, and the causal arrows in such a complex relationship seem to run in both directions. Candidates themselves have added to the muddle by distorting the role of their political supporters, exhibiting "congratulation effects" if they have been successful, and assigning blame if they have lost (Kingdon 1968; Huckshorn and Spencer 1971). Furthermore, it is often unclear how support is distributed during the prenomination phases of candidacy, because this is a relatively invisible, unconscious, and uncoordinated process that takes place over a long period of time (Fowler and McClure 1989).

Given these many ambiguities, the absence of a theoretical framework for thinking about the interaction of candidates and elites has contributed to a long and, so far, fruitless debate over the measurement of "quality" candidates in congressional elections, which I shall take up in the next chapter. It is possible to ascertain after the fact whom elites regarded as strong candidates by examining their pattern of campaign contributions (cf. Abramowitz 1991; Jacobson 1990a), and it is simple to pick winners after the election is over. But such tautological thinking hardly advances the capacity of scholars to ascertain how and why competitive candidates appear at a particular place and time. Thus, candidacy cannot be fully understood unless this simultaneous process of approval and elimination is addressed. As Fishel has observed, "For better or worse, political systems are as distinguished by who they reject as who they accept" (1973, 2).

Last, and perhaps most important, the rational actor paradigm gives us a static view of the decision to run for Congress. The way the equation is set up, it provides a snapshot of the prospective office seeker's utility calculus at a particular moment. It lacks any provision for predicting how the individual calculus of office seeking has changed over time. Moreover, it leaves out the systemic affects of social and economic transformations that can affect the aggregate choices of candidates. In this respect, the rational actor approach to candidacy fails to account for long-term trends associated with eligibility, motivation, elite influence, and institutional structures.

This is a failing common to purposive models in general, because the logic of utility maximization leads to the search for an equilibrium. In any given election cycle, the static quality of the theory is not a particular problem because the rules of the game do not change very often or very rapidly, and short-term shocks such as presidential popularity or the state of the economy are easily identified, even if they have turned out to be difficult to measure. But over time, local contexts do change with redistricting and population shifts, organizations and activists do alter their strategic objectives and tactics, and patterns of social stratification do evolve. The example of Mike Espy in Mississippi taught us that.

As a practical matter, scholars who use the rational actor theory of candidacy have endeavored to overcome some of the shortcomings of the cost-benefit formulation in their empirical work. Most have used contextual variables as surrogate measures of candidates' subjective probablity estimates or their assessment of the costs and benefits of running. Rohde (1979), for example, showed how the overlap in constituencies affects the likelihood that House members will run for the Senate. Stewart (1989) used a similar measure to predict the frequency of experienced Senate candidates. Brace (1984) and Abramson, Aldrich, and Rohde (1987) found significant relationships between the decision to seek higher office and such variables as the availability of other opportunities or the presence of political liabilities, such as freshman status. Furthermore, several scholars have found that party strength in a state or district is significantly related to the quality of House and Senate challengers (Stewart 1989; Canon 1990b; Bond, Covington, and Fleisher 1985; Krasno and Green 1988; Jacobson 1990b). Finally, Jacobson and Kernell (1981) demonstrated that national events, specifically the popularity of the president and the performance of the economy, exerted a powerful pull on candidate ambitions (see also Jacobson 1987b and 1989).

These efforts rest primarily on a commonsense reading of what matters to politicians, however, rather than a theoretical construct that specifies the relevant independent variables and their relationship to candidacy. We might be satisfied with such tinkering under certain conditions: if ambition were randomly distributed throughout the population; if it were fixed early in life by psychological need or social experience, so that it could be treated as a constant; or if the rules of the game operated neutrally for all candidates. Then we might be happy with the parsimony of a model that frames candidacy as the act of autonomous political entrepreneurs. But we have seen from the discussion of other scholarly traditions, as well as from the rational choice scholars, that there are sound reasons for presuming that ambition varies with the social and political environment and the individual's relation to that environment. In sum, the cost-benefit approach to ambition has proved extremely useful in making predictions about the likelihood of career shifts among well-defined pools of incumbent officeholders. But taken as a whole, it has had the effect of removing from the equation most of the interesting variation in candidates' decisions to run.

The Rule-Based Tradition

Recently, several scholars have begun to modify the rational actor theory of office seeking by incorporating rules and institutions into their models of candidate behavior. This perspective is a natural outgrowth of the "new institutionalism" that has arisen among formal theorists in the discipline, and it is an obvious throughback to Schlesinger. One study, by Banks and Kiewiet (1989), is a sophisticated mathematical analysis of the impact of primaries on prospective House candidates. The other, by Canon (1990b), is a more impressionistic treatment of how external influences on the supply of prospective candidates shape the capacity of individuals to run for Congress. Although both analyses focus primarily on the individual candidates' decisions to run, each offers interesting perspectives on how candidacy is contingent on the size and composition of the candidate pool and how the pool in turn is affected by external constraints and structures.

Banks and Kiewiet (1989) started with a paradox: that inexperienced candidates are more likely than experienced candidates to challenge incumbent House members even though they have a lower probability of success. They argued that the cost-benefit formulation of candidacy accurately predicts the propensity of experienced officeholders to wait for an open seat when the chances of victory are higher. But they noted that it only fits the case of inexperienced challengers when scholars posit unusually large rewards from the act of running or assume that challengers are more likely to delude themselves about the true value of p, B and C (cf. Fowler 1979 and 1980). In short, the cost-benefit model accounts for the candidacy of the largest group of competitors—inexperienced challengers—by treating them as less rational than other types of candidates.

The two scholars resolved this puzzle by exploiting the sequential nature of the candidacy decision created by party primaries. Because so few candidates ever get elected to Congress through write-ins and virtually all open seat races have primaries, the problem for the inexperienced candidate is gaining his or her party's nomination. In this two-stage process, the likelihood of beating an experienced opponent in the primary is so low that the rational amateur who wants to run for Congress will bypass the open seat race and take the low odds of challenging the incumbent. In short, the *conditional probability* of winning for inexperienced candidates is higher when they do not have to compete in a primary. An analysis of primaries between 1980 and 1984 confirmed this expectation, for inexperienced candidates seldom contested primaries in which experienced candidates were present while they predominated in races against incumbents (Banks and Kiewet 1989, 1011). Furthermore, the great majority of amateurs elected to Congress obtained their offices by defeating an incumbent—often on the second try (1989, 1012).[7]

Banks and Kiewet derived a plausible explanation for a seeming anomaly among congressional candidates through the use of game theory. In effect, they constructed a two-person game in which an inexperienced candidate calculates a mini-max strategy against a more qualified opponent in his or her party. Furthermore, they demonstrated that no matter what strategy an inexperienced candidate chooses, it is always optimal for an experienced contestant to wait for the open seat. Their work suggests a promising avenue for richer and more complex theories of candidate strategies—theories that encompass the competitive interaction of maximizing individuals under conditions of uncertainty. More generally, their successful exploitation of the sequential nature of candidacy in calculating the probability of success gives their model a dynamic character that is typically lacking in conventional rational actor models.

Canon (1990b) incorporated political institutions and contexts into a model of political change that attempts to account for the emergence of strong Republican contenders for Senate seats in the South. His concern was the secular realignment in the region—the gradual shift in party attachments among voters toward the Republican Party—and how it has changed the career calculations of prospective Senate candidates. In effect, Canon tried to integrate a macrolevel phenomenon that shows up in aggregate voting behavior with an individual-level change in the competitiveness of Republican candidates for the Senate. He did this through the simple schematic diagram shown in figure 3.1.

In Canon's view of party realignment, competitive candidates arise when a variety of local electoral contexts combine to create a greater likelihood of winning, such as the increase in partisan identification and the development of an effective organization. When short-term effects, such as national conditions or changes in the incumbent's performance, combine to favor prospective candidates with

---

7. See also Squire and Smith's (1984) analysis of the success rate of repeat challengers.

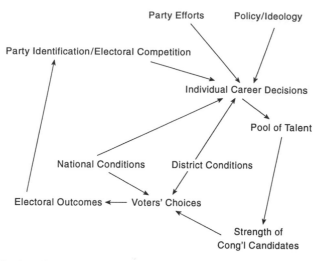

Fig. 3.1. A model of elite-driven secular realignment. (*Source:* Canon 1992, 79.)

certain political beliefs, then the pool of talent expands. But as the strength of candidates increases, Canon argued, this reinforces the trend toward realignment by encouraging voters to stick with the new party and its attractive standard-bearers.

Canon's model of the connection between candidates and electoral change is intriguing, even though it is not rigorously specified. Three features of this model make it particularly significant for the development of a more comprehensive theory of candidacy. First, it imbeds the individual candidate in a complex but realistic context, giving explicit recognition to the dynamic aspect of ambition. In doing so, it enables us to begin to think systematically about the various types of influences that induce politically active people to extend themselves into the realm of candidacy. Second, it links electoral outcomes to changes in the candidate pool in explicit recognition that parties, no matter how favored by national events or local conditions, cannot beat somebody with nobody. Third, it offers an intriguing causal connection between the capacity of parties to field strong candidates and their ability to turn voter predispositions into more permanent attachments.[8]

---

8. Several other researchers have begun to think about the connection between the political environment and the quality of the candidate pool as it pertains to the likelihood of state legislators seeking congressional seats. See research proposals by Fowler et al. (1988) and Francis (1991).

Implications

Several generations of scholars have attempted to develop a theory of candidacy. The recruitment theorists have stressed the systemic, environmental, and procedural determinants of candidacy, whereas the ambition theorists have emphasized the strategic calculations of individual candidates. Taken as a whole, their work provides a framework for thinking about congressional candidates both as products of a particular social setting, time, and place and as strategic actors. But it does so in a piecemeal fashion and without specifiying the connecting mechanisms that link the two aspects of candidacy together.

Moreover, both groups of theorists have shared a common focus: the description and explanation of career paths of incumbent officeholders. They took this path early and have pursued it consistently for many years, in large part because of constraints on the observation and measurement of prospective candidates. Incumbents could be analyzed, whereas potential office seekers, who were winnowed out before the public competition of nominating conventions and primaries, proved elusive. However, scholars paid a price for such convenience because they forwarded a conception of ambition that was incapable of dealing with changes in the supply of candidates.

Some might label these two features of the theoretical literature as defects, but I take them as evidence of how difficult it is to construct a comprehensive theory of candidacy. Candidates not only are purposive actors in the American system but also are acted on by numerous participants and events in the electoral arena. In this sense, their ambition for office is conceptually analogous to partisan identification among voters—it determines behavior while responding to actions of political elites and to conditions within the economic and social environment.[9] To push the analogy one step farther, the inability of scholars to reconcile the purposive and conditional dimensions of candidacy is quite similar to the conflict among students of voting behavior about the rational versus social origins of partisanship and the long-term relationship of party identification to governmental performance. Thus, acknowledging the separate strands of recruitment theory, just as with partisan identification, may not necessarily lead to their synthesis into a new paradigm of candidacy.

Yet there are several avenues of inquiry that may move us closer

---

9. I am indebted to an anonymous reviewer of this manuscript for suggesting this analogy.

to the integration of the diverse intellectual traditions that the theoretical literature on candidates comprises. First, there is a great need to recast theories of ambition to encompass the full range of candidate behavior beyond the progressive ambition of incumbents. In effect, that means greater emphasis on the supply side of candidacy. What differentiates potential candidates from declared candidates? What factors determine the size and composition of the pool of potential candidates, and what makes it vary across constituencies? What structures and contexts account for variation in political experience among prospective officeholders? Finally, how does the supply of candidates for Congress adapt over time to broad social and institutional changes, such as the professionalization of state legislatures or the political mobilization of women and ethnic minorities?

Equally important is an understanding of the interaction of candidates with other actors. A model of the sequence of decisions to run for Congress could be fruitful in two respects: first, in explicating the decision nodes that set ambitious politicians on one office-seeking path as opposed to another and, second, in illuminating the relationship of time-dependent personal characteristics, such as age or experience, to existing opportunity structures. In addition, it is critical to pursue the strategic calculations of candidates within an N-person environment. Given the multiple steps that typically lead to candidacy for Congress, ambitious politicians constantly assess and reassess the motives and strategies of potential supporters and rivals. It is therefore imperative that scholars understand the configuration of payoffs at various stages of candidates' deliberations that affects their ability to pursue elective office.

A possible starting point to merge the structural and strategic aspects of candidacy is to reexamine Schlesinger's work on ambition. For too long, scholars have focused on the goal-oriented logic of his model of opportunity structures, but the larger lesson in his classic study is the idea of institutional constraint—that politicians can only achieve their objectives when institutions favor their ambitions and when they match their strategies to the existing rules of the game. Schlesinger confined his analysis to the office-seeking behavior of incumbents, but his logic could readily be adapted to the supply side of candidacy. Similarly, he considered only a few of the possible structural constraints on candidacy, but his list could be easily expanded to include a broader set of factors.

As I survey other domains of the congressional literature, I see models of constrained goal-seeking behavior developing under the rubric of the *new institutionalism*. With the notable exception of the

Banks and Kiewiet (1989) study, a similar analytical approach has been conspicuously absent from the literature on candidacy and recruitment. Should the new institutionalism take root in this corner of American politics, however, it will surely need to be less concerned with finding stable equilibria and more attuned to explaining change—in the ambitions of prospective office seekers, in the supply of eligible competitors, and in the environment that governs their emergence.

Perhaps we will never truly understand how the microlevel calculations of individual candidates respond to macrolevel conditions, but until scholars make an effort to ground candidacy within the broader social and political contexts that affect ambition, they will get no further than the rather limited theory of incumbent careerism that characterizes the literature at present.

CHAPTER 4

Candidates and Congressional Elections

> . . . if a group of planners sat down and tried to design a pair
> of American national assemblies with the goal of serving members'
> electoral needs year in and year out, they would be hard pressed
> to improve on what exists.
>
> —David Mayhew, *Congress: The Electoral Connection*

By constitutional design and long practice, congressional elections
have allowed the public to vent its feelings about the national government. Every two years, voters can use House and Senate elections as a
referendum on the president's performance, the health of the economy, or the general state of the union, and they have availed themselves of this opportunity for much of the nation's history. The referendum pattern has been less pronounced in Senate races because of
the chamber's staggered terms, but it has been quite prevalent in
House contests. Such trends as the coincidence between presidential
and congressional shares of the two-party vote, the phenomenon of
midterm loss for the president's party and the connection between
party fortunes and various economic indicators have all tended to
confirm Lord Bryce's observation of a century ago that "the election
of every second Congress . . . enables the people to express their
approval or disapproval of [the president's] conduct by sending up
another House of Representatives which may support or oppose the
policy he has followed" (quoted in Jacobson and Kernell 1981, 60).

Contemporary congressional elections, however, no longer fit
this simple characterization. In many respects, they now operate according to their own rhythms and rules—an increasingly idiosyncratic
mix of individualism, incumbency, and localism that makes many
electoral contests both uncompetitive and unresponsive to the public
mood. Indeed, the results of congressional elections today are nearly
the opposite of what the framers intended, with the House enjoying
extraordinary reelection rates and one-party dominance and the Senate
experiencing relatively higher turnover and more frequent shifts in
party control.

In attempting to assess the transformation of congressional elections from national referenda to idiosyncratic events, scholars have examined three closely related phenomena, each of which is closely connected to candidacy: (1) the decline of competition in House elections, (2) the role of political elites in nationalizing congressional campaigns, and (3) the persistence of divided party control of the federal government. The power of incumbency is a common concern in each of these literatures, but what distinguishes them is the relative independence attributed to challengers and voters in determining electoral outcomes. At issue is whether candidates—particularly incumbents—control their own political fates or whether they are constrained by patterns of recruitment and public expectation that are beyond their control.

The scholars working in this field subscribe nearly unanimously to the rational actor paradigm of candidacy. Their research agenda therefore focuses on the strategic aspects of individual candidacies and tends to produce explanations of election results that are either incumbent driven or challenger driven. Consequently, contexts and rules are generally ignored, and interactive effects among competing elites are typically overlooked in this literature. A heavy reliance on cross-sectional data and relatively short time-series further limits the scope of the research. Thus, although scholars have endeavored to account for the decoupling of congressional elections from national trends, they have given limited attention to local factors other than incumbency. And although their studies are aimed at explaining long-term patterns in congressional elections, their methods rarely yield dynamic models of electoral change.

Such shortcomings are inherent in the rational actor theory of ambition, as I have noted in the previous chapter, but taken together, they create a strikingly ambiguous portrait of candidates in congressional elections. In some of the analyses I review here, candidacy appears as an exogenous influence on electoral outcomes, while in others it is clearly endogenous, and in still others, it seems to be both. Over the long run, resolving these contradictions will require a more comprehensive theory of candidate decision making. In the short run, however, it is necessary to examine the various ways that candidates figure in the literature on congressional elections.

The Decline of Competition

The decline of competition in congressional elections is manifest in high reelection rates for incumbents, lopsided margins of victory, and increasing numbers of uncontested House races. Although the variance in the outcomes of presidential elections has declined, signifying a relatively uniform sweep of national forces across the country, just the opposite phenomenon has occurred in House elections (Kawato 1987, 1241). Presidents have diminished coattails and have consequently suffered fewer losses in the off year. Indeed, the estimated district-level component of the two-party vote has reached unprecedented highs over the past two decades (Jacobson 1989 and 1990b, 56), and partisan defections have heavily penalized challengers (Jacobson 1992b, 115). Thus, for most of the 1980s incumbents were relatively immune from the ebb and flow of popular sentiment, and even though their election margins diminished in 1990 and 1992, they still won in overwhelming numbers.

From a historical perspective, the decline in competition represents a significant departure from the traditional role congressional elections have played in reflecting economic and political currents in the polity. Although House elections have always had a sizeable local component (Vertz, Frendreis, and Gibson 1987), they have also evidenced long-standing statistical relationships between economic performance and the two-party division of the vote (Kramer 1971; Tufte 1975) as well as the shift in seats (Oppenheimer, Stimson, and Waterman 1986; Marra and Ostrom 1989; Waterman 1990; Simon, Ostrom, and Marra 1991). An even longer historical connection existed between the presidential and congressional vote, punctuated, of course, with periodic realignments that gave one party a dominant position in both branches of government (Brady 1988). The reduction of such strong regularities in the American political landscape has therefore become a source of considerable scholarly concern (cf. Burnham 1982; Fiorina 1984).

The referendum effect occurred in the past because partisanship exercised such strong influence over the vote decision in congressional elections. Survey research in the 1950s, for example, revealed voters to be so ignorant of their representatives in Congress and so disinterested in their lawmakers' roll calls that the voting decision seemed inseparable from partisanship. According to the "surge and decline" theory of voting in congressional elections (Campbell 1967), citizens were drawn to the polls by the excitement of presidential politics and cast their vote in accordance with their preferences for the top of the ticket. Two years later, they either stayed home or returned to the party fold to which they had been socialized as children. As Stokes and Miller noted in their study of the 1958 election, "The condition of no information [in House elections] leads to fairly unrelieved party-line voting" (1967, 204). Indeed, they reported that roughly 84 percent of all House votes "were cast by party identifiers supporting their parties" (1967, 198).

More recently, however, the influence of party has waned, and the emphasis on candidates has become more pronounced. Voters appear to be moved by the individual attributes of the contestants, such as their name recognition, experience and personality traits (Mann 1978; Mann and Wolfinger 1980; Hinckley 1980; Jacobson 1987b and 1992b; Cain, Fiorina, and Ferejohn 1987; Abramowitz 1975 and 1988). Not only do citizens' likes and dislikes about individual candidates carry more weight than party in some estimates of the vote choice (Jacobson and Kernell 1981, 16), but their satisfaction with the constituency service provided by the legislator increasingly leads to a "personal vote" that depends less on national policy concerns (Cain, Fiorina, and Ferejohn 1987). Moreover, as House and Senate contests have grown more complex and expensive, the candidates' skill in overseeing a sophisticated organization of pollsters, fundraisers, direct mail experts, and volunteers is a critical election variable (Stewart 1989; Herrnson 1989; Squire 1991). Both the electorate's choice and the caliber of the campaign thus increasingly depend on who runs.

The impact of candidate-centered politics is manifest in the increasing frequency of divided results at all levels of government—for the House and the president, state legislators and governors, and even senators of the same state (Jacobson 1990b; Fiorina 1991; Cox and Kernell 1991; Westlye 1992). Moreover, it is expressed in the shrinkage of the base party vote in House constituencies, despite the fact that party identification increased during the 1980s (Jacobson 1990b, 42). In fact, these patterns have led Gary Jacobson to speculate that citizens increasingly take their cues about partisanship not from their family or social milieu but from their perceptions about the relative attractiveness of candidates at the top of the ticket (1990b, 128).

Yet vestiges of the old regularities have remained as partisanship and national tides continue to influence both particular races and aggregate outcomes. Party identification is still a strong predictor of the vote choice (Jacobson 1992b; Keith et al. 1992, 72), and presidents still have some coattails (Campbell 1990; Jacobson 1992b, Simon, Ostrom, and Marra 1991). Major issues, such as the economy, continue to shape attitudes toward candidates and parties (Jacobson 1990a and 1992a; Wyckoff and Dran 1992). Indeed, in a comparison of five different levels of election—Senate, House, governor, and upper and lower state legislatures—Simon, Ostrom, and Marra (1991) found the most pronounced referendum effects for the House. However, they concluded that the considerable variation in the relative strength of the variables across equations indicated that other influences were also at work (1991, 1188). The combination of these old and new patterns raises perplexing questions for congressional scholars: how much have individual candidacies transformed House and Senate races and what is behind the apparent shift?

Some scholars see the changes as quite significant and attribute them to reelection-minded incumbents. Members of Congress, they argue, have become consummate entrepreneurs who use the perquisites of their office to create a demand for their services and who control campaign resources so disproportionately that they suppress the supply of challengers. By manipulating voter preferences and potential competitors, incumbents are able to insulate themselves from shifting partisan tides and national events. In this model, ambition for reelection among incumbents is the prime mover of electoral change and all else falls before it.

The empirical case for incumbent-driven outcomes depends on two different types of evidence: period effects in the pattern of electoral competition, which presumably coincide with alterations in incumbent goals, and manipulation by incumbents of electoral resources and voter preferences. However, neither of these explanations has proved conclusive, and each has serious drawbacks. Consequently, some congressional scholars have turned to the phenomenon of weak challengers as an explanation for the decline in electoral competition.

These analysts contend that the supply of prospective candidates has diminished, or at least is poorly matched against available opportunities to run for Congress. They do not deny the power of incumbency as an influence in the willingness of qualified candidates to run, but they tend to regard it as a necessary rather than sufficient condition for decreasing competition. However, weak challengers have derived their explanatory power in the literature partly through default as researchers have eliminated various structural impediments to competition, such as redistricting, from the list of possible causal variables. But they have also gained credibility as scholars have explored comparisons between House and Senate elections. Nevertheless, this line of attack remains largely speculative because the reasons for weak challengers remain unclear. In general, then, the absence of compelling evidence about many aspects of candidate recruitment leaves unresolved the entire debate about the relative importance of incumbents and challengers in accounting for declining competition.

Incumbents as Causal Agents

As everyone knows, the incumbency effect in House elections has produced reelection rates above 90 percent in the past two decades and over 98 percent in 1986, 1988, and 1990. Although House incumbents suffered a record number of nineteen defeats in the 1992 primaries, even in a year of such exceptionally high turnover, 93 percent of incumbents who competed in the general election won. Incumbent senators typically have lower reelection rates than House members, dropping to 55 percent in 1980, but senators' reelection performance has averaged a little better than 80 percent over the past two decades and came close to the rate for representatives in the last three elections. Is this incumbent success a well-deserved reward for members' hard work and responsiveness to their constituents, or is it the result of manipulation of electoral resources and voter preferences?

House incumbents seeking reelection have always been good at it, even during periods of high turnover in the nineteenth century (Kernell 1977). But something happened in the 1960s and again in the mid-1980s to ensure even greater success. These are identifiable thresholds that show up quite clearly in time series analysis (Jacobson 1990b). Although all House members appear to have increased their efforts to woo constituents, newcomers seem to have been particularly adept, giving rise to the well-known "sophomore surge" (Mayhew 1974b). Studies by both Born (1979) and Collie (1981) suggested the presence of pronounced generational effects behind the growing margins of incumbents, although Alford and Hibbing (1981) and Hibbing (1991a) documented increases in electoral security for incumbents of all age cohorts. Nevertheless, these scholars too marked the mid-1960s as a watershed, as did Krehbiel and Wright (1983). Furthermore, junior members have managed a higher probability of retaining their seats than senior representatives who enjoyed large vote totals in prior elections (Jacobson 1987a; Hibbing 1991a), and junior members have been less prone to make the costly mistakes that lead to defeat (Bauer and Hibbing 1989).

A variety of statistical estimates have measured the value of incumbency, which appears to add anywhere from 3.6 percent (Erickson 1972), to 4.9 percent (Alford and Hibbing 1981), to 7.0 percent (Jacobson 1992b), 11.6 percent (King and Gelman 1991) to an incumbent House member's share of the vote. Moreover, many studies have demonstrated how incumbents have brought about this result through skillful use of the perquisites of office (Cover 1977; Johannes and McAdams 1981; Yiannakis 1981; Cover and Brumberg 1982; Fiorina 1981a; Rivers and Fiorina 1989; King 1991; Serra and Cover 1992)[1] and through careful cultivation of home styles that stress lawmakers' personal identification with the constituency and disassociation from the institution (Fenno 1978). Not surprisingly, then, voters report high approval levels for incumbents (Jacobson 1992b), find many things to like about them even when they cannot remember their names (Mann 1978; Abramowitz 1975; Jacobson 1992b), and tend to view them more favorably than the opposition (Jacobson 1992b; Mann and Wolfinger 1980; Parker 1981; Abramowitz 1988).

However, an incumbent-based theory of declining competition lacks satisfactory answers for why these changes took place and why they occurred within a particular time period. There is no compelling reason, for example, to equate diminished party ties with preferences for incumbents, and the evidence that voters developed a taste for incumbency as a voting cue is inconclusive (Ferejohn 1977). Indeed, Jacobson's analyses suggest that the preference for incumbents is largely a function of their greater familiarity to voters and contact with them (1992b, chap. 5). Moreover, incumbent-based voting seems to conflict with the compelling evidence Fiorina (1981b) has developed for a retrospective model of electoral behavior based on the past performance of the parties in managing the economy. Furthermore, voter preferences for incumbents occurred across all levels of party identification, not simply among independents and weak identifiers, as we might expect (Krehbiel and Wright 1983, 152). Finally, the possibility that voters are caught in a Prisoner's Dilemma in which it is individually rational for them to support lawmakers who provide constituency service—even though they dislike the collective result of large government that service-oriented representatives provide (Fiorina 1977; Fiorina and Noll 1979)—demands a level of pessimism about democracy that is difficult to accept.

In the absence of any convincing explanation for declining competition grounded in public attitudes toward incumbents, some

---

1. Johannes and McAdams (1981) argue that casework is not as electorally rewarding as many studies suggest because the average recipient of such services has a low probability of voting. In response, Fiorina (1981a) argues that casework has reputational benefits that extend well beyond the actual recipient. His argument is supported by Serra and Cover's (1992) research, which indicates that voter satisfaction with casework enhanced incumbents' recognition and positive evaluations among voters.

scholars have concluded that members of Congress have become more motivated and adept in the pursuit of reelection. Despite the outpouring of research on the incumbency effect, which invoked Charles Jones's now-famous primal scream (1981), this proposition has not been seriously tested. Regrettably, little of the firsthand observation of candidates or incumbents in the mid-1960s looked for changing career motivations when the incumbency effect came into full flower. The major campaign studies of the period paid scant attention to candidates' motives in running and their experiences in obtaining nominations, other than to assert that congressional candidates were primarily self-starters (Kingdon 1968; Leuthold 1968; Huckshorn and Spencer 1971; Fishel 1973).[2] In addition, interviews with a small sample of members in the 1960s did not reveal any particular intensification of the drive to remain in office (Clapp 1963), although such a change in career attitudes did surface a decade later (Bibby 1983). Finally, the higher incidence of retirements among Republicans suggests that they have less ambition for House careers than Democrats, although they are just as successful in winning reelection as their Democratic colleagues (Gilmour and Rothstein 1991).

Nevertheless, the electoral histories of House members elected between 1966 and 1974 showed a strong, positive, and very nearly linear relationship between increasing tenure and the percentage of the vote (Hibbing 1991a, 39–41). However, the problem is that for the next cohort of legislators, elected between 1976 and 1984, the relationship between length of service and electoral margin is virtually nonexistent (Hibbing 1991a, 45). These differences are significant on two counts. First, the earlier generation of lawmakers appeared to be much like its predecessors in learning how to cultivate the constituency as it gained experience, whereas the second cohort apparently came into office knowing how to secure the constituency from the start. Thus, although newcomers to the House did manifest a different type of electoral career, their emergence seems to have lagged the threshold date for the incumbency effect by nearly a decade. Second, the more recently elected House members have managed to secure safe seats while spending relatively less time at home than their predecessors because of changes in the way travel allowances were allocated in the House (Hibbing 1991a, 136). In other words, these mem-

---

2. These studies did document a perception among candidates that they were largely self-starters and perceived themselves as being responsible for their own election margins, but they did not ask respondents to differentiate themselves or their strategies from other individuals who sought the nomination. Nor did they inquire about perceived career paths in getting to Congress.

bers did better electorally while engaging in less of the behavior that was thought to be a prime factor in the incumbency effect.

In the absence of other evidence linking the manifestations of incumbent success—vanishing marginal districts, sophomore surges, or enhanced reelection rates—to changes in their motivations and patterns of recruitment, we are left with several questions. Why, for example, did the incumbency effect show up in the mid-1960s when both the 1964 and 1966 elections were characterized by exceptionally high turnover? What accounts for the sudden surge in reelection success in the late 1980s, again in the wake of two elections—1980 and 1982—in which a relatively large number of incumbents were defeated? Why did high reelection rates for incumbents persist in the South even though the region became more hospitable to the GOP for other types of federal office? Most puzzling perhaps is the issue of why periods of highest election turnover in the contemporary House were those marked by the largest percentage of successful amateurs, who presumably had the fewest skills for cultivating the constituency (Canon 1990, 120).

Weak Challengers as Causal Agents

Not everyone has been persuaded that incumbents have single-handedly brought about their own reelection successes. In a perceptive critique of this literature, Jacobson drew on some of his earlier research to point out several anomalies in the incumbency interpretation of declining competition (1990b, chap. 3). First, he noted that incumbent reelection rates for the House were quite stable throughout the 1970s and early 1980s despite the disappearance of marginal districts (see also Jacobson 1987a and 1992b, 34–37).[3] Second, he demonstrated that the previous year's vote total has lost its predictive power in estimating incumbent reelection success and that the variance in electoral margins has grown over time, producing far more unpredictable outcomes in the statistical sense even in the midst of high reelection rates. A disproportionate percentage of incumbent defeats, for example, occurred not in marginal districts but in those won by better than 60 percent of the vote in the previous election. Ansolabehere, Brady and Fiorina (1988) have also confirmed this increased volatility with respect to prior margins. Finally, Jacobson pointed out that at least one index of the incumbency advantage attained its peak value in 1966 (see King and Gelman 1991, 115), a year

---

3. Hibbing (1991a) makes a similar point.

of record defeats for incumbents. These patterns, he suggested, are at odds with the notion that incumbents are masters of their electoral fate. Instead, Jacobson and others have turned to the phenomenon of weak or nonexistent challengers as the source of incumbent success.

Any number of measures leads to the conclusion that fewer and fewer House races attract strong competition. The phenomenon of weak challengers first drew widespread recognition in the wake of the 1978 election survey by the Center for Political Studies (CPS) at the University of Michigan. Not only did voters have difficulty recognizing challengers' names, but they had fewer contacts with them and identified fewer positive attributes in connection with their candidacies (cf. Hinckley 1980; Mann and Wolfinger 1980; Ragsdale 1981; Jacobson 1987b). Challengers were typically underfunded (Jacobson 1980), and in recent years, they suffered increasing discrimination from PACs (Abramowitz 1991). Moreover, the electoral return for each campaign dollar spent by challengers has declined (Abramowitz 1991.) Lacking visibility, resources, and a saleable image, few challengers have been able to offer the electorate a genuine alternative to incumbents. This pattern strongly contrasts with Senate elections that have produced more incumbent defeats and have drawn more competitive challengers into the fray with the very attributes of name recognition and money that their counterparts in House elections have lacked (Hinckley 1980; Abramowitz 1988; Squire 1989a; Stewart 1989).

Some scholars have suggested that House challengers are not quite as bad as they appear in public opinion surveys (Eubank and Gow 1983; Gow and Eubank 1984; Eubank 1985), while others contend that competitive Senate races have been oversampled by survey researchers (Westlye 1983 and 1992). Furthermore, Wright (1990) has discovered a strong incumbent bias in surveys of Senate voters resulting from the size of the winning margin and the time lapse between the election and the interview.[4] Since the tendency to overreport voting for the winner is connected to the context of the election and the National Election Study (NES) methodology, it presumably occurs in surveys of House voters as well.[5] Nevertheless, even if voter perceptions, or the way we measure them, are biased toward incumbents,

---

4. Gronke (1992) disputes Wright's findings about over-reporting on measurement grounds and argues that it is not statistically significant if one examines the winner's vote total rather than the Republican percentage of the two-party vote.

5. In fact, in a rebuttal to Gronke (1992) in the same issue of *Legislative Studies Quarterly*, Wright (1992) indicates that over-reporting of the vote for winning candidates does occur in House races if one looks only at contested races.

several other patterns suggest that competitive challengers are scarcer than they used to be.

In the late 1980s and early 1990s, the number of uncontested races (Squire 1989b) and lopsided contests (Fowler and Maisel 1991) rose steadily. After dropping noticeably in the mid-1960s because of the increased GOP strength in the South (Schlesinger 1985), the frequency of House races with no opponent increased by 45 percent in the past decade, from fifty-six contests in 1982 to eighty-five in 1990 (Fowler and Maisel 1991, 14).[6] When combined with the number of races in which the challenger got less than 30 percent of the vote, fully three-fifths of all incumbents running in the elections between 1984 and 1988 attracted little or no opposition (Fowler and Maisel 1991, 16). Nor were races dominated by House incumbents the only contests marked by a lack of competition. Throughout the 1980s, roughly 40 percent of the open House seats have been won by a margin of two to one or more (Fowler and Maisel 1991, 31). These figures improved somewhat in 1990 as an antiincumbent backlash added a few percentage points to many weak challengers' margins. Then in 1992, the number of uncontested races dropped precipitously to 6 percent, and the magnitude of incumbent vote totals shrank noticeably. Nevertheless, most political observers seem inclined to treat 1992 as an anomaly rather than as the beginning of a more competitive environment for House elections.

The decline in competitive challengers is partially connected to the decline in the number of candidates who have had prior officeholding experience. Green and Krasno (1988) reported, for example, a strong relationship between the vote and their index of candidate quality, a largely experiential measure. Jacobson, too, found that previous experience in public office has had an increasingly strong statistical relationship to challengers' victories (1989, 782). Moreover, changes in the percentage of seats won by Democratic candidates were strongly correlated with differences in prior officeholding experience between Democratic and Republican challengers (Jacobson 1989, 777). In short, Jacobson asserted that challengers in the 1980s, especially GOP challengers, were such an unusually weak group that they were destined to lose (1990b, 102).

The problem with attributing declining competition to weak, inexperienced challengers is twofold. First, we have Canon's (1990a)

---

6. Along with Schlesinger (1985), they counted general election races in Louisiana as uncontested even if there were candidates from both parties in the primary. Squire (1989b) does not include such contests. At issue are six to eight seats that are relatively constant throughout the period and do not affect the trend.

data, which point to a high incidence of amateurs winning seats in both the House and the Senate. Canon noted that the number of incoming freshmen without prior experience in public office has averaged about one-fourth in the House from 1930 to 1986 and during the 1980s has been as high as 40 percent (1990a, xii). Moreover, he demonstrated that landslide presidential elections have a high probability of bringing large numbers of amateurs into the House. Second, some studies have disputed the premise that candidate experience is related to their performance at the polls. Neither Abramowitz (1984) nor Born (1986), for example, found a significant relationship between candidate officeholding experience and voters' likelihood of selecting a challenger. Nor did Mack's (1992) analysis of repeat challengers find much of a benefit for candidates who had previously run for Congress. Third, there is little consensus among political observers about why the frequency of uncontested seats and weak challengers increased in the 1980s. Several very different and quite plausible explanations have been put forward to account for this phenomenon. Some attribute it to gerrymandering, others to campaign finance practices, and still others to voter preferences. Thus, even if we accept the phenomenon of weak challengers as the cause of decreased electoral competition, we are still a long way from understanding why it has occurred.

Early in the debate on incumbency, several scholars speculated that the decline in competition arose from partisan districting practices. Tufte (1973) pointed to the decline in the swing ratio (the ratio of total seat shifts to total vote shifts) as a sign that local districts were becoming disconnected from changes in the national two-party vote. But several scholars have disputed his view, pointing out that there was little difference between races involving incumbents who had been redistricted and those who had not (Ferejohn 1977; Cover 1977) and that the partisan effects of redistricting failed to show up in the presidential vote returns (Fiorina 1977). Subsequent research uncovered a modest impact from redistricting (Abramowitz 1983; Gopoian and West 1984; Cain and Campagna 1987), although Born's research (1985) suggested that these relationships were largely a phenomenon of the 1960s.

In the 1980s and early 1990s, redistricting has been resurrected as a factor in explaining weak challengers from Repubicans who charged that the Democratic party has benefited from its disproportionate control of state legislatures, which have responsibility for reapportionment, to create districts where GOP candidates have no hope of success. However, this argument is hard to square with the Democrats' disproportionate share of victories in recent senatorial and gubernatorial races, where the constituency boundaries do not vary (Fiorina 1991). Nor does it jibe with the fact that Democrats have done disproportionately well in contesting open seats (Jacobson 1990b). Although there have been instances of partisan advantage conferred by redistricting—notably in California (Cain 1985), Indiana (Niemi and Wright 1990), and a handful of other states (Brady and Grofman 1991)—the overall pattern of Democratic victories in the House does not show a statistical effect from redistricting (Jacobson 1991, 64). Furthermore, there are relatively few states (about one-fifth) in which one party controls both the legislative and executive branches and is therefore able to impose a partisan bias in congressional races (Fiorina 1991).

Finally, a simple measure of partisan bias, calculated as the share of seats a party wins with 50 percent of the vote, reveals that until the mid-1960s the electoral system favored Republicans, not Democrats, and since then has been relatively neutral between the parties (Jacobson 1990b, 93–94). Other analyses of partisan bias do show a small advantage for Democrats, which seems to be connected to wasted Republican votes in the South (Brady and Grofman 1991) and the Democrats' ability to win seats in districts with low turnout with relatively few votes (Campbell 1991).

These conclusions are reinforced by King and Gelman (1991). Although the two scholars do not calculate estimates of their incumbency advantage immediately following legislative reapportionments, their similar measure of partisan bias is at or near zero from the mid-1960s to the early 1980s (1991, 127)—precisely the period when redistricting was supposedly most favorably skewed toward Democratic incumbents. King and Gelman also noted the absence of any strong single-year change in their measure of electoral responsiveness, particularly in 1970–72 or 1980–82. They concluded that redistricting "may have had large effects in particular states and may account for some of the election-to-election variability in these figures, [but] it seems an unlikely candidate for directly explaining long-term systematic trends across the country" (1991, 130).

The argument over the impact of redistricting is further confounded by recent work on the partisan impact of reapportionment plans on state legislatures by Niemi and Jackman (1991). Presumably, state legislators would be more inclined to create a partisan bias for their own seats than for House members' districts, and they ought to be more adept at strategically configuring constituencies with which they are familiar. If gerrymandering is instrumental in reducing electoral competition, then its influence should be most pronounced in state legislative races. Yet Niemi and Jackman do not find systematic evidence that state lawmakers have favored their own parties when they control both branches of government or that they have helped incumbents when they share power with the opposition. This is true whether the measure of advantage is the swing-ratio or the party's proportionate change in seats relative to its proportionate share of the two-party vote. Curiously, what little bias they uncovered favored Republicans and was largely confined to the 1970s.

It may be that gerrymandering strategies differ according to whether the state is losing seats or gaining them. A legislature that is compelled to redistribute voters among a smaller group of officeholders is engaged in a zero-sum game and may not have the opportunity to create party fiefs under pressure from anxious incumbents. In contrast, lawmakers with the responsibility for creating new districts are engaged in a cooperative bargaining situation and may have more leeway to act strategically in the reapportionment process. We know from game theory that these two situations yield different types of equilibria, yet scholars have modeled them as if the processes were the same. Indeed, the lack of explicit controls for fundamentally different strategic situations among the legislative players means that the analyses cited above are misspecified and may therefore yield unreliable coefficients. However, even without taking such strategic considerations into account, the weight of so much evidence against redistricting as a major factor in the weak competition for House seats suggests that we look elsewhere for explanations about weak challengers.

If gerrymandering lacks a direct effect on the declining competitiveness of House elections, it remains to be seen whether or not it has an *indirect* influence on the calculations of prospective congressional candidates because it has increased the costs of running (Fowler and McClure 1989, chap. 3). Redistricting has the potential to disrupt media markets, and such fragmentation tends to depress voter recognition of candidates (Campbell, Alford, and Henry 1984; Niemi, Powell, and Bicknell 1986; Stewart and Reynolds 1990). At the same time, it reduces the effectiveness of television as a campaign tool, because candidates can buy less time and receive less coverage (Goldenberg and Traugott 1984, 120). When that happens, voter recognition and response diminishes (Goldenberg and Traugott 1984, 157–58) and incumbents benefit (Stewart and Reynolds 1990, 511).

Redistricting also tends to alter the overlap of constituency boundaries between stepping-stone local offices and the House. Since some estimates of the size of the candidate pool have yielded significant coefficients in predicting challenger quality (Canon 1990a; Stewart 1989), any connection between redistricting and the reservoir of eligible candidates has potentially adverse consequences for electoral competition. At the very least, redistricting makes districts more complex by amalgamating counties and disparate communities. In the 1980 reapportionment, for example, the frequency of single-county districts declined according to my rough count by about 20 percent. Such a trend could enhance electoral competition by creating more heterogeneous constituencies, but it also accentuates the difficulties of organizing a coalition and coordinating party efforts. Furthermore, it raises information costs by increasing the level of uncertainty about the district's likely political orientations. Indeed, Krasno and Green (1988) speculated that the increased predictive power of what they termed "local forces" in accounting for the emergence of quality challengers from 1974 to 1980 could be related to the improved information available to candidates after several postreapportionment electoral cycles have taken place. "Over time, as the nature of the redrawn district becomes better known," they argued, "the effect of the local political climate on challenger quality grows" (1988, 930).

None of these possibilities has been subjected to systematic investigation for their influence on the type of candidates who contest House seats. But Canon reports that an advantageous redistricting plan is a highly significant variable in predicting whether or not experienced challengers will run for the House (1990a, 107). Thus, the cumulative effects wrought by redistricting in changing the financial, organizational, and informational costs of running seem worth investigating as factors in the recruitment of noncompetitive candidates.

A related argument pertinent to the high frequency of lopsided House races, and one also increasingly voiced by Republicans, is that incumbents have prospered because challengers cannot raise money to run against them. Several findings in the literature give credence to this view, but others suggest that low challenger spending is a symptom rather than a cause of their poor showing at the polls.

It is a well-established fact that challengers benefit disproportionately from campaign expenditures in comparison to incumbents (Jacobson 1980; Thomas 1989; Abramowitz 1991; Kenny 1992), a pattern that holds, incidentally, for Senate candidates as well (Stewart 1989). Money buys name recognition and organizational capabilities—resources that incumbents already possess by virtue of their office. Furthermore, challengers who do defeat incumbents have typically spent in excess of $500,000, which is well above the $135,000 the average challenger could muster (Abramowitz 1991). In estimates of incumbents' margins of victory in 1984 and 1986, for example, challenger spending was the single most powerful variable, and it figured strongly in a model distinguishing between incumbent victory and defeat (Abramowitz 1991, 41–42, 46). Indeed, Abramowitz estimated that a $500,000 expenditure by a challenger reduced an incumbent's margin by 23.5 percent (1991, 43). Moreover, the rate of challenger spending also appears to positively affect voter attitudes, with early money yielding the highest return (Kenny 1992). Not surprisingly, therefore, serious challengers are typically defined as those who raise and spend large sums (Bond, Covington, and Fleisher 1985; Ragsdale and Cook 1987; Wilcox 1987; Jacobson and Kernell 1990).

It is an equally well-established fact, moreover, that challengers raise far less than incumbents and that their ability to assemble a campaign war chest has significantly eroded in the past decade. Abramowitz noted, for example, that challengers' share of total spending in House elections varied between 39 and 42 percent during the 1970s but began a long slide in 1980 that left them with only 24 percent of campaign expenditures by 1988. PACs have contributed ever smaller percentages to challenger campaigns—just 9 percent in 1988 (Ornstein, Mann, and Malbin 1990, 105) and 6 percent in 1990 (Ornstein, Mann, and Malbin 1992, 100). Thus, while incumbents tripled their outlays in this period, challengers did not even keep up with inflation (Abramowitz 1991, 48–49). Instead, financial resources in both parties have been concentrated on a few open-seat and marginal races (Jacobson 1990b, 70). A preliminary analysis of the 1992 elections indicated that although challengers raised more money in the aggregate, their relative share of the total remained relatively constant (Sorauf 1992, communication to author).

Goldenberg, Traugott, and Baumgartner (1986) suggested that the financial advantage incumbents enjoyed was a weapon they could use to scare off strong challengers, thus making money an indirect rather than a direct factor in declining competition. Incumbents' spending does seem to have a positive relationship to their vote margins in several studies (Green and Krasno 1988; Thomas 1989; Jacobson 1990b, 53; Green, Robins and Krasno 1991), although by no means in all (Jacobson 1980; Jacobson 1990a; Abramowitz 1991; Kenny 1992). It also appears to reflect an incumbent's sense of vulnerability, expecially after a narrow win in the previous election (Goldenberg and Traugott 1984; Green and Krasno 1988). Yet the only direct test in the literature of the capacity of incumbents to preempt strong challengers is negative. Krasno and Green (1988) regressed their index of challenger quality for 1978 first on incumbent receipts and then on incumbent expenditures in the year before the election with controls for party tides and the previous challenger's vote margin. Their statistical results were negligible and led them to conclude that early fundraising by incumbents was not responsible for the emergence of weak challengers (1988, 931).[7] Coincidentally, preemptive spending did not protect Senate incumbents from strong challengers, either (Squire 1991).

But Krasno and Green (1988) admitted that their aggregate results may mask a good deal of variation in the success of incumbents' efforts because of differences in the quality of each district's candidate pool. For example, they noted that incumbents in districts with a large supply of top-quality challengers might appear to be wasting money on preemptive expenditures when compared to an incumbent in a district with a small supply of strong competitors (1988, 931). In that instance, the first incumbent might actually succeed in preventing the emergence of a tough opponent, but the relationship would be rendered insignificant if the second incumbent had secured a weak opponent by spending nothing.

If the impoverished state of challengers' campaigns is beyond dispute, it is unclear whether they have been discriminated against by political elites or whether they raise sums appropriate to their credentials and experience. After all, contributors want to spend their money on likely winners and to avoid wasting resources on contestants who have little or no chance of victory, Of course, these judgments become something of a self-fulfilling prohecy, for strong candidates attract funds that in turn enable them to make a vigorous appeal to voters, while weak ones languish in the obscurity that inevitably leads to a poor showing at the polls. Thus, the 1990 voter backlash against incumbents produced so few defeats because the year's unusually weak crop of challengers had so little money to capitalize on public disaffection (Jacobson 1992c), Nevertheless, the existing evidence does not particularly support the notion that prospective donors have treated challengers unfairly.

The most vigorous proponent of the view that challengers' financial deficits are a function of their poor election prospects is Gary Jacobson (1990b). Although he did not scrutinize the direct impact of campaign receipts on challenger quality as Krasno and Green did, he made a strong circumstantial case for his view. First, he asserted that in the great majority of elections, Republican incumbents and chal-

---

7. The emerging literature on challenger and incumbent spending in Senate elections contrasts sharply with this literature.

lengers have on average outspent Democrats to a considerable degree and that the incumbent bias in PAC contributions is greatest for Republican incumbents in all years but 1982 and 1984. Next, he demonstrated that in open-seat races, the Republicans have had a financial advantage throughout the 1980s. Then, he showed that in every year except 1980, prior officeholding experience had a positive influence on the variation in challengers' campaign spending, when party and marginality of the seat are controlled, and that its predictive power became more pronounced in recent years (1990b, 101–2). In sum, Jacobson concluded that Republicans have not been starved for resources in contesting House elections and that when they have had competitive candidates, they have been able to fund them.

However, Jacobson's explanation for the impoverishment of challengers' campaigns leaves unanswered the issue of why the nominees of both parties have become so starved for funds in the past decade. This question is difficult to resolve statistically because of the simultaneity of money and votes, which is manifest in several different ways (Jacobson, 1990a). First, incumbents' spending in one election period is strongly conditioned by their spending in prior elections (Green and Krasno 1988 and 1990). This pattern may reflect their general predispositions toward fundraising and judgments about what constitutes an adequate war chest in their particular district (Green and Krasno 1988 and 1990). Or it may be a function of the challenger's quality in the last election (Jacobson 1990a). If the latter, the statistical impact of the previous challenger could result from the incumbents' perceptions of their general vulnerability, or it could indicate the depth and strength of the candidate pool in the district.

Second, it has been impossible to develop a reliable measure of the challenger's expected vote before the election, and this failure has hindered statistical efforts to sort out how much direct influence money exerts over House election outcomes and how much it reflects the competitiveness of the challenger. There are two issues here: One is that high quality challengers seem to get a better return in votes from what they spend (Green and Krasno 1988 and 1990). The other is that a challenger's ability to raise money is correlated with how contributors think he or she will do. This problem occurs whether one uses early money, as Green and Krasno did (1988 and 1990), or total spending by challengers, as Jacobson has done (1990a). The problem is that any variable that influences the final vote will also influence campaign contributions; thus, it becomes impossible to correctly identify a simultaneous equation model that specifies the interaction of these two mutually reinforcing phenomena (Jacobson 1990a). As Jacobson observed,

> If all of the available exogenous variables influence both spending and votes, reciprocal effects can never be untangled using [two-stage-least-squares] techniques. Indeed, without additional information, we cannot be certain that campaign spending has any effect at all on election outcomes because we cannot prove conclusively that the strong, stable [ordinary-least-squares] results are not merely an artifact of well-informed contribution strategies that funnel the most money to the best challengers, who would do just as well without it. (1990a, 342)

Second, it is extremely difficult to model donors' perceptions of candidate viability in congressional races. Although research on state legislative elections has indicated that the level of PAC contributions to challengers and open-seat candidates is influenced by their prior ability to raise money from individuals (Cassie, Thompson, and Jewell 1992), no comparable studies exist on patterns of congressional fundraising. Thus, we do not have a clear picture of how individual donors calculate which candidates to back, especially in a primary in which partisanship is, in effect, held constant. Given the apparent sensitivity of voter preferences to the timing of challenger spending (Kenny 1992), the lack of models to explain the dynamics of contributions and their connection to candidate emergence is a serious deficiency in the literature.

Third, the absence of empirical research on the size and quality of the pool of prospective candidates hinders any assessment of how the relative difficulty of acquiring adequate resources influences potential challengers' decisions to run. For example, the variation in campaign costs across districts for lower-level offices can affect how prospective candidates evaluate preemptive spending by incumbents or the general difficulty of funding a congressional race. If they have been accustomed to raising large sums to contest a state legislative seat or a major county office, as in California, New York, or parts of Texas, they may not be as intimidated by an incumbent's early bankroll or by the generally high cost of House races. Indeed, Squire and Wright (1990, 94–95) reported that former state legislators from large constituencies raised significantly more money than candidates with the same experience from small legislative districts, and they did substantially better at the polls on election day.

Finally, it is important to control for the fact that although the timing of candidates' decisions to run is related to their capacity to raise money, the opposite pattern also holds. For 1982 and 1984, over 50 percent of those who raised more than $400,000 had filed with the Federal Election Commission before the beginning of the election year (Wilcox 1987), and this pattern continued through 1988 (Wilcox and Biersack 1990). But whether the early start indicated their potential strength or enabled them to do better than they might have otherwise done is unclear. We simply do not know enough about how prospective candidates size up their fundraising prospects to do more than guess.

The issue for congressional scholars, then, is not whether incumbents buy their offices because of bias in the campaign system but how money figures in the recruitment of prospective candidates. One might consider, for example, the factors that account for differences between well-financed amateurs and under-financed but experienced candidates. Or one might investigate the marginal return on campaign dollars in different types of districts or examine the variations in states' finance regulations and party practices to see if some areas are inherently more expensive or more hospitable to raising money. Finally, one might map the flow and timing of funds to various types of races to analyze the momentum of of candidate fundraising or look for bandwagon effects. The point is that there is a wealth of information in the public domain about campaign funds, and almost none of it has been tapped to look beyond the connection between money and the final vote tally. We need to start at the beginning of the "money chase," to use Magleby and Nelson's term (1990) and examine its early impact on candidate recruitment instead of focusing solely on its end product.

If structural features of House races fail to account for weak challengers, comparisons with Senate contests nevertheless provide reasons to continue looking at candidacy as a cause of declining electoral competition. Scholars initially examined the greater competitiveness of Senate elections and concluded that the greater visibility and resources of Senate candidates were responsible (Hinckley 1980; Mann and Wolfinger 1980; Abramowitz 1988; Stewart 1989). Overall, the majority of Senate candidates have been experienced and well funded, they have been more exposed to public scrutiny, and they have been held more accountable by the voters for the state of the nation. They are neither protected by gerrymandering nor shunned by contributors. Far from being able to insulate themselves from political issues and trends, as their House colleagues have done, senatorial candidates are more susceptible to partisan considerations (Abramowitz 1988; Stewart 1989), to economic trends (Kuklinski and West 1981; Abramowitz and Segal 1986; Lewis-Beck and Rice 1986); to issue voting (Wright and Berkman 1986; Miller 1990); and to ideological evaluation (Erikson 1990b; Franklin 1991b). There is even some speculation that senators are victims of the greater exposure they receive from the news media (Robinson 1975). Complementing these patterns is a long-term shift in party organizational strength, particularly in the South. Where senate seats were once sinecures for one party or the other, all states now have competitive Senate elections on occasion (Schlesinger 1985).

One analysis of Senate challengers from 1980 to 1988 provided some clues about how individual candidates affect voter attitudes during the election. Squire (1992a) documented the impact of two personal attributes on voter attitudes—the candidates' level of political experience and their reported political skill.[8] Both were positively related to various measures of the traits voters liked about the candidates, as well as the voters' thermometer ratings of them. In addition, both attributes were positively related to the challengers' eventual vote (1992a, 256–59).

A telling example of how individual candidates shape the competitiveness of Senate races occurred in the 1986 California campaign involving Democratic incumbent Alan Cranston and former Republican House member Ed Zschau (Jacobson and Wolfinger 1989). Over the course of the campaign, voter attitudes were highly susceptible to the claims made by the two candidates. First, the seemingly indestructable Cranston fell precipitously in public esteem and then succeeded in casting doubts on his opponent. Eventually, Cranston narrowly won, but his slim victory testifies to the power of skillful and experienced opponents backed by abundant campaign resources in shaping the voters' eventual choices.

However, not all Senate contests fit the Cranston-Zschau model. During the 1990 election, for example, a seasoned House member, Republican Lynn Martin, took on a seemingly vulnerable incumbent, Democrat Paul Simon, with full financial backing of the Republican party and its then-popular president. But for all her name recognition, skills, and money, Martin was unable to develop an exploitable issue against Simon, and she lost badly (Wyckoff and Dran 1992). Her experience contrasted starkly with that of Christine Todd Whitman, a little known challenger whose incumbent opponent, Democrat Bill

---

8. Franklin (1991a) also developed an index of the strategic behavior of Senate candidates' which has a statistically significant impact on voter perceptions.

Bradley, outspent her twelve to one in the same election year. Whitman came close to winning, despite her underdog status, because of voter disaffection with New Jersey's Democratic governor.

The Martin-Simon and Whitman-Bradley races were not merely flukes but rather indicated the variability of Senate races. A decade ago, for example, the Senate was awash with amateurs who won despite their lack of credentials and name recognition (Canon 1989b).[9] Over a sixteen-year span, fully 22 percent of the Senate challengers lacked previous officeholding experience and 14 percent of the open seat candidates were inexperienced (Westlye 1992, 27). Disparities in fundraising also existed, with incumbents—particularly Republicans—enjoying a considerable financial advantage over their challengers (Stewart 1989). Moreover, media coverage of Senate candidates has varied significantly across states with predictable consequences for the electorate's knowledge about the campaign (Westlye 1992, 51–57). Overall, fully 43 percent of all Senate races from 1968 to 1984 have been uncompetitive (Westlye 1992), and in recent years 58 percent have had outcomes in which the margin of victory was better than two to one (Ornstein, Mann, and Malbin 1992, 62).

In a recent analysis of 304 Senate races, Westlye (1992, 25) attributed the variation in Senate election outcomes to differences in the level of intensity and information in campaigns—what he termed either hard-fought or low-key contests.[10] He found that open seat elections fit the conventional view, with 81 percent falling into the hard-fought category. But incumbent races satisfied the hard-fought definition only 48 percent of the time (Westlye 1992, 25). Most important, he came to some unexpected conclusions about the role of prior political experience, noting that previous officeholding bore "little relation to whether candidates actually won. . . . Running against incumbents, former governors and senators did little better than state legislators and barely outdistanced the least experienced candidates" (1992, 29). Indeed, the most successful challengers appeared to be candidates closely tied to party organizations, despite their lack of elective office. For these candidates, the success rate was 38 percent (Westlye 1992, 29)! Among open-seat candidates, a lack of experi-

---

9. Several of these same senators did not survive their first attempt at reelection, because they failed to tend their electoral coalitions (Frendreis and Overby 1992).

10. Westlye's classification scheme is based on *Congressional Quarterly's* preelection synopses of Senate races, supplemented by postelection campaign expenditure data. Whenever the ratio of candidate spending exceeded two to one, he considered the race to be low-key, despite Congressional Quarterly's interpretation.

ence was somewhat penalized, but the level of officeholding did not show any consistent relationship with eventual success (1992, 29). Westlye also made extensive use of statewide polling data to examine the level of voter information and contact with Senate candidates. This approach compensated for the tendency in the CPS and NES surveys to undersample certain large states in selected years (1972, 1978, and 1984) and to undersample small states in all years. As it turned out, many of the findings of previous research on Senate voters were based on an unacceptably small and unrepresentative N. More important, the survey bias against small states, which have produced a large percentage of the low-key Senate races, tended to exaggerate the contrast between Senate and House elections in terms of voter contact with and information about the candidates (Westlye 1992, 92–97).

Although Westlye's findings are sometimes at odds both with the conventional wisdom about Senate races and with the prevailing views about how candidates' office-holding experience affects election results, his research nevertheless reinforces the preoccupation in the congressional literature with candidacy. In his view, candidates determine the competitiveness of Senate elections because their personal attributes—background, political skill, and prior record—attract the media attention and elite backing that make for a hard-fought race. Absent opponents with such newsworthy traits, the election will command little coverage, the candidates will fail to develop sufficient name recognition, and the voters will have little opportunity to learn about the issues. Senate candidates, in Westlye's view, define the intensity and themes of the race, which, in turn, enable voters to make decisions on the basis of partisanship and policy preferences. This model of electoral competition, Westlye asserted, is the only one that is compatible with several different patterns he found in Senate elections: the high incidence of split-party delegations; the lopsided margins for candidates of different parties in consecutive races in the same state (1992, 9); the failure of statewide variables, such as population and prior party vote totals, to predict election outcomes, except in the very largest states (1992, 154–55); and the differing rates of voter defection to incumbents, particularly in states with skewed party distributions (1992, 165).

If Westlye's (1992) research makes a compelling case for individual candidates as defining features of Senate elections, it nevertheless leaves the issue of causality unresolved. One reason for this ambiguity lies in his measure of campaign intensity. Based on two types of information—assessments of the closeness of a race by political observers in *Congressional Quarterly*'s autumn campaign summaries and total campaign expenditures—this variable may be appropriate for classifying campaigns after the fact, but it cannot be used for predicting outcomes. To employ it in a causal sense is to engage in tautological explanation, in other words, to say the final vote was close because it looked close at the end of the campaign is to say very little.

A second problem in assessing the causal implications of Westlye's (1992) analysis stems from the particular alternatives on the ballot. Although Westlye argued that candidates' personal qualities and skills are the factors that generate the media attention and money necessary to give voters a genuine choice, he offered no clues about how or why individual nominees obtained their party's nomination. Nor did he examine which factors led the *Congressional Quarterly* reporters and the campaign contributors to judge races as hard fought or low key. In effect, Westlye asked us to accept the variation in campaign intensity as a given to focus on its consequences.

This is a reasonable research strategy, given his primary interest in voter decision making, but it leaves us with a partial explanation of electoral competition. Unfortunately, the existing literature on the emergence of Senate candidates does little to fill in the gaps. For example, recent efforts to predict the quality of Senate candidates have produced contradictory results. Squire (1989a) found that the level of experience among Senate candidates is primarily a function of the size of the candidate pool and the population of the state. Stewart (1989, 574), however, discovered that favorable party registration favors the emergence of strong challengers but does not seem to deter them, and he noted that the incumbent's prior electoral margin is most significant in accounting for challenger quality. These confusing patterns are compounded by the contradictions between the results of Rohde (1979) and Brace (1984) and those of Copeland (1989). The former two scholars found House members' decision to run for the Senate to be primarily a function of the opportunity structure in the state and the likelihood of success, whereas the latter concluded that lawmakers' personal circumstances where much more effective predictors of House members' progressive ambition for the Senate.

In the absence of clear-cut patterns of candidate recruitment to Senate elections, it is difficult to interpret several of Westlye's (1992) most interesting findings. What, for example, accounts for the fact that prior officeholding experience is less important to Senate challengers than it seems to be in House races or that party offices are more effective stepping stones for Senate challengers than elective posts? What explains the higher incidence of low-key races in middle-sized states? Far from diminishing the impact of Westlye's important study, these unresolved questions provide further impetus to the study of candidacy. But they leave us with the same puzzle we encountered in House elections: are competitive candidates exogenous factors in electoral competition, as Westlye assumed, or is their presence on the ballot a function of political processes that remain obscure?

In sum, both incumbency and challenger quality undoubtedly figure in the pattern of declining competition in congressional elections. In the absence of more information about candidate emergence, however, we simply cannot say how much incumbents create demand for their own particular brand of representation and how much they depress the supply of likely opponents through their attentive behavior to the constituency. More important, we cannot ascertain how much structural factors inhibit competition by deterring likely challengers from running and how much they actually constrict the pool of available talent.

Strategic Elites as Nationalizing Influences

If declining competition accounts for the decoupling of congressional elections from national political tides, then what accounts for the continuing influence of partisanship, economic issues, and presidential performance in such a candidate-centered environment? Some scholars have turned to political elites as instruments of aggregate partisan change in the Congress (Jacobson and Kernell 1981). Strong candidates, they reasoned, make strategic calculations to run when national conditions are favorable, thereby giving national parties and PACs a wedge into local politics. The resources the activists provide, in turn, enable high quality candidates to wage competitive campaigns that offer voters an appealing alternative to the status quo. Voters can choose the most attractive candidate and consequently tap into the national trend without being aware that they are doing so. Their preferences for experienced and locally oriented candidates thus add up to a significant net advantage for one of the parties in Congress.

This view of candidacy as a nationalizing force stands in stark contrast to the one canvassed in the previous section. Instead of de-coupling congressional elections from national concerns, candidates in the Jacobson and Kernell (1981) model act as mediating agents between local concerns and national trends. In effect, their calculations of political advantage turn House elections into national referenda and therefore serve to reconcile the discrepancy between scholarly analyses of aggregate election results and cross-sectional studies of voter attitudes. As the research on strategic politicians has matured, however, a paradox has developed in which candidates and elites, still acting strategically, now seem driven by local conditions. Thus, the literature has come full circle with Jacobson's most recent studies (1990b, 1992a, and 1992c), which now stress how strategically motivated candidacies weaken the national component of congressional elections.

In the strategic politicians literature, the causal agents are challengers, open-seat competitors, and activists rather than incumbents. Again, like the research on declining electoral competition, the evidence is inconclusive. Most of the scholarly debate has focused on whether or not high quality candidates time their decisions to run in accordance with favorable national events or whether they primarily consider local and personal circumstances in seeking congressional office. Adding to the conflict are disputes over the relevant variables and how to measure them. Yet underneath the methodological issues is a far more serious problem of model misspecification. The treatment of candidacy as both an endogenous and exogenous factor in congressional elections prevents scholars from ascertaining the relative strength of political elites as nationalizing influences.

A validation of the Jacobson and Kernell (1981) strategic politicians hypothesis requires two sorts of tests: (1) an analysis of prospective and declared candidates to ascertain if they timed the decision to run or not run in accordance with national tides and (2) an analysis of voters' decisions to see if they evaluated one party's challengers vis-à-vis opposing incumbents more favorably than the other when national trends favored it. The former test has never been undertaken because a lack of survey data on candidates or prospective candidates has made such inquiries impossible.[11] Instead, most of the work published on stragetic politicians has been devoted to testing the model's assumption that relatively higher quality candidates are mobilized to run when national tides favor their party. Two scholars have attempted the latter test on voter attitudes: Abramowitz (1984) and Born (1986), who assessed the relative importance of candidate qualifications and national issues in citizens' voting decisions.

The various attempts to confirm or disconfirm the Jacobson and

---

11. The most recent surveys were done in the 1978 election by Maisel (1982), who studied primary candidates, and Goldenberg and Traugott (1984), who investigated campaign managers, and in the 1984 election by Herrnson (1988). These studies did not ask about the influence of national events on the decision to run.

Kernell (1981) hypothesis present a confusing picture because much of the evidence is indirect and little of it is strictly comparable. Differences in the time periods examined, the choice of independent variables, and the measurement of both dependent and independent variables raise questions about the appropriateness of various indicators and require caution in interpreting the results. To help the reader follow the discussion, I have summarized the major features of each of the studies on strategic politicians in Table 4.1, grouping them according to the type of dependent variable explained.[12]

Jacobson and Kernell (1981) marshaled two types of evidence. First, they reworked Tufte's (1975) econometric model, which predicted the parties' share of the standardized national two-party vote on the basis of changes in real disposable income and presidential popularity. Having achieved a better fit by measuring changes in income and presidential popularity in the first quarter (March) of an election year rather than the period right before election day, they inferred that candidate decision making, rather than national issues, affected the vote totals. That was true, they argued, because candidates made up their minds about running or not running in the spring, whereas voters made their choices in the fall. Second, the two scholars presented a detailed analysis of the 1974 and 1980 elections, which were marked by significant differences in the level of prior officeholding experience and fundraising success among challengers of different parties and candidates for open seats. In each case, the differences were related to the party tides favoring the Democrats in 1974 and the Republicans in 1980. Subsequently, they noted that a Republican debacle was averted in 1982 during the worst economic recession since the Depression because the party took the unusual step of recruiting and funding particularly strong challengers (summarized in Jacobson 1987b).

Let us start with Born's (1986) replication of Jacobson and Kernell's (1981) original analysis and subsequent extensions by Jacobson. Here the dependent variable is the Democratic share of the national two-party vote for the House, principally for off-year elections. The key argument is whether one obtains a better fit of the model through the measurement of the independent variables—changes in real disposable income and presidential popularity—early in the election cycle and, if so, whether that means candidates are behaving strategically. Several contradictory aspects are associated with this test. First,

---

12. Open-seat races generally attract more competitive candidates, irrespective of national tides. Although Jacobson and Kernell (1981) and Fleisher and Bond (1992) report the influence of national indicators on the degree of competition for open seats, the strategic politicians literature has primarily focused on challengers.

TABLE 4.1. A Summary of Research on Strategic Politicians in the House

	Time Period	Dependent Variable	Independent Variables
The Aggregate Vote Test (off-year elections)			
Jacobson and Kernell (1981)	1946–80 (off-year)	Democratic percentage of two-party vote	Real disposable income (first quarter/first quarter); presidential approval (average January–March)
Born (1986)	1946–82 (off-year)	Democratic percentage of two-party vote	Real disposable income (first quarter/first quarter); presidential approval (average August–October)
Jacobson (1987b)	1946–84 (off-year)	Administration party percentage (moving average)	Real disposable income (first quarter/fourth quarter); presidential approval (first quarter/fourth quarter)
Jacobson (1987a)	1946–84 (all)	Democratic percentage of two-party vote	Challenger's public office; percentage difference in experienced party challengers
Jacobson (1990b)	1948–88 (all)	Percentage administration party seats	Real per capita income (fourth quarter/fourth quarter); party exposure; presidential approval (October–October)
The Individual Vote Test			
Abramowitz (1984)	1980–82	Voter picks challenger	Challenger's public office; challenger's party; challenger's money; presidential thermometer (1980); economic scale (1982); voter party identification; voter ideology
Born (1986)	1966–82 (off-year)	Voter picks challenger	Challenger's public office; challenger's party; previous challenger's margin; presidential thermometer; economic dummies (4); voter party identification
Jacobson and Kernell (1990)	1986	Voter picks Democratic candidate	Party identification; challenger's money; issue index; interaction of issue index and challenger's money

The Challenger Margin Test			
Jacobson and Kernell (1981)	1974	Challenger's margin	Challenger's public office; challenger's money
Jacobson (1990b)	1946–88 (all)	Challenger's margin; challenger's win	Challenger's public office; previous challenger's vote; shift in two-party vote; trend
The Candidate Quality Test			
Bianco (1984)	1974–80 (all)	Challenger's public office	Challenger's party; real disposable income (by state/one year before filing); previous challenger's margin; presidential vote (four-year average); Watergate; retiring incumbent's party
Bond, Covington, and Fleisher (1985)	1980	Challenger's money; challenger's experience (three-point scale); composite	Incumbent's previous vote; incumbent's party; normal vote; district diversity; incumbent's ideological differences; advertisement/casework
Krasno and Green (1988)	1974–80 (all)	Challenger's experience (seven-point scale)	Previous challenger's vote; party dummy; scandal; incumbent's money
Canon (1990a)	1972–88 (all)	Challenger's experience (four-point scale)	Real disposable income (by state/one year before filing); state unemployment; previous challenger's margin; normal vote; Watergate; scandal; open primary; redistricting; institutions (four); challenger's age; incumbent freshman
Jacobson (1990b)[a]	1946–88 (all)	Challenger's public office	Real disposable income (second quarter/second quarter); presidential approval (average April–June); administration's party; previous Democratic vote; previous party control; candidate pool
Jacobson (1990b)	1946–90 (all)	Percentage experienced challengers	Real disposable income (second quarter/second quarter); presidential approval (average April–June); administration's party; previous percentage Democratic win

[a]Jacobson published similar analyses in 1989, but I have focused on the more up-to-date results.

Born obtained a better fit using income change over eighteen months (the first three months of the preelection year to the last full quarter before the mid-term election) and the average presidential approval for the three months right before the election. Moreover, he noted that when Jacobson and Kernell added 1982 to their initial formulation, they lowered the R-square of their original model. In addition, Born tested the relative capability of both models to forecast an election based on the results for all prior elections and found a lower predictive error for his model than for Jacobson and Kernell's. Finally, he pointed out that the trend for both models is in the wrong direction, that is to say, the strategic explanation of election outcomes ought to become more pronounced after 1966 when the incumbency effect kicked in, but it actually modestly diminished in his formulation and sharply dropped in Jacobson and Kernell's.[13]

Jacobson's subsequent analyses do not answer these criticisms, but in his (1987b) model predicting the effect of challenger officeholding experience on the national two-party vote, he obtained a fit roughly as good as the economic-presidential estimation. A later study showed an even stronger effect for experience in later years (Jacobson 1990b). Nevertheless, these later efforts do not directly connect strong candidates to national forces, for the percentage or distribution of quality candidates is not included in the majority of these models.

Moreover, in the more recent studies, several changes have been made in the variables. For example, Jacobson changed the time period for measuring presidential popularity to the last quarter of the election year (1987b and 1990b). This change is puzzling in its implication that politicians respond strategically to the economy but not to the president's performance. Since the election takes place in November and the indicator runs through December in the first study and right before election day in the latter, it is hard to see how politicians (or voters) can react to such late-breaking events. Furthermore, in the more recent work (1990b), Jacobson measured changes in real per capita income in the year before the election, by which I assume he means fourth quarter to fourth quarter. The fit presumably is better with this income variable, but he did not explain the switch.

A related issue is whether the March-to-March time frame, or

---

13. Erickson (1990a) demonstrated that the change in real disposable income, however measured, employed by Tufte and then by Jacobson and Kernell might not signify pocketbook voting because this variable loses its significance in the equation when the presidential party's previous share of the two-party vote is incorporated in the equation. The implications of his results for the strategic politicians hypothesis are unclear.

some other variant, provides the most accurate cues for prospective candidates. One could plausibly pick the date when declared candidates file with the Federal Election Commission (FEC), which occurs after March of an election year for roughly two-thirds of nonincumbent House candidates (Wilcox 1987; Wilcox and Biersack 1990). Yet this information tells us nothing about when candidates decide whether or not to run. Moreover, half of the strongest candidates in terms of fundraising made up their minds to run in the fourth quarter of the year before the election (Wilcox 1987; Wilcox and Biersack 1990), and in a survey of candidates conducted in 1978 at least 40 percent of primary contestants made up their minds to contest a House seat in the year before the election (Maisel 1982). Since Jacobson got the poorest fit when this time frame is used (1987b), one is forced to ask whether the strongest candidates are the most strategic, as he assumed, or whether such aggregate measures simply have too much noise in them to be good estimators of individual-level behavior.

In the absence of any systematic inquiry into the actual timing of candidates' decisions to run, this issue remains open to disagreement. However, it is instructive that other scholars working in this field have chosen different measures. Both Bianco (1984) and Canon (1990a) used the yearly change in the state income data calculated from six months before the filing deadline for candidates. And no other scholars, except Jacobson (1990b) employed the presidential approval data in subsequent analyses.

Perhaps the most telling test of the strategic politicians hypothesis is the one undertaken by Abramowitz (1984) and Born (1986), because it is the most direct. These scholars attempted to assess the influence of challenger strength on voters' decisions in comparison to their partisanship and attitudes toward the economy and the president's performance. Although they used slightly different independent variables, neither one obtained significant results for the challenger's prior experience in elective office. Abramowitz reported that even when challenger spending was included in the equation, it was not nearly as significant as the economic issue and party variables.

However, in a subsequent analysis of forty-seven districts in the 1986 election, Jacobson and Kernell (1990, 74) reported that the strength of the challenger did exert an independent effect on the vote intention. Their article attempted to move beyond the simple dichotomization of the vote choice in House elections as being either candidate centered or issue centered by examining how the quality of candidates affected the salience of issues. Issues are most relevant to voters, they reasoned, when strong challengers are in a position to elevate them in the public consciousness, and in this way, strong national tides will show up in heightened issue voting among constituents by bringing competitive candidates into the fray.

Serious limitations of the data obtained from an ABC News/ *Washington Post* panel study constrained the applicability of these findings, for it oversampled marginal and open seat races and lacked any evaluative questions about the candidates other than the voter's choice. It was therefore unclear if voters perceived the candidates as actually holding the positions they favored. In addition, the survey inquired about respondents' vote intentions rather than their eventual choice. Furthermore, by some quirk, it yielded candidates who had raised a lot of money, or very little, and had no races with moderately competitive challengers. Nonetheless, it is instructive that when competitive candidates (defined as having raised more than $450,000) challenged incumbents or faced each other for an open seat, both their quality and the citizens' attitudes toward such issues as the Strategic Defense Initiative affected the vote choice. More important, these variables appeared to be mutually reinforcing (Jacobson and Kernell 1990, 77 and 83). At the same time, so few competitive candidates emerged to raise issues that voters had relatively few opportunities to consider them.

However, what is most telling about this particular test of the strategic politicians argument is that Jacobson and Kernell emphasized *local* political conditions rather than *national* ones as stimuli to the emergence of strong candidates. They asserted that "regardless of national conditions, local circumstances have the strongest effect on political career strategies (1990, 70). Strong candidates, they concluded, were most likely to run in districts in which their parties' candidates for the House and presidency had previously done well and in which voters' partisanship and approval of the president was favorable to them. In short, Jacobson and Kernell concluded that House elections still serve their function as a referendum on the performance of the national government, but only in a few cases and *only if local conditions encourage the emergence of the right candidates.*

These mixed results from survey data contrast strongly with much of Jacobson's other work. In some equations, for example, he predicted that an experienced candidate on the ballot was worth an additional 2.8 percentage points to the aggregate vote (1990b, 54); and in other equations that predicted challengers' margins, victories, or both, previous officeholding experience is significant, even when the challenger's vote in the previous election is included. Thus, we confront a dilemma similar to the one Jacobson and Kernell originally set out to resolve, that survey findings and aggregate results are inconsistent.

Last, we have the disparate analyses evaluating the key assumption in the Jacobson and Kernell (1981) hypothesis regarding the influence of national events on experienced politicians' decisions to run. Several aspects of this research are important. The first is the finding by both Bianco (1984) and Canon (1990a), using quite different measures of candidate experience and somewhat different independent variables, that national events are associated with experienced candidates in races with incumbents but not in open seats. Moreover, Jacobson (1990b, 65) reported that both parties are fielding more experienced candidates in open seats, although the Democrats have a considerable edge.

The second consideration is Jacobson's (1990b) discovery that Democratic candidacies seem to respond to national forces but that Republican candidacies do not. Given the GOP's status as a minority party with a weak local base for most of the period scrutinized, one would expect that Republican politicians would be more rather than less susceptible to national tides because they need the boost that a popular president and healthy economy give to their less advantageous starting point. Indeed, Born (1990) found that Republicans do benefit from strong candidates at the top of the ticket and lose ground in the off years. Taken together, however, this research suggests that the Jacobson and Kernell assumptions about when strong candidates run holds only for Democratic challengers—or roughly a third of all congressional candidates—and that those candidates most likely to benefit from behaving strategically—Republicans—fail to respond to such opportunities.

The third and most significant aspect of this body of research is the overwhelming strength in all the models predicting the emergence of experienced candidates—defined in myriad ways—of variables used to measure the local partisan tendencies of the district. These range from several versions of the normal vote to the challenger's or incumbent's vote in the preceding election. Some other decidedly local factors, such as a scandal involving the incumbent, an incumbent with freshman status, a disadvantageous bout of redistricting, and a provision for an open primary, all have larger coefficients than the national tides variables (Canon 1990a). Jacobson (1989) himself uncovered a strong trend in the postwar years toward the separation of national tides and local electoral outcomes, especially since 1972. Moreover, he found that the most powerful influences for the emergence of experienced challengers in both parties are variables that control for local party strength in the previous election, specifically a shift in the control of the seat and the vote total of the challenger's party. He concluded, "A successful challenge is now far more contingent on local circumstances—on particular candidates and campaigns—than it once was." (1989, 789).

It is unclear at this point to what extent the independent variables used to test the strategic politicians model are truly surrogates for local events. Some certainly capture district-level phenomona, such as a scandal or an open primary. But others, such as the previous vote, could bear some connection to national events. Yet in the absence of better information about what types of local influences and contexts affect recruitment, it is difficult to know what these measures truly stand for or what other types of indicators would be more effective.

The 1990 election, however, suggested just how important it has become to understand the local component of candidate recruitment. That year marked the worst crop of challengers to run for Congress in modern times, yet incumbents across the board lost points from their vote margins, even though few actually lost (Jacobson 1992c). Only 10 percent of the challengers had ever held public office. As a group they spent less money than in any year since 1974, while their incumbent opponents raised record sums. Indeed, when the election was over, incumbents had twice as much cash on hand in unspent funds as challengers had put into the entire campaign (Jacobson 1992c). Despite this mismatch in resources, fourteen challengers received between 45 and 49.9 percent of the vote while spending less than $200,000.

How did experienced prospective challengers and their potential supporters miss the anti-incumbent backlash of 1990? Why did they overlook those fourteen vulnerable incumbents? Why did *Congressional Quarterly* identify only half of the fifteen incumbents who lost as "vulnerable" or "potentially vulnerable" less than a month before the election? Jacobson concluded that today's strategic politicians are so fixated on incumbency that they have diverted all of their resources to a few marginal and open seat races. Consequently, they overlooked the challengers who did well despite their meager funds and ensured that such promising contenders would lose. Thus, not only do elites seem to have given up their function as nationalizing influences in congressional elections, but they may actually have dampened the force of national tides.

As the strategic politicians literature has matured, the research agenda has increasingly shifted to voter attitudes. Without actually abandoning the strategic politicians argument, Jacobson nonetheless switched from the timing of candidacy to the message of candidates. In his (1990b) book, he argued that Democrats are the majority in Congress because they field more experienced candidates, but he also suggested that these more seasoned contenders offer voters more appealing alternatives than their Republican opponents. In this sense, Jacobson came full circle to the original question proposed in *Strategy and Choice* (Jacobson and Kernell 1981): how much do issues influence congressional elections and what role do candidates play in framing them for the public?

In sum, the Jacobson and Kernell (1981) hypothesis rested largely on inference from a model of the aggregate share of the two-party vote that has since been seriously compromised by questions of measurement. A more direct test of voter behavior yielded mixed results, and the various efforts to predict the emergence of experienced candidates produced some support for the influence of national tides on candidate recruitment. But on balance, the decision among experienced candidates to seek a seat in the House appears to be strongly connected to other, presumably local, partisan factors. Equally important, national elites no longer seem as effective nationalizing agents as they have been in the past. Finally, it is clear that as a determinant of the vote choice candidate quality is probably not the independent force it was first thought to be but rather interacts with voters' party identification and issue preferences.

Has the strategic politicians literature been a dead end, given so many contradictory and inconclusive results? I think not, for it has been an area of research that looks remarkably like real science, if one excuses the absence of genuine replication. Yet the debates over measurement and the arguments about the relative importance of local versus national factors in candidates' decisions to run have obscured the most important feature of the strategic politicians hypothesis. What has gotten lost is the simultaneity implicit in Jacobson and Kernell's (1981) view of candidacy. If one goes back to the logic of their model, it is apparent that candidates are both endogenous and exogenous factors in the electoral system. In other words, candidates are drawn into the political arena because of political influences, which they, in turn, reinforce and amplify through their campaigns.

Viewed from this perspective, I think it is fair to say that the strategic politicians hypothesis has never been properly tested. Scholars have usually examined only one side of the equation—either the decision of experienced candidates to run or the voters' preference for experienced candidates favored by partisan tides—but they have never put the two relationships together in a unified model. A more appropriate specification would be a system of equations that connects each dimension of candidacy to the other rather than a single, linear model. Even with a more appropriately specified model, however, scholars must still take one further step backward and ask, where did the candidates come from and how do communities differ in their supply of strategic politicians?

Divided Government

However one assigns the responsibility for declining competition and the localism inherent in congressional elections, the results of these long-term trends seem clear: a nearly permanent condition of divided government. The phenomenon of divided government poses a somewhat different puzzle because it involves both presidential and congressional elections. Leaving aside the matter of whether or not divided party control of the executive and legislative branches is good or bad for the country (cf. Mayhew 1991; Cox and Kernell 1991), it is clear that at least one source of division is the chronic inability of the Democrats until 1992 to nominate competitive candidates for the presidency (Petrocik 1991; Wattenberg 1991a).[14] However, it is the other aspect of the split—the Democratic hegemony in the House and to a lesser extent in the Senate for nearly four decades—that is of concern to congressional analysts.

One explanation for the congressional contribution to divided government is virtually indistinguishable from the argument over incumbents, challengers, and declining competition. On the one hand, we have incumbents manipulating voters and resources so successfully that no rational politician would consider a challenge even with the powerful electoral pull of a popular presidential candidate at the top of the ticket. In this way, the numerical advantage gained by the Democrats, when the GOP was in trouble nationally during the 1960s and 1970s, became a self-perpetuating majority because more Democratic incumbents have run in every subsequent election cycle. On the other hand, the perennial inability of the Republicans to recruit competitive candidates in so many House districts has clearly limited the party's ability to capitalize on its strong presidential showings in recent years.

Several political observers dispute both interpretations in favor of other causal factors. Some stress the fact that an ideology of activist

---

14. One might argue, in fact, that the Clinton nomination of 1992 was a continued manifestation of this problem and that the Republicans handed Democrats the presidency because of bad judgment and an exceptionally poor campaign.

government gives the Democratic party an inherent edge in developing a pool of strong congressional candidates while others believe that it fits comfortably with voter expectations about the representational functions of the Congress. The key in either case is the recruitment of candidates who are eager to provide a particular mix of constituency service, localized benefits, and personal access to voters. Yet empirical proof that the root causes of divided government lie in the ideological attitudes of prospective members of Congress is sketchy at best, so this piece of the congressional election puzzle remains unresolved as well.

Jacobson (1990b) has stressed the issue preferences of voters as a primary cause of divided government. As his strategic politicians argument became more problemmatic, he began to shift his emphasis from the timing of candidates' emergence to voters' assessment of their message. In a subsequent article (1991), he mustered further survey data indicating that voters wanted policy outcomes from the Congress that were very different from what they expected from the president. Given their desire for localized benefits, personal attention, and responsiveness to organized interests, he suggested that voters tended to prefer candidates who satisfy these preferences. Because Democratic candidates for Congress find such positions philosophically compatible with their personal views, they inevitably have the electoral advantage.

Ehrenhalt (1991, 218), too, contended that Republicans are a permanent minority in Congress because they are unable to recruit candidates who appeal to the electorate. Ehrenhalt depicted the contemporary officeholder as someone so intensely engaged in public life that only the most single-minded and committed politicians are willing to pay the costs of running for and holding onto elective positions. These total politicians drive out the amateurs, partly because they develop superior entrepreneurial skills in appealing to voters and partly because they tend to believe in government as a way of life and as an institution. Over time, then, the combination of competition and self-selection elevates a type of politician who is a governmental activist, a trend that gives the Democratic party a "natural majority" among the pool of prospective candidates, if not in the electorate. Ehrenhalt concluded, "The Democratic party is the party of government in the United States, or more precisely, the party that believes in government. . . . As such, it is the obvious magnet for people who think running for office is worth the sacrifices it entails" (1991, 224).

Fiorina (1991) arrived at a similar conclusion by a different route. He argued that voters deliberately cast their votes for legislators of the opposite party to correct the ideological extremism in the executive branch that is the inevitable consequence of the current nomination system. Given that direct primaries tend to produce candidates who are too far from the median voter, voters compel the adoption of moderate policy choices by placing the legislature in the hands of one party and the executive in the hands of the other. The sophisticated logic of Fiorina's analysis is partly born out by survey research that shows voters more accepting than they used to be of divided government. (See also Jacobson 1990b, 119). On the other hand, it stretches the bounds of credibility to suggest that voters, who cannot recognize their own legislators or make basic judgments about the ideological stances of presidential candidates, would resort to such a complex, constitutional calculation at the polls. Indeed, Segura and Nicholson (1992) have recently argued that one manifestation of divided government, split-Senate delegations, is more likely attributable to the increasing frequency of candidate-centered campaigns.

If such theories provide an intriguing case for the permanent minority status of Republicans in the House, they fail to account for the loss of competitiveness among Democratic candidates. As noted earlier, throughout the 1980s both parties suffered an increase in uncontested races and a surge in noncompetitive challengers. But Jacobson (1990b) and Ehrenhalt (1991) could account for only the Republican part of the deterioration in the candidate pool. Fiorina (1991), on the other hand, postulated an outcome—divided party control—that assumes the elevation of extremists for executive and legislatitve nominations but does not indicate why this bias should operate in a conservative direction for presidents but not governors and in a liberal direction for lawmakers in Congress but not necessarily in state legislatures.

Finally, all these analyses have assumed that voters' preferences for candidates depend on political issues. There is some support for this notion in the literature, for example, Fiorina 1981b, Kiewiet 1983, Born 1986, and Uslaner and Conway 1985. But Petrocik's (1991) research on the role of issues in divided government suggests two severe limitations on this interpretation. First, voters were able to connect issues they perceived as important with either of the two national parties' presidential nominees with some frequency, but they hardly ever made the connection between such problems and House candidates. Indeed, fully 71 percent of the respondents in the 1988 NES survey could recall no issue as being a factor in the House campaign (Petrocik 1991, 32). More significantly, voters who had some party-related issue information tended to give incumbents only a slight bonus beyond what would be expected on the basis of their partisanship, but the large majority, who had no information, gave Democratic incumbents a twenty-nine-point edge and Republican incumbents a 24-point edge (Petrocik 1991, 33). This suggests that such factors as name recognition, experience, and money are more important than median issue positions as contributors to divided government.

Undoubtedly, the voters' information deficit is related to the lack of competitiveness in most House races, a factor that Petrocik (1991) failed to consider. An examination of the electoral fortunes of legislators who supported highly unpopular deficit reduction package in 1990 suggests just how important the interaction between challenger quality and issue positions can be under conditions of divided government (Jacobson 1992a). Voters penalized House members who voted for the deficit reduction package, but only if they could recall the challenger's name. For the NES sample of House elections, this represented just 3.7 percent of self-reported voters (1992a, 12). What is more telling, however, is that senators who were running for reelection and had significant opposition did not vote for it (1992a, 14). Boschwitz was the lone exception: he seems to have underestimated his opponent, voted for the bill, and lost.

In the end, the arguments about what citizens are choosing with their ballots rests at least in part on the capacity of candidates to frame alternatives in ways that are compelling to voters, whether it be particularized benefits and attentiveness, a particular view of governmental activism, or median policy outcomes. But this brings us back to recruitment and forces us to ask once again; Where do these candidates come from? How do their political ambitions lead them to choose one set of electoral strategies over another? How do political institutions and norms foster or hinder the emergence of individuals with a particular mix of policy orientations?

Implications

What conclusions about candidacy flow from this rich and complex literature on congressional elections? We can certainly speak with more certainty on some topics than on others, but the big issue—the causal role of candidates—remains elusive. Throughout this chapter, we have observed candidates in various guises, both responding to given incentives and strategic situations and creating opportunities and choices on their own. Their dual role presents empirical challenges that cannot be resolved with the simple linear models most scholars working in the field currently employ.[15] Complex interactions occur between incumbency, candidate quality, national and local political contexts, and voter decisions. Their estimation perforce becomes more complex, particularly when one of the endogenous variables—candidate quality—often takes on ordinal values. Although economists have developed techniques for simultaneous equation models using discrete dependent variables (see, for example, Manski and McFadden 1981), to my knowledge, few political scientists have ventured onto this methodological terrain.

But even as scholars employ more sophisticated methods to unravel what is cause and what is effect, they will need to address at least three other pressing methodological questions: the definition of candidate quality, the specification of local contexts, and the control for changes across time.

At present, candidate quality has the same status in the congressional literature that pornography enjoys in the opinions of the Supreme Court; that is to say, scholars recognize a quality candidate when they see one, but they disagree about just what individual attributes are most salient to the definition. For some scholars, such as Jacobson (1990a and 1992b) and most recently Fleisher and Bond (1992), what matters is prior office-holding experience, irrespective of when it occurred and what level of responsibiltiy it entailed. Others, such as Canon (1990a), Krasno and Green (1988), Segura and Nicholson (1992), Squire (1991 and 1992a), and Stewart (1989), also rely on experience as the most salient aspect of candidate quality, although they differentiate among types of offices held. Still others— such as Goldenberg, Traugott, and Baumgartner (1986); Bond, Covington, and Fleisher (1985); and occasionally Jacobson and Kernell (1990)—have employed campaign expenditures, or some mix of money and experience, to capture the political strength of candidates. Finally, some scholars, such as Canon (1990a) or Herrnson (1991), have attempted to differentiate among candidates lacking officeholding experience by treating party officeholders, legislative staffers, or repeat challengers as special cases or by acknowledging their celebrity status as media figures, astronauts, or sports heroes.

Each of these definitions endeavors to encompass the different dimensions of successful candidacy—political ambition, voter appeal, name recognition, organizational and coalition-building skills, and fundraising ability. What differentiates them, however, is the

---

15. One exception is the study by Green and Krasno (1988 and 1990) that employs a two-stage least-squares procedure to estimate the endogenous relationships of money and candidate quality on House election results.

degree to which they assign a weight to the various components. For example, the simple dichotomization of officeholding experience makes no pretense at sorting out the relative importance of candidate characteristics: having won public office before is prima facie evidence that a candidate has all or enough of the important attributes to win again.

This approach obviously assumes away a great deal of variation that is significant to both candidates and voters. Politicians need more ambition to run for Congress than for dogcatcher, they need current exposure to voters more than a reputation from the past, they need better skills to construct a district-level or statewide coalition than to capture a county legislative seat, and they need to attract a different type of donor for a national office than for a local one. Moreover, voters expect a different quality of representation from their members of Congress than from their members of city council. To ignore all these differences is to lump individuals of widely divergent political caliber in one category as "quality" candidates and to relegate some very promising politicians to the residual category. Measurement error is the inevitable consequence.

Any efforts to distinguish more precisely among candidates has risks, however. First, no two indices of candidate quality have yielded the same rank ordering of candidates, because they give different priority to particular offices and distinguish among nonofficeholders in a variety of ways. Scales can range from a low of three to a high of eight, and they can place state party officials or television stars near the top of the pecking order or closer to the bottom. Second, most indices rely on information about candidate attributes available before the election, but some depend on ad hoc judgments, particularly in the case of amateurs. Third, none of the indices attempts to specify the intervals between categories of candidates, even though they are typically used in statistical analyses as if they were cardinal measures. Fourth, none of the schemes controls for regional differences in the relative importance of various kinds of experience. Fifth, none of the indices incorporates nonexperiential qualities—ambition, energy, empathy, and policy concerns—all characteristics that matter a great deal to candidates themselves and to the elites who back them (Fowler and McClure 1989).

In the face of such limitations, it is reasonable to ask whether the considerable effort needed to construct a complex measure of candidate quality is worth the effort, yet not a single scholar has seriously attempted to assess the trade-offs involved with various measures of candidate quality. Jacobson (1990a) reported a correlation of .8 between his dichotomization of candidate experience and Green and Krasno's (1988) eight-point scale for only the 1978 election. But as Green and Krasno subsequently pointed out, this means that between 20 to 35 percent of the variance in Jacobson's variable is "random noise" (1990, 370). Significantly, the disagreements between these authors have major consequences for their widely divergent findings about whether or not incumbent spending matters in House election outcomes. Moreover, information regarding relationships between the rival indices for other years is unavailable, and comparisons among other scales are nonexistent. Thus, we have no idea which candidate rankings have changed most in the postwar period or which are the best predictors over time.

Equally important, none of the indices of candidate quality has been matched against actual candidates. In the absence of any systematic observation of candidates' attitudes and campaign styles, there is simply no way of assessing whether any of the experiential measures adequately tap the qualities that make a candidate successful. For example, different levels of officeholding presumably signify different degrees of aptitude for coalition-building, but this assumption has not been systematically tested.

Finally, experiential measures of quality candidates have not been evaluated in terms of the opinions of elites and voters. Although scholars have a pretty good understanding of how voters assess the declared candidates at the time of the election, they have little information about why voters arrived at those opinions or which attributes produced the greatest change in the like-dislike variables. Moreover, they have no data whatsoever about how elites—party and interest group activists, contributors, and campaign volunteers—arrived at their decisions to back a particular candidate or how relevant the various experiential indices were to that choice.

Candidate quality is not the only methodological issue confronting congressional scholars, however. Equally pressing is the development of a more complex treatment of the constituency context. A variety of studies in the strategic politicians literature has identified various indicators of party strength as significant predictors of experienced challengers. Some have used the previous vote margin of the incumbent or challenger, while others have used some form of the normal vote. It is extremely important to control for the partisan dispositions of the constituency because 75 percent of the congressional electorate still consists of party-line voters (Keith et al. 1992, 202). Furthermore, the number of defections that take place over the course of a campaign are relatively small, even when challenger spending is taken into account (Jacobson 1990a). But in choosing a measure of the constituency's partisan orientation, it is probably preferable to adopt the normal vote because it is less likely to reflect the quality of the previous year's challenger and the fundraising activity of the past campaign.

Partisanship is an important contextual variable in other respects as well. A number of scholars have indicated that party organizations are involved in the recruitment of congressional candidates, even if they cannot control who actually runs (Tobin and Keynes 1975; Kazee and Thornberry 1990; Haeberle 1985; Kunkel 1988). It is therefore important to ascertain the relationship of measures of party organizational strength already in the literature to the emergence of competitive candidates (cf. Mayhew 1986; Cotter et al. 1984) and to consider alternative possibilities.

In addition, it is important to estimate the pool of prospective candidates. Both Canon (1990a) and Stewart (1989) have developed indices of the number of officeholders per constituency that have proved statistically valid. But the most likely office seekers, state legislators, do not always run (Robek 1982). Thus, far more work is needed to understand which factors affect the local supply of potential candidates and their likelihood of running. Some of the more promising variables that emerged from McClure's and my case study (1989) of candidate decision making in Upstate New York included the following: the degree of overlap between constituencies for lesser offices with House and Senate constituencies, particularly as it changed under successive reapportionments; the configuration of local media markets; the opportunity structure of lower-level offices, especially those leading to the state legislature; and the level of professionalization of local and state government. Many of these variables turn out to be significant in other districts as well (Kazee 1993).

This kind of research has high opportunity costs because the data are not readily available and many variables change for House districts every ten years, but it is an important and feasible task for anyone with the will and a sufficient number of graduate students. A far more difficult methodological task, however, is documenting and controlling for the dynamic aspects of candidate emergence.

A great deal of the existing research on congressional candidates relies on cross-sectional data. Most of the time series analysis has been conducted by scholars working on the question of strategic politicians and to a lesser extent by those studying campaign finance. But the investigation of many important aspects of candidate emergence has been limited to a single year or a few years at most, even though the political environment in which candidates make their decisions to run for Congress has radically changed over the postwar period. We have already seen that there are identifiable thresholds (the mid-1960s and the mid-1980s) that mark changes in the competitiveness of House elections, but there are more subtle changes at work that are both harder to spot and more troublesome to control.

First, scholars need to find a way to account for the changing trends in uncontested races. Before the mid-1960s, it was relatively easy to deal with this problem because single-candidate elections were largely confined to the South, although most scholars simply ignored the situation altogether by eliminating such races. But the frequency of cases continued to grow substantially during the 1980s, and instances of uncontested races cut across parties and regions in relatively unsystematic ways. King and Gelman (1991, 121) noted that eliminating uncontested seats introduces selection bias into the analysis and that assigning some arbitrary number or the last contested result generates measurement error. Instead, they adopted a method for calculating an *effective vote* by creating a density function based on each party's congressional vote in the previous election to estimate what the district vote would have been in that year if an opponent had run. But to do this, they had to assume that there were no systematic differences in the two parties' ability to contest seats and no systematic biases in local communities that depressed the supply of opposing candidates for one party or the other. From various studies cited throughout this chapter, it is not clear that such assumptions are warranted. The main point, however, is not whether King and Gelman have introduced a new source of bias in their analysis of House elections in attempting to control for uncontested seats but that such bias exists and is extremely complex to control.

Second, there is increasing evidence that prospective candidates must consider a variety of changes in the political environment that have taken place quite rapidly. For example, congressional campaigns are now more open to nationalizing influences because of the resurgence of the national parties, the rise of political consultants, and the growth of PACs. Whether these actors actively promote particular candidacies or simply loom in the background as prospective supporters, their control over the flow of campaign resources makes them highly significant to the emergence of congressional candidates. With continuing increases in the absolute cost of House and Senate campaigns and in the relative proportion of money coming from outside the constituency, the influence of national elites is likely to grow (cf. Eismeier and Pollack 1988; Grenzke 1988).

At the same time, the opportunity structures shaping the career paths of members of Congress have been under enormous pressures from such forces as reapportionment, the professionalization of state and municipal government, and developments in local party organizations. None of these trends has taken place uniformly across the nation, and so each potential candidate confronts a unique set of circumstances that may be more or less conducive to candidacy. In an analysis of the entry of former state legislators to Congress, Berkman (1990) provided data that indicated a striking amount of variation in the recruitment of a key group of prospective lawmakers. The percentage of House members with prior experience in the state legislature has increased gradually for both parties since 1959, rising from about 36 percent to slightly over 50 percent by 1988. But some state delegations actually experienced a decline in the proportion of former state lawmakers, while others had large increases. In small states, in particular, the state legislature declined significantly as a political base for prospective House members.

Finally, it is likely that in attempting to assess the role of congressional candidates in fostering electoral competiton, scholars will be aiming at a moving target. But as many of the long-term relationships of interest to congressional election scholars change over time— particularly those concerning election margins, money, and national economic conditions—they become subject to a variety of problems likely to hinder statistical analysis. These probably vary in magnitude. Autocorrelation, for example, is quite pronounced in electoral data. The electoral margin in a district at time t is closely correlated with the margin at t-1, but this relationship has weakened in recent years and with various local circumstances that are not altogether clear (Ansolabehere, Brady, and Fiorina 1988). Complicating these factors is the level of the parties' exposure in terms of the number of seats obtained in the last election or the number of open seats. When parties are more exposed, their candidates fare worse at the polls and thus their performance in one election cycle depends on how well or badly they did last time (Oppenheimer, Stimson, and Waterman 1986; Waterman 1990). Thus, the statistical signifance of an incumbent's or a challenger's previous margin in affecting experienced House and Senate candidates' decisions to run may be misleading.

All these lag effects can produce a correlation of the error terms in econometrically estimated models, which in turn yields biased coefficients and large sample variances. Under such circumstances one can obtain some curious results, such as Erikson's (1990a, 386) bizarre finding that the magnitude of the winning party's electoral triumph determines subsequent economic growth, rather than the other way round. Erikson wisely rejected this argument, but the occurrence of the relationship suggests how perilous it is to deal with the dynamic elements of congressional electoral data.

Change is not confined to electoral data but seems to be associated with economic data as well. In the 1970s and 1980s, evidence has emerged to suggest that the connection between local economies and national conditions may be weakening (Owens and Olson 1980; Radcliff 1988). Erikson (1990a) further indicated that economic voting is largely confined to presidential election years because voters tend to hold the president rather than the Congress responsible for the economy, and he argued that one finds economic voting at the midterm only under rather extraordinary circumstances. If these scholars are correct, then they raise a host of complicated issues about how prospective candidates judge the mood of the electorate and its general impact on their electoral fortunes and how differences between presidential and off-year elections shape the recruitment process.

None of these issues of candidate quality, constituency context, and dynamics can be completely resolved without access to survey data about prospective and declared candidates. Regrettably, little information is available on this score. With the exception of Maisel's (1982) study of primary challengers in 1978 and Herrnson's (1988) survey of the major party candidates in the 1984 general election, both of which used mailed questionnaires, there has been almost no empirical work on the attitudes and strategies of congressional candidates. Incidentally, neither of these efforts contained more than a few items on the motivations and decisions to run; and of course, neither obtained information on potential nominees. Kazee (1983) did interview a few potential challengers in his assessment of the deterrent effect of incumbency, and my own case study with McClure (1989) examined the decision to run in an open seat. More recent case studies undertaken for the candidate identification project organized by Kazee (1993) have generated a much richer understanding of how the candidate pool arises in roughly a dozen different constituencies. But other than this handful of analyses, the most recent and extensive survey on candidacy remained a mail survey conducted by Baker and Bennet (1991) of 400 nonincumbent primary contestants. Indeed, a national survey of primary candidates in the 1992 election by Norris and Darcy (1992) is a long-overdue effort to tap candidates' attitudes toward running for Congress.

This meager range of information, all gathered on a shoestring budget, imposes serious limits on the questions scholars can raise about candidacy over the past two decades. Given the wealth of resources devoted to surveying the mass public, I find such deficiencies disturbing.

In sum, once electoral competition is tied to individuals rather than parties—whether incumbents, challengers or contestants in open seats—the outcomes only make sense if we understand how one set of alternatives instead of another ends up on the ballot. As we have seen, the last decade has sparked a variety of inquiries that bring us closer to understanding the myriad ways in which candidacy affects congressional elections, but in doing so, it has also revealed how much more remains unknown. Before the ambiguous status of candidacy is resolved, many important methodological issues require attention. Furthermore, many of the parameters we recognize as influencing candidate decision making are in a state of flux. These circumstances create significant opportunities for new research while at the same time they lend a certain urgency to the investigative enterprise. If scholars fail to understand candidate emergence in the present context, they may limit their capacity to explain it in the future.

CHAPTER 5

Candidates and Representation

The requisites in actual representation are that the Representatives should sympathize with their constituents; should think as they think and feel as they feel. . . .
—George Mason, Remarks at the Constitutional Convention

Wherever there is representative democracy, there is potential for distorting the popular will. Bias comes not just from the delegation of authority or the process of collective deliberation, but also from the means of designating lawmakers. This was why early republics chose legislators by lot and why even today the principle of random selection is thought to produce the purest form of democratic assembly. Modern legislatures, by drawing their members from a relatively small and homogeneous political elite,[1] have strayed far from the ideal of serving as microcosms of the general public. Consequently, lawmakers' social and political origins and their effect on representation are questions of long-standing interest. Particularly in the contemporary Congress, members' individual attributes are connected to two different aspects of the institution's representativeness: its failure to reflect the political mobilization of women and various ethnic minorities and its seeming imperviousness to the partisan realignment in the South.

Given the rapid changes in the past two decades in the status of women, in the enfranchisement of African-Americans, and in the growing ranks of citizens of non-European origin, the demography of the Congress ought to look quite different—more female, more racially heterogeneous, and more culturally diverse. But the entry of women to Congress has not kept pace with the expansion of female participation either in politics generally or in the professions and public offices that have been the traditional stepping-stones to Capitol Hill. Nor has the presence of major ethnic groups in Congress, African-Americans and Hispanics in particular, increased propor-

---

1. For an excellent overview of how recruitment affects the representativeness of legislative bodies, see Aberbach, Putnam, and Rockman 1981 and Eldersveld 1989.

tionately relative to their numbers in society. Moreover, the general underrepresentation of African-American voters is compounded because the majority of African-American citizens in the United States live in the South while most African-American representatives come from the North.

Yet it is not simply the demography of Congress that has proved resistent to change; the partisan balance, too, should look quite different in light of the economic and social transformation of the South in recent years. Many of these changes have worked their way into the political arena and are now manifest both in the liberalization of the Democratic Party and the revival of the GOP. The presence of intensely loyal southern African-Americans in the Democratic coalition has moved the region's officeholders into the national mainstream of the party. At the same time, the migration of northern Republicans and the shift of the region's conservatives away from the Democrats have made southern Republican candidates viable enough to dominate presidential contests and to win statewide offices. But Republicans have been unable to capitalize on their strength at the top of their party's ticket to get more Republicans elected to the House and, to a lesser extent, the Senate. Thus, the partisan realignment long predicted for the South is only partially reflected in the region's congressional delegation.

Each of these developments has a different implication for the nature of representation practiced inside Congress. The most obvious, of course, is the relationship between the demography of the institution and its capacity for descriptive representation. But such trends have an effect on the policy aspects of representation as well.

By *descriptive representation,* I mean the extent to which lawmakers are like the people they serve. In this view, according to Pitkin (1967, 60–61), true representation occurs when the legislature's composition "corresponds accurately to that of the whole nation" and when individual legislators mirror their constituencies. Thus, representation is judged not as "acting for" the citizenry but as "standing for" its salient characteristics, although, of course, action presumably reflects this correspondence between representatives and constituents. Eulau and Karps (1977) use the term "symbolic responsiveness," and Fenno (1978) refers to the "identification" between legislators and constituents in discussing the empathetic dimensions of representation. Unlike Pitkin, however, these scholars suggest that legislators can create a sense of similarity through gestures and attitudes even though they do not mirror the citizens they serve.

By *policy representation,* I mean the extent to which legislators reflect the basic political orientations of the people who elect them. This type of representation is often discussed in terms of the delegate-trustee dichotomy in which the legislator must choose whether to be the constituency's messenger to Congress or to exercise independent judgment about what is in the long-term interests of the citizens and the nation (Pitkin 1967, chap. 7). When applied to Congress, policy representation is more typically defined as the congruence between members' roll call votes and citizens' preferences on specific policies (Eulau and Karps 1977). Such a view has been widely attacked as an extremely narrow conception of representation that has been poorly specified in theory and badly measured in practice (cf. Achen 1977 and 1978; Erikson 1978), that demands more information from voters than they are likely to possess (Bernstein 1989), and that requires a degree of certainty about constituency attitudes that legislators seldom experience (Fenno 1978). Nevertheless, the very essence of accountable representation is that legislators make decisions that are responsive to the wishes of their constituents (Pitkin 1967, 209–10). This need not require agreement on every vote but rather a general accord on broad principles of public policy. Thus, I take partisan congruence rather than issue-by-issue congruence to be a necessary condition for policy representation.

To some extent, the ability of Congress to satisfy these different dimensions of representation is inseparable from the incumbency effect discussed in the previous chapter. If incumbents cannot be beaten and they refuse to retire, then newcomers will be kept out of Congress whatever their gender, ethnicity, or partisan appeal. But some of the resistance to change could be linked to the rules and norms governing nominations, the opportunity structures within particular constituencies, and the perceptions among prospective candidates that women, members of minority groups, or southern Republicans, such as themselves, can strive for congressional office in their particular communities. In understanding the social and political orientation of the contemporary Congress, then, it is important to establish how much the institution's marriage to the status quo is traceable to current practices of recruiting candidates.

By and large, the literature examining the representational aspects of candidate recruitment has concentrated on descriptive representation. The social biases of candidacy, as we saw in chapter 3, were heavily canvassed by early scholars. But when this avenue of research failed to yield useful predictions about legislative roles or voting behavior (cf. Matthews 1983; Prinz 1989; Canon forthcoming), such lines of inquiry gradually disappeared from the scholarly agenda.

In reopening the discussion of how candidate emergence influences representation, however, it is not my intention to resurrect the sociological paradigm of candidacy. Rather, I concentrate on developing the connection between representation and candidates' motives and methods of attaining congressional office. What emerges from this fragmented and ambiguous literature is a clear sense that scholars' neglect of candidate recruitment has cost them an opportunity to examine broad questions of political change.

Candidates and Descriptive Representation

The ideal of descriptive representation is behind the long tradition of inquiry among legislative scholars into the backgrounds and social characteristics of the people who serve in Congress.[2] Not only were lawmakers examined for their likeness to the people they governed, but their characteristics as members of the governing elite provided evidence about the tendencies toward hierarchy and rigidity in the class system of American society. In addition, legislators' social backgrounds were regarded as factors in shaping the roles that legislators would adopt, particularly the classic distinction between trustees and delegates (Wahlke et al. 1962; Davidson 1969; Jewell 1970). In summarizing the research on social background and experience, Matthews (1983) noted that their relationship to legislative behavior was weak. He concluded, "Viewed as independent variables [this approach to recruitment] has been pretty much a wash" (1983, 42). Canon (forthcoming) further observed that analyses of the social bases of recruitment provided few clues about who among the pool of eligibles might actually become a candidate. Indeed, in a study of the recruitment of British members of Parliament, Norris and Lovenduski (1992) reported that the applicant pool and the eventual nominees were quite similar in demographic terms.

It is hardly surprising that personal attributes provided such weak explanations of politicians' behavior, because lawmakers have been such a homogeneous group. For nearly two centuries, members of Congress have come from the same social and professional stratum and have been almost exclusively male and of European ancestry (Bogue et al. 1976), so that there was almost no variation in the independent variables. Although the institution has begun to adapt to growing political participation among women and ethnic minorities,

---

2. For a summary of this literature, see Matthews 1983, Prinz 1989, or Canon. Forthcoming.

many political observers question whether an institution that continues to be dominated by one segment of the population can responsively legislate on behalf of a highly pluralistic society. Their view is gradually gaining support from studies that trace differences in political behavior to gender and ethnicity.

In studies of roll call voting, for example, female lawmakers are consistently more liberal than their male colleagues, even when party affiliation is controlled (Welch 1985; Poole and Ziegler 1985; Carroll 1985). Moreover, in a longitudinal analysis of male and female party activists in California, Costantini (1990, 766) found marked differences in issue attitudes between the two groups, and he concluded that women inside the parties were more issue oriented and more likely to take positions that would lead to further polarization of the parties. Furthermore, in state legislatures that have a relatively high proportion of female members, female lawmakers are more likely to introduce and pass bills dealing with issues relating to children, families, and women's well-being (Thomas 1991; Center for the American Woman and Politics 1992). There is some anecdotal evidence that they pursue different issue agendas inside Congress as well. In the aftermath of the 1992 election, for example, National Public Radio's congressional reporter, Cokie Roberts, observed that women in Congress tend to take the issues from the bottom of the pile that men often consider less important.

Similar patterns are evident among African-American legislators, who have constituted the most liberal and cohesive voting block in the Congress (Greene 1991) and whose alternative budget has become a rallying point for advocates of reduced military spending and increased attention to human resources. The number of Hispanic or Asian legislators in Congress is presently too small to make generalizations about the relationship between their backgrounds and policy decisions. There is some evidence, however, that the cultural diversity among Latinos will lead to significant differences in partisanship and ideology among legislators from different Hispanic backgrounds (Hero 1992).

In addition to different policy priorities, women and ethnic minorities often bring different occupational backgrounds to Congress. Compared to the total House figure of 183 lawyers in the 102d Congress, for example, there were relatively few female and African-American lawmakers who have legal backgrounds: only three of the twenty-eight women and four of the twenty-five African-Americans (compiled from Barone and Ujifusa 1991). Moreover, among the women contesting House seats in 1992, including the incumbents, only 9.5 percent reported the law as their profession. An additional 28 percent claimed business and financial backgrounds, and 12 percent had experience in government and public affairs, but a relatively large percentage of candidates were in less typical occupations: education (17 percent), media and public relations (10 percent), community activism (8 percent), health and social services (8 percent), and clerical (2 percent) (National Women's Political Caucus 1992).

Such life experiences probably contribute to the differing agendas that women and ethnic minorities pursue in Congress, but they also raise questions about differing approaches to the legislative craft. Eulau and Sprague (1964), for example, have suggested that the dominance of lawyers in American legislatures springs from a congruence of norms and skills in the two fields. If they are correct, then women and ethnic minorities may be less effective legislators inside Congress because they have had different training; or they may transform the business of legislating when their numbers become large enough to have an impact on the culture of the House and Senate.

The level of representation for women and various ethnic minorities is presented in table 5.1. Steady improvement over the past few decades is apparent for all groups, but with the exception of the 1992 election, it has not been as rapid as we might expect or some people might wish. Various explanations for the slow rate of progress have been advanced, ranging from voter discrimination to conspiracy among white male elites to prevent women and ethnic minorities from seeking congressional office, to structural impediments arising from the American electoral system, to a lack of political ambition among the disadvantaged groups. Much of this literature does not directly pertain to the Congress, for it has tended to concentrate on other types

TABLE 5.1.   Gender and Ethnicity in the U.S. Congress

	1961	1971	1981	1991	1993
House (N)[a]					
Female	18	13	19	28	47
African-American	3	13	17	25	38
Hispanic	2	5	6	10	17
Senate (N)					
Female	2	1	2	2	6
African-American	0	1	0	0	1
Hispanic	0	0	0	0	0

Source: Compiled from Ornstein, Mann, and Malbin 1992, 38–39; Barone and Ujifusa 1991; New York Times, November 5, 1992, B1.; U.S. House of Representatitves Hispanic Congressional Caucus 1993.

[a]Does not include nonvoting representatives from the District of Columbia and U.S. Territories.

of offices and electorates. Scholarly investigations of women officeholders, for example, have largely examined their role in state legislatures, while those directed at ethnic groups are heavily concentrated in the urban politics literature. Furthermore, considerably more research has been published on leadership among women in politics, for example, than on leadership within ethnic communities. It is therefore problematic how much one can infer about recruitment to Congress from such disparate sources. Yet despite these limitations and imbalances, it appears that the impediments to candidacy for women are somewhat different from the factors affecting the political advancement of ethnic minorities.

The Dearth of Women in Congress

Until recently, the most common route to Congress for women was widowhood (Bullock and Heys 1972; Gertzog 1979). Party organizations often nominated the wife of a deceased representative to run for his unexpired term, or governors appointed a spouse to serve her late husband's remaining time in the Senate. If she was successful, the powers that be occasionally supported her continuance in office. Sometimes these congressional widows became powerful politicians in their own right, such as Representative Lindy Boggs (D—La.), but more often they had relatively brief and uneventful legislative careers, such as Muriel Humphrey (D—Minn.).

When women began winning seats in Congress on their own in the 1970s, many observers took this as a sign of a new era of political equality, even though the more immediate effect of women's newfound political independence as candidates was a *decline* in their numbers inside Congress. But progress in achieving public office at lower levels of government was not matched by comparable advances by women into Congress, and it began to appear that parity between men and women in the nation's legislature would take centuries. Indeed, Andersen and Thorson (1984) estimated that given prevailing rates of electoral success among women candidates and continuing levels of incumbent retirement and reelection, the number of women serving in Congress by 2000 would increase by about 1 percent. Until 1992, their predictions proved only a little more pessimistic than the reality.

As scholars have attempted to account for the slow pace of change in congressional membership, they have gradually ruled out many of the stereotypical, but nonetheless plausible, explanations for the dearth of women in Congress.[3] They established that voters were relatively accepting of female candidacies and did not appear to discriminate against women (Darcy and Shramm 1977; Darcy, Welch, and Clark 1987). They discovered that women were as able as men to obtain campaign funds, once appropriate controls for incumbency and party status were taken into account (Burrell 1985; Uhlaner and Schlozman, 1986), and that women were as experienced, visible, and aggressive candidates as men, again when the relevant constraints were controlled (Darcy, Welch, and Clark 1987; Burrell 1991). They determined that women in lower-level offices were as ambitious for political advancement as their male colleagues (Carroll 1985). They demonstrated that the primary process, which had been thought to discriminate against women in favor of younger, more ambitious men (Bernstein 1986), was not a particular barrier to female candidacies (Burrell 1991).

To be sure, there is solid evidence of bias against women that makes their candidacy for Congress more difficult. Discrimination within local party organizations in the South, for example, has hindered women from obtaining nominations (Nechemias 1987), although in other instances, women seem to have benefited from party support (Deber 1982) and generally seemed to obtain as much help from the party as men (Burrell 1991). Pronounced differences in the way newspapers treated male and female candidates for the Senate not only have denied women equal time but have cast them in a more negative light (Kahn and Goldenberg 1991). Disadvantages in raising early money and in attracting contributions from large donors have further contributed to the difficulties female candidates have experienced (Mandel 1981; Fowler, Rupprecht, and Tamrowski 1987), although this handicap all but disappeared in the 1992 election. Harmful stereotyping has continued in the minds of voters, which shows up both in experimental situations (Sapiro 1981–82) and in public opinion polls (Wyckoff and Dran 1992). The fact that until the 1992 election women were typically ten years older than men when they were first elected to Congress suggests that their family responsibilities have tended to delay their political careers (Fowler and McClure 1989).[4] But taken altogether, the facts do not add up to a wholesale denial of women to public office because of their sex. As

---

3. For readers interested in exploring these issues in greater depth, see the excellent volume by Darcy, Welch, and Clark (1987) or the detailed overview of the literature on women's political careers by Carroll (1989a).

4. Again, 1992 is an exception. Freshmen legislators as a group were a good bit older than the norm, and women on average were only a year older then men entering the House.

Darcy, Welch, and Clark concluded, "when women run, they are treated like similar male candidates by voters and political elites" (1987, 91). The issue, then, is why so few women run for Congress. There are three possible strategies for answering this question: the first is to look more deeply into the recruitment process for other types of gender bias, the second is to investigate possible structural barriers that prevent women from seeking congressional nominations, and the third is to peer inside women's heads to see if they are predisposed against congressional careers.

Although gender differences in party support, campaign funds, electoral recognition, and so forth wash out at the general election stage, Carroll (1989a) has suggested that they may be present at earlier stages in the recruitment process. Just because women who make it to the final hurdle are politically indistinguishable from men, she argued, does not necessarily mean that discrimination is absent at the nomination stage or even earlier. Prospective female candidates may be disadvantaged among donors and party elites (Wilhite and Theilman 1986; Fowler, Rupprecht, and Tamrowski 1987), or the primary electorate may take a different view of women candidates than does the general electorate. Why have women, for example, experienced difficulty raising early money? Do they fare worse in crowded primary fields? Is their relatively low level of participation in open-seat races simply an artifact of how few women run for Congress, or does it signal a continuing tendency for women to serve as sacrificial lambs? At present, there has been little research into such issues, and Carroll has urged further analysis of the pattern of early money in congressional races and the emergence of party front-runners in primaries before we declare congressional recruitment to be gender neutral.

The structural explanation showed early promise, because the number of women in the U.S. Congress is so disproportionately small compared to most other national assemblies. When we look at the educational and professional attainment of women in this country vis-à-vis other democracies, we would expect the Congress to have one of the largest proportions of female members, when in fact it has ranked at the bottom of the list with the British Parliament (Darcy, Welch, and Clark 1987, 67). Only after the 1992 election brought a record number of women into the House and pushed the percentage to 10.8 did women in the United States achieve the average rate of representation for European democracies.

This has prompted some scholars to suggest that single-member districts are inherently discriminatory against women (as they are known to be against ethnic minorities (Grofman and Handley 1989; Polinard and Wrunkle 1991)) because they require a plurality of votes and because they inhibit ticket-balancing strategies among party leaders. When the election is an all-or-nothing affair, the argument goes, then women inevitably lose a place on the ballot to men. From studies of municipal and state legislative elections, Darcy, Welch, and Clark (1987, 116–24) found some support for this argument, as did Bledsoe and Herring (1990). But other research on subnational, multi-member constituencies in the United States and Great Britain indicated that the effects are quite limited and localized (Welch and Studler 1990; Studler and Welch 1992; Bullock and MacManus 1991).

An additional structural argument concerns the mismatch of the supply of women candidates and the available opportunities to run for Congress. If we consider who is eligible to compete for a congressional seat, it is obvious that we have to look first at the entry of women into the relevant professions and stepping-stone offices. Women's entry into the legal profession, for example, rose from about 3 percent to about 13 percent between 1970 and 1984 (Darcy, Welch, and Clark 1987). The percentage of female state legislators was slightly higher for both periods—4 percent and 14 percent, respectively. Both lines of increase have nearly identical slopes (Darcy, Welch, and Clark 1987, 101), which suggests that women's rate of professional advancement in society is also related to variables that affect their political advancement.

A similar constraint is evident when we consider women's position in state legislatures, which are traditional training grounds for members of Congress.[5] The number of women serving in such posts, as noted above, has more than quadrupled in the past two decades from 4 percent to 17 percent in 1991 and 20 percent in 1993. But the rate of increase has been far slower for women in Congress, rising from 3 percent in 1970 to about 6 percent in 1991. Generally, women's significant gains in state government led to much more modest increases in congressional representation until 1992's substantial rise to 10 percent.[6]

Undoubtedly, the differential effects of incumbency at the state and federal levels account for the slower rates of advancement to Congress. Although the frequency of uncontested races and the re-

---

5. Approximately 50 percent of incumbent members of the House have served in a state legislature at some point in their careers (Fowler and McClure 1989).

6. This figure is for both chambers of Congress.

election rate for incumbents in many states are similar to those in the House of Represenatatives (Maisel et al. 1990, 143 and 145), some state legislatures are nevertheless still marked by relatively high rates of retirement and defeat among incumbents. In these states, the more plentiful opportunities for women to run successful campaigns have led to rather rapid gains in the state house. In Colorado, Washington, Arizona, Wisconsin, and several other states, women now constitute more than a fifth of the membership. Unfortunately, the low retirements and exceptionally high reelection rates in Congress from 1984 to 1990 diminished the chance that women could compete successfully for congressional office in such states. It was not until the 1992 election that a record number of sixty-six retirements and nineteen primary defeats created sufficient opportunities for women to make serious inroads in the House.

A closer look at the dynamics of 1992 reveals what a major barrier incumbency has been to the advancement of women in the House. Of the one-hundred-six women who ran, forty-one survived the primary season to run as challengers and thirty-nine obtained major party nominations in open seats (National Women's Political Caucus 1992). Among the eventual winners, two women defeated incumbents and twenty-two, or better than half, succeeded in the open seat contests. Even more striking, four of the five women contesting open seats in Florida and two of the four women competing in Washington's open seats won, while five women in the eight open California districts in which female candidates were running also secured seats.[7] In short, except in Texas, women were successful in states that experienced unusually large numbers of open-seat races and where they had made substantial inroads in the state legislature.

Nevertheless, the distribution of female state legislators is skewed in such a way that even if incumbency were less of a barrier to Congress, women would still arrive on Capitol Hill at a slower rate than they enter their state capitals. For reasons that are unclear, a disproportionate number of female state lawmakers comes from small states. In the early 1960s, for example, almost one-half of the 350 women serving in state legislatures were from Connecticut, Vermont, and New Hampshire (Nechemias 1987, 130). By 1988, the bias was not nearly as pronounced, but ten states still accounted for 38 percent of the female state legislators. Moreover, these ten states held only 9 percent of the House seats in the nation. Thus, the largest pools of

---

7. California's Thirty-sixth and Forty-ninth Districts were among four open-seat races in which both major party nominees were women.

eligible female congressional candidates are located in places where there are relatively few chances to run for Congress.

Where the opportunities are greatest—in California, Pennsylvania, Texas, New York, and other large states—there are relatively few women serving in the state legislature. Indeed, Squire (1992b) has reported that the more highly professionalized the state legislature, the lower its percentage of female lawmakers. Furthermore, highly stable patterns of tenure because of high reelection rates and low levels of retirement offer few prospects for rapid change of this situation, and it will therefore take a long time for women to move into positions in these states from which they can advance to Congress. Incidentally, such patterns have led most political observers to conclude that instituting term limitations for state and federal legislators—whatever else they might accomplish—would probably lead to greater representation for women in the nation's assemblies. However, it is noteworthy that none of the seventeen nonincumbent women running in the general election for the U.S. House in California had served in the state's legislature.

A simple example in table 5.2 illustrates how the skewed distribution of eligible female candidates can slow the advancement of women to the House of Representatives. In New Hampshire, a state with the largest number of female state lawmakers, the probability of a female legislator being elected to the House is .00013. This figure reflects the fact that New Hampshire has only two seats and almost never draws its federal representatives from the state legislature. But the odds are not much better in New York State at .0003. Here the

TABLE 5.2. The Probability of a Female State Legislator from New Hampshire or New York Securing a Seat in the U.S. House of Representatives, 1988

	New Hampshire	New York
Ratio of women in state legislature	138/424	22/221
National rank based on percent women in legislature	1	34
Probability of female legislator	.33	.10
Probability of open/marginal seat in House (average over 1982–88)	.125	.16
Probability of female legislator in open/marginal seat	.04	.016
Probability state legislator runs in open/marginal seat	.01	.50
Probability state legislator wins if runs in open/marginal seat	.001	.33
Probability of female state legislator entering House	.00013	.0003

Source: Data from Center for the American Woman and Politics 1988, and Ujifusa 1984 and 1988.

likelihood that a state lawmaker will run for Congress in an open or marginal district and win is quite high at .33, but so few women are positioned to take advantage of such favorable odds that the probable outcome is quite similar to what is likely to occur in New Hampshire. Again, women's experience in the 1992 election appears consistent with this analysis. Six women sought House seats in New York State, none had state legislative experience, and the two who were successful had experience in New York City politics.[8] Five women sought House seats in Texas, the only successful one, Eddie Bernice Johnson, was also the only state legislator. In Texas, senate constituencies are actually larger than House districts, so when Johnson used her position as chairperson of the senate's reapportionment committee to draw herself a favorable district, she was able to create one that closely aligned with her existing constituency. In Pennsylvania, only one woman ran for Congress in the entire state, and again, she had no state legislative experience but managed to win in a dead heat against a county commissioner. In the large midwestern states with low turnover in the state legislature—Illinois, Ohio, Michigan—we see the same pattern: very few women contesting House seats in the so-called year of the woman, none of them state legislators, and all losers with the notable exception of a female judge in Ohio's Fifteenth District.

In a longitudinal analysis of the percentage of female lawmakers in state legislatures, Nechemias (1987) discovered that a variety of contextual factors in the states were correlated with their levels of female representation. Levels of education among the electorate and party control of the legislature both were related to the percentage of women in the legislature. But these relationships were highly unstable across time and grew weaker in the 1980s. Nechemias concluded, "we are losing explanations for state-to-state disparities in the proportion of women representatives more rapidly than we are formulating new ones" (1987, 136). Presumably, as it gets more difficult to account for the different rates of women's entry into the statehouse, it will become harder to account for their progress onto Capitol Hill.

A further structural factor in the rate of female recruitment to Congress is the relative position of women inside the two national party organizations. In the 1970s and 1980s, Democratic women have outnumbered Republican women in the House,[9] as one might expect

---

8. Representative Nydia Velazquez, (D—N.Y.) was a community activist before defeating Representative Stephen Solarz in the primary for a newly created Hispanic district. Carolyn Maloney (D—N.Y.), had a seat on the New York City Council when she defeated incumbent Bill Green.

9. In 1991–92, 68 percent of the female House members were Democrats.

given the Democrats' majority status. But Republican women were more numerous in the state legislatures, and their presence enabled the GOP to field experienced and capable female candidates for Congress. More recently, however, there is some evidence of gender differences in the recruitment of women inside the two parties, with women becoming more visible among prospective Democratic candidates and less frequent in the Republican ranks.[10] In the 1992 election, for example, the Democratic party had nearly twice the percentage of female candidates for open seats as the Republican party, and its nominees typically had more political experience. Not surprisingly, then, the women of the 103d Congress were disproportionately Democratic, with a ratio of thirty-five to twelve in the House and five to one in the Senate.

This pattern may be linked to the gender gap within the electorate (Nechemias 1987) or to the difference in party cultures (Freeman 1986), or it may be connected to the emergence of feminist organizations as major agents in the recruiting and funding of female candidates, groups whose agendas strongly conflict with the Republican party platform on abortion, the Equal Rights Amendment and affirmative action. However, if the two parties continue to differ in their ability to field strong female congressional candidates, this tendency will add another level of complexity to an already convoluted mix of structural factors affecting the recruitment of women to Congress. Given that reapportionment will continue to allocate seats to states in Texas, Florida, California, and other parts of the Sunbelt, where Republicans are relatively strong, differentials in the parties' recruitment of women at the state level could translate into a long-term liability for women in Congress.

Still, it is difficult to imagine that either party organization would be hostile to the candidacies of women, at least at the national level, because the parties themselves now have many prominent women in high positions. In contrast to the 1970s, when women of both parties believed that men actively prevented them from assuming leadership roles (Jennings 1990), women no longer get stuck with the coffee and the envelopes but instead are serving in the party hierarchy. Most important, they make up a significant percentage of the campaign professionals in both parties (Burrell 1992, 6–8). From these vantage points, women will be able to recruit other women as candidates and steer political resources in their direction.

---

10. The opposite was true in the 1970s, when it was the Democratic Party that was most resistent to the political advancement of women (Burrell 1992, 11).

Some scholars are not satisfied that structural explanations will suffice to explain the level of female representation in the House and Senate. Although there is an understandable reluctance among feminists to blame the victim for her lack of political power in the nation's legislature, there is also some evidence to suggest that women's slow rate of entry to Congress is partly a matter of socialization or personal choice. In Great Britain, for example, the primary obstacle to women in Parliament was found not in the actual selection of party nominees from the pool of applicants, although there was some bias against women in the Labour Party. Rather, the problem lay in the smaller percentage of female party activists who became certified applicants, especially in the Conservative Party (Norris and Lovenduski 1992, 24).

It is not clear why women are less inclined to put themselves forward as candidates. But Costantini (1990, 751–54) has demonstrated that at the level of party activist, women are still less ambitious than men for elective office, although the ambition gap has narrowed considerably. Certainly, feminist writings suggest that women place a higher premium than men on personal integration, family roles, and empathetic connections with friends and significant others. For this reason, the demands of public life in general and of Congress in particular may appear more costly for women than they are for men, or at least require a price that women are less willing to pay (Sapiro 1982).

In an intriguing study that compared male and female council members' decisions to pursue higher office, Bledsoe and Herring (1990) found gender differences in the way men and women interpreted their political environment and the way it affected their aspirations. Among men, ambition was the single most important predictor of whether they pursued another office, whereas ambition alone did not play as strong a role for women. Instead, women's likelihood of running for another position was conditioned by their electoral security and whether or not their council seats were at large. Bledose and Herring suggested that the greater importance of contextual variables in women's decision calculus may derive from their relative lack of social and business connections in the community or their tendency to be less single-minded in pursuit of career goals. If their speculations are valid, then existing theories and variables typically associated with political ambition may predict office-seeking behavior for only half the population.

Whatever the barriers—elite, structural, or psychological—hindering women's advancement to Congress, the problem of increased representation is fundamentally a numbers game. The 1992 election is a case in point. Widely hailed as the year of the woman candidate, not only did this election see a record number of women candidates in both House and Senate races, but it witnessed an unprecedented success rate of 64 percent for women in obtaining primary nominations. The result was one-hundred-six women running for the House—up from a high of sixty-nine in 1990—and eleven women running for the Senate—up from a high of ten in 1984. But when the twenty-eight female incumbents seeking reelection are subtracted from the totals and the five races in which women ran against each other are taken into account, 1992 appears less remarkable. If women were victorious in every House race they contested, they could have won no more than 43 percent of the open seats and 8 percent of the incumbent-held seats. Incidentally, ten of the eventual victors were African-American and Latina women who were assured victory in their newly drawn districts once they got past the primary. This means that only slightly more than half of the newly elected women gained their seats without the benefit of judicial intervention. In the Senate, three women contested the eight open seats, and all of them won. But of the eight women challenging the twenty-six incumbents up for reelection, only one was victorious.

What was unusual about 1992, then, was the high rate of success for women in open seats and newly drawn minority-majority districts. The extraordinary number of vacancies created unprecedented opportunities, and women were poised to take advantage of them, especially in the key states of California and Florida. But such openings are not likely to arise again for another decade, and women will once again be forced into the situation of identifying and picking off vulnerable incumbents one by one. Thus, although the year of the woman produced a net gain of nineteen seats in the House and four in the Senate, it did not produce the revolution in congressional representation that many predicted. Until many more women are in a position to contest House and Senate races, the gender bias in the Congress and the conservative policies that flow from it are likely to continue. For ethnic minorities, however, the situation is somewhat different.

The Descriptive Representation of Ethnic Minorities

A quick glance back at table 5.1 indicates that minority representation in Congress increased significantly in the wake of the 1992 reapportionment, with the number of African-American legislators increasing from twenty-five to thirty-eight and the number of Hispanics increasing from ten to seventeen. Indeed, until this past election, ethnic minorities have done relatively better than women in increasing their representation in Congress. Collectively, African-Americans, Hispanics and Asian-Americans made up roughly one-quarter of the population and accounted for approximately 8 percent of House and Senate seats in the 102d Congress and roughly 14 percent in the 103d Congress. While far from parity, the level of underrepresentation for such groups is half what it is for women. To my knowledge, there has been so little empirical work on the recruitment of various ethnic group members to Congress that we have no way of telling why the pattern is as good—or as bad—as it is.[11] The existing literature on minority representation has focused on the characteristics of minority communities, on structural variables such as multimember districts, or on the electoral behavior of various minority groups—almost all in urban areas (Barker and McCorry 1980). While this research gives a good picture of the conditions that lead to minority electoral success, it does not explore how or why particular types of individuals in the minority community run and win (Guerra 1989, 2).[12] For example, Carol Swain's (1993) insightful examination of home styles among black legislators in a variety of districts, from historically black constituencies to white majority districts, analyzes how these members maintained themselves in Congress but of necessity relies on the members' recollections of how they were recruited. Finally, the existing literature on African-American politicians neglects the special difficulties women of color confronted until 1992 in achieving congressional office (Prestage 1977 and 1980; Williams 1982; Wilhite and Theilman 1986; Darcy and Hadley 1988).

However, no examination of minority recruitment can begin without recognizing the substantial impact of the amendments to the Voting Rights Act passed in 1982 and their subsequent interpretation by the federal courts on the representation of disadvantaged groups. Before 1982, districting plans could not be held unconstitutional unless they *intentionally* diluted the voting strength of disadvantaged minorities.[13] Since then, plans can be overturned if they have the *effect* of weakening the electoral clout of minority groups. By forbidding the outcome of dilution, Congress created grounds for using race

---

11. Canon (Forthcoming, 8) attributes the lack of research to the fact that social background analysis of office seekers occurred in the 1950s and 1960s, when the percentage of African-American members of Congress was less than 1 percent.

12. Guerra's (1989) research focuses on gatekeepers and political networks in Los Angeles, and he reports that among ethnic officeholders, one of the most significant stepping-stones to higher office is as a political aide.

13. For a clear and concise discussion of the law governing reapportionment, see Butler and Cain 1992, chap. 2.

and ethnicity as legitimate criteria in establishing constituencies, and the courts have often interpreted this to mean that state legislatures should define constituencies in such a way as to create minority-majority districts. In some instances, such as Mike Espy's Second Congressional District in Mississippi, that meant taking account of differences in voting participation rates rather than simply considering the total percentage of African-Americans in the community. In the 1992 reapportionment, ten states tailored districts with the express purpose of creating new African-American or Hispanic constituencies to satisfy the 1982 act.

One consequence of these practices is to solidify a trend that was already well under way before the 1982 amendments—the election of African-American or Hispanic legislators from predominantly African-American districts or Latino districts. Grofman and Handley (1989, 275) have argued, in fact, that African-Americans must be at least 40 percent of the district population before African-American candidates have a significant chance of being elected to Congress. Moreover, Welch and Hibbing (1984) have observed that this necessity places a ceiling on Hispanic representation because Latino citizens are concentrated in a few states (Florida, Texas, California, and New York). In the 1980s, they noted, Hispanics constituted a majority in only eight districts and made up one-fourth of the population in an additional twenty-seven districts. Thus, although Hispanics are the most rapidly growing ethnic group in the nation and comprise about 7 percent of the population, their prospects for comparable representation in Congress seem dim.

Does the creation of such homogeneous constituencies create distinctive patterns of recruitment among African- American and Hispanic politicians? A cursory look at the careers of African-American House members suggests that they have often followed different routes to Congress. First, many African-American lawmakers have started their political careers as ministers, because of the unique role of the church in local African-American communities and its involvement in the civil rights movement. Second, the great majority of African-American members have come from large northern cities, where they have had to contend with entrenched party machines. In some instances they have entered politics as insurgents bent on overturning the status quo, whereas in others they have obtained congressional nominations as rewards for party loyalty. Third, they have all been Democrats, with the exception of Edward Brooke during the 1970s in the Senate and Gary Francks during the 1990s in the House. Hence, they have had to pursue their ambitions among Democratic elites and supporting constituencies. Finally, African-American politicians in Congress are distinctive for their electoral safety and their seniority in the House. They are seldom challenged by the opposition party and rarely turned out in primaries. On the other hand, they have rarely run for the Senate.[14] In sum, the particular nature of the constituencies that elect African-American representatives seems to lead to career paths that are quite distinctive and stable.

One consequence of this unique pattern of recruitment, however, is an increasing mismatch between the rapidly growing pool of eligible candidates and the opportunities for contesting House seats. In 1990, 7,370 African-Americans held elective office in the United States, which represents a 500 percent increase in just two decades (Bositis 1991, 6). The largest increases among African-American public officials have been in the South, which is where one finds the greatest number of African-American citizens. But African-American House members come predominantly from districts in the North. In other words, the underrepresentation of southern African-Americans is greatest for Congress and least for state and local offices.

This pattern appears to be an artifact of political geography, according to Grofman and Handley (1989). Given prevailing patterns within the electorate, African-American legislators typically require large numbers of African-American voters to secure public office, as noted above. In the North, large metropolitan areas provide a political base for prospective members of Congress because they have large concentrations of African-American voters and because segregated housing patterns facilitate the grouping of African-Americans into a minority-majority district. In the South, however, only six cities have African-American populations over 200,000, and only 15 percent of all African-American citizens live in such large urban areas (Grofman and Handley 1989, 275). Consequently, although the distribution of African-American citizens in the South is sufficient to support the election of African-American politicians to lower-level offices, it is not adequate to create constituencies that will foster their recruitment to Congress.[15] More important for the long run, however, is the development of the largest pool of eligible congressional candidates in

14. The exceptions are Harvey Gantt in 1990 (N.C.) and Carol Braun in 1992 (Ill.).

15. This problem was evident in North Carolina during the 1992 reapportionment where African American citizens constituted a large enough percentage of the population to warrant two congressional seats but their distribution was sufficiently dispersed to make the design of a second district extremely difficult. The solution the state legislature eventually adopted created the Twelfth District that slashes diagonally across the entire state and that is as narrow as the super highway that links it together in some places and at one point even changes lanes (Canon, Schousen, and Sellers 1992)!

an area where it is still difficult for African-Americans to get elected to Congress.

Compounding the difficulties of political geography is the pattern of what Bullock and Campbell (1984) termed "racial" voting. The strong tendency among whites and African-Americans to support candidates of their own race not only makes it difficult for African-American candidates to win primary elections in predominantly white districts but also has created strategic difficulties for African-American office seekers even in court-mandated minority-majority districts (cf. Parker 1991). In the South, for example, where runoffs may be required unless a candidate gets 50 percent of the vote, an African-American candidate might have a plurality of votes in the first round but lose to the white candidate in the second round as white voters unite behind one of their own. When North Carolina recently changed its rules to limit runoff elections to cases in which no candidate received at least 40 percent of the vote to make it easier for African-American candidates to win primaries, a different problem arose. Then, any time more than two African-American candidates contested the primary and split the African-American vote, the white candidate could obtain the nomination with a plurality.

It is difficult to say what impact racial demography and racial voting have on the ambitions of African-American politicians. Preliminary analyses of new districts in North Carolina expressly created in the 1992 reapportionment to promote African-American candidacies, for example, had wildly different results. In the new First District, there was a large pool of candidates, which created a serious coordination problem for African-American activists and raised the prospect of a primary victory for the sole white candidate (Canon, Schousen, and Sellers 1992). In the Ninth District, however, the reapportioners' efforts to satisfy the Justice Department's demand to create a second district containing a majority of African-American citizens reduced the base of support for any Democrat—irrespective of race—to run (Kazee and Roberts 1992).

More important, however, is the extent to which current practices of creating African-American districts with overwhelming majorities—the commonly used standard is 65 percent—will choke off opportunities in the future for African-American legislators. By packing African-American into homogeneous constituencies, the reapportioners not only dilute their political strength in a state's overall congressional delegation but diminish the number of communities in which prospective African-American candidates could build on a sizeable minority base. Indeed, Swain (1993, chap. 10) contends that more African-American legislators have demonstrated an ability to attract white voters and more would be encouraged to do so if districts were less lopsided.

Although the geographic distribution of African-American citizens and the practice of racial voting have uncertain consequences for descriptive representation in Congress, it has the more immediate consequence of affecting the election of liberal Democrats in the South. Grofman, Griffin, and Glazer (1992) have compiled data indicating that as the percentage of African-American voters in a district increases so does the likelihood of electing liberal Democrats.[16] They calculate that in the South, the optimum strategy for electing liberal Democrats would be to create as many districts as possible with African-American populations of 20 to 30 percent (1992, 374). Thus, if African-American voters are concentrated in minority-majority districts, fewer are available to anchor liberal coalitions in white majority districts. Republicans clearly had this in mind when they pushed for the creation of an additional African-American district in North Carolina during the 1992 reapportionment.

Nevertheless, it seems clear that until African-American politicians are able to create a base among elites and voters in predominantly white communities their numbers on Capitol Hill are unlikely to grow significantly (Swain 1993). Certainly, one obstacle standing in their way is the inability of prospective African-American candidates to raise money (Smith 1988), and others may be found in the party organizations. Most important, however, is the relatively small size of the African-American middle and professional class. Not only does that depress the pool of would-be candidates, but as Hero (1992, 17–18) observes, it creates problems of "validation" for African-American politicians in which they must prove themselves to two very different types of constituencies within a district—one white and relatively well-off and one African-American and relatively disadvantaged. (Baird [1977] notes a similar difficulty for Latino candidates.) Although there is almost no research on how these issues affect the political advancement of ethnic minorities to Congress, Swain (1993) has begun the task by closely studying the careers of three House members who bucked the prevailing pattern and secured election in predominantly white districts.

Ethnic voting raises a somewhat different problem for prospective Latino candidates, which has scarcely been analyzed. Lacking the

---

16. This pattern did not always prevail, especially in the South in the 1970s and 1980s, when Republicans were more likely to be elected if the African-American population was between 30 and 40 percent (Grofman, Griffin, and Glazer 1992, 371).

cohesiveness within the electorate that African-American politicians enjoy and hindered by the lowest participation rates among all ethnic groups, Hispanic candidates are even more susceptible to primary losses, particularly in their potential stronghold states—New York, Florida, California, and Texas—where the rules give the nomination to the plurality winner. Furthermore, Latino candidates increasingly find themselves in competition with African-American candidates in urban areas where there are large concentrations of both ethnic groups. Politicians in these areas are engaged in the equivilent of a zero-sum game in which the gain of a seat for one ethnic group often comes at the expense of the other. McClain and Karnig (1990) not only demonstrated the presence of such political competition in large cities but indicated that Hispanics are the net losers, particularly when the city has an African-American majority or plurality.

It is difficult to know what to make of the partial and confusing picture of the recruitment of women and ethnic minorities to Congress. Scholars can all agree on the simple fact of their absence from Capitol Hill, but they are far from understanding the impediments to greater descriptive representation. The literature is too fragmented for anything more than speculation about either the motives or means of women and ethnic minorities who could be running for Congress but remain on the sidelines. The state of scholarship is equally sketchy when we turn to the role of candidates in furthering policy representation in the South.

Recruitment and the Solid South

In 1984, Ronald Reagan carried 121 of the 129 congressional districts in the South and won more than two-thirds of those House constituencies by more than 60 percent of the vote (Rohde 1989b, 137). Reagan also captured all thirteen southern states, yet when he began his second term, his party commanded just forty-seven of the House seats in the region and twelve of the Senate seats (compiled from Ornstein, Mann, and Malbin, 1990, 11 and 15). What's more, the conservative House Democrats, or Boll Weevils, who had provided him with a working majority early in his first term had turned away from the GOP. Reagan had a popular mandate in the South, but he lacked the congressional support in the region to convert his conservative beliefs into public policy. Four years later, George Bush suffered a worse fate, with four fewer southern Republican seats in the House and three fewer in the Senate.

It is not uncommon for voters to select presidents of one party and congressional candidates of another: such split results occured in 34 percent of all House districts in 1988 (Fiorina 1991, 13). But the inability of Republican candidates to capitalize on growing GOP strength in the South reflects more than ticket-splitting tendencies among the electorate. First is the GOP's failure to build a grass roots organization that can field strong candidates for the House. Second is a gradual realignment within the southern wing of the Democratic party, which has fostered more moderate and progressive candidacies for federal office based on a coalition of African-Americans, rural populists, and working people. This latter trend, along with the emergence of more centrist legislators in the north, has enabled the Democrats in the House to present a more united front in Washington. Both trends have significant consequences for the perpetuation of divided government in the United States.

The rise of Republicanism in the South is unmistakable. In their comprehensive analysis of the transformation of the region, Black and Black (1987, 276–83) provide a mass of evidence pointing to increased two-party competition, which has enabled the GOP to achieve striking results in gubernatorial and senatorial races. Party organizations have developed in many southern states, from small groups of committed amateurs (Key 1949) to more professionalized groups of office seekers (Bullock 1988). Prominent officials who began their careers as Democrats have switched to the GOP (Canon 1990b). Voter attitudes reflect the growing viability of Republicanism in the South (Petrocik 1987; Stanley 1988), and the erosion of Democratic hegemony is evident both in increased identification with the Republican party and rising numbers of Independents who are receptive to Republican candidates.

Despite these dramatic changes in party competitiveness and voter behavior, the GOP's southern strategy has performed poorly when applied to the House. Although the party has contested virtually all open seats in the 1980s, it has been unable to field challengers against large numbers of incumbents. Uncontested seats in the South rose in the past decade after dropping steadily since the 1960s, with the result that fully 40 percent of all House contests in the region had no GOP candidate (Canon 1990b, 35). Moreover, the party has had mixed success in contesting new districts and open seats. Of the twenty-five new seats created in the South since 1972, the Republicans gained eleven—or less than half (Canon 1990b, 27). Over the same period, the GOP had a net gain of just seven open seats in comparison to the Democrats (Canon 1990b, 27).

Party switchers have been the most reliable source of new Republican House members, and twenty of the forty-eight Southern Republican senators and representatives in the 101st Congress had once been Democrats in their careers (Canon 1990b, 21). Once elected, Republican incumbents have been effective in creating safe seats (Canon 1990b, 28).[17] Yet, the Republicans have been far less successful in developing a stable of prospective candidates inside the party. This is evident in southern state legislatures, which consistently remain in the hands of Democrats throughout the region (Fiorina 1991, 31).

The relative failure of the GOP to match its success at the state level in fielding competitive candidates limits the capacity of citizens to express their Republican impulses in their local communities, but it also has national implications. Because the Republicans have not had enough qualified House candidates in the region, they have been unable to capitalize on their strength at the top of the ticket. According to Campbell (1990), the president's wasted coattails in the South were the principle cause of the weakened surge and decline effects in American politics that began with Richard Nixon's landslide in 1972.

While the Republicans have struggled to adapt to the altered political environment in the South, the Democrats have not been idle. Local party officials have wooed potential defectors to remain in the fold, and the national party organizations have begun reflecting the political needs of elected officials in the South who have relatively conservative constituencies through such mechanisms as the Democratic Leadership Conference. At the same time, both Democratic newcomers and seasoned incumbents from the South have begun to express the liberal beliefs of the sizeable numbers of African-American voters in their constituencies (Whitby and Gilliam 1991). Consequently, southern legislators in the House have become more and more like their Democratic colleagues from the north—far more liberal, not just on racial issues but on questions of national defense and social welfare policy. The effect, according to David Rohde (1989a and 1991), is a remarkable decline in the divisions that have plagued the party throughout the postwar era.

Both national parties, then, can trace their current levels of partisan strength in the House to patterns of political recruitment that have occurred—or failed to occur—across the region. Given this fact, it is striking how little research has been undertaken to make sense of the underlying processes in the South that have produced such results.

---

17. The three Reagan Republicans elected to the Senate in 1980 are a notable exception, and their defeat in 1986 is viewed by Frendreis and Overby (1992) as a failure to pay attention to the basics of politics—constituency service, responsive voting records, and strategic use of committee assignments.

The comprehensive study of Southern politics by Black and Black (1987), for example, altogether ignored the question of recruitment. Despite detailed treatments of demographic, economic and social change in the old Confederacy, the authors made no attempt to link these trends with variations in the opportunity structures or the pool of eligible congressional contestants. Other scholars have treated the prospects of southern realignment primarily as a phenomenon of the mass electorate (e.g., Petrocik 1987; Stanley 1988). Yet Carmines and Stimson's (1989) theory of partisan change implied a role for candidates in differentiating party positions on new issue cleavages. According to these authors (1984, 136), the American party system can experience several different types of realignment: impulse-decay, critical election, secular realignment, and what they term dynamic growth. It is the latter type of realignment that they see occuring within the parties on the dimension of racial attitudes.

In a dynamic realignment, the party system receives an initial shock, but what defines its special character is the subsequent polarization of the parties over a prolonged period of time—a combination of a critical election and a secular realignment. In this respect, the emerging cleavage pattern entails both rapid mobilization of the electorate around an issue and generational replacement by which older voters who cling to their long-standing party affiliation are succeeded by young voters who find the new cleavage salient (Carmine and Stimson 1984, 140). Although this type of realignment starts with attitudinal changes in the mass public, it eventually shows up in Congress. According to Carmines and Stimson, polarization between House Democrats and Republicans along racial lines lagged behind divisions within the electorate. Such delays were unavoidable given the influence of incumbency in congressional elections. But gradual change in issue cleavages did finally surface, and Carmines and Stimson described it as a necessary condition for sustained realignment. They concluded, "the driving force of continuing mass realignment is continuing elite realignment" (1984, 151). Having demonstrated the emergence of a new cleavage on racial issues in Congress, however, the authors were unclear how it came about other than to attribute it to generational replacement.

David Canon (1990b) provided some insight into the problem of elite realignment in his study of congressional candidates in the South. Canon demonstrated that Republicans running for the House today are significantly more experienced than they were in the past and that the level at which they hold office is now on a par with Democratic candidates in the region (1990b, 34). He also found a significant increase in the number of Republican primary contests, in races with both incumbents and open seats. And he noted that a higher proportion of Republican primary contestants have previous office-holding experience (1990b, 36–37). Canon did not make the connection between racial polarization and the changing pattern of candidate recruitment explicit, but he nevertheless saw the pattern within the GOP as evidence of a secular realignment in the South, which is elite driven rather than voter driven. In Canon's view, then, the experience of the region is a superb opportunity for scholars to abandon the big bang theory of realignment typified by the 1932 election and examine more gradual types of realignments, similar to the one that took place in New England in the first half of the twentieth century.[18]

In a more recent article, Canon and Sousa (1992) pushed the realignment argument further by suggesting that the electoral disturbances characteristic of realigning elections alter legislative career patterns. In their examination of the New Deal period of 1932–36, they found that the realignment era was initially marked by a high incidence of successful amateurs in the Democratic party, a greater likelihood of low seniority House Democrats contesting Senate seats, and an increased frequency of Democratic politicians who had interrupted political careers returning to legislative office. All these features of the New Deal realignment toward the Democrats now are evident in the recruitment patterns of GOP legislators in the South.

The 1992 election offered striking evidence that the GOP has continued to improve its capacity to recruit congressional candidates, at least in some respects (see table 5.3). The number of uncontested seats in the region was only 10 percent, with the GOP accounting for most of the failures to field a candidate. The number of lopsided contests in which the loser received 30 percent or less of the vote was about 21 percent, and more important, the frequency of marginal contests was fully 41 percent. Despite these encouraging signs, however, the GOP picked up just 39 percent of the open seats—not nearly as well as they had hoped to do after redistricting created significant numbers of open seats and moved concentrations of African-American voters into newly created minority majority districts.

Still, the southern wing of the Republican party confronts major obstacles in developing the elite support that will enable it to capital-

---

18. The change in electoral opportunities for Republicans in the Mountain States and for Democrats in the Northeast suggests that a similar line of inquiry might prove fruitful in other regions as well (see Bullock 1988).

TABLE 5.3. Electoral Competion in Southern House Races, 1992

State (Number of Seats)	Total Uncontested	Total Lopsided (30%)	Total Marginal (60%–40%)	GOP Share of Open Seats
Alabama (7)	0	2	3	2/2
Arkansas (4)	0	2	2	2/3
Florida (23)	2	3	13	5/10
Georgia (11)	0	2	8	2/6
Louisiana (7)	4	1	1	0/1
Mississippi (5)	0	2	1	none open
N. Carolina (12)	0	2	5	0/2
S. Carolina (6)	0	1	1	0/1
Tennessee (9)	1	2	3	none open
Texas (30)	4	8	9	0/3
Virginia (11)	1	1	5	1/3
Total (125)	12	26	51	12/31

Source: Compiled from *New York Times,* November 5, 1992, B14–B15.

ize on voters' propensities to choose Republican presidents. The GOP remains remarkably dependent on amateurs for contesting House elections in the South, and this handicap may account for the relatively weak gains made during the past three presidential landslides and Bush's dominance of the South in 1992. More important, this deficit in experienced politicians is likely to continue in light of the continued Democratic dominance of state and local offices, including three-fourths of all state legislative seats and most of the statewide offices below the gubernatorial rank (Canon 1990b, 29). Given large concentrations of loyal African-American Democrats in most southern states and districts, this pattern is likely to persist unless the GOP can attract overwhelming numbers of white voters. As Petrocik (1987) has shown, Republicans must win 65 percent of the white vote in state-wide contests whenever the African-American population exceeds 20 percent (which is in most southern states.)

Thus, we might speculate about why the GOP has failed to make inroads in local offices and state legislatures. Or, we might hypothesize about how changes in the Democratic party's constituency base prompted adaptations among local elites in how they defined eligible candidates. But in the absence of systematic research, that is as far as we can go. Given the importance of these issues for both local and national politics, as well as for theories of political change, it is imperative that scholars look deeply at the patterns of recruitment that have developed in the South over the past two decades.

Implications for Representation and Research

Although much of the linkage between recruitment and representation remains unclear, it appears that candidates are implicated in the social and political composition of the Congress in three very different ways. For women, the problem appears to be a general shortage in the supply of female candidates and a poor fit between the pool of eligible women and the opportunities for electoral success. For African-Americans and Latinos, the barriers to advancement seem linked to the skewed geographic distribution of ethnic voters and the high incidence of racial voting among European-Americans. For southern Republicans, the chief obstacle to visibility in Congress appears to be rooted in the inability of local parties and elites to create an organizational basis for grooming candidates in local offices. Whatever the political implications for these particular groups of citizens, their inability to gain access to the nation's legislature has important consequences for democratic politics and for the discipline of political science.

Undoubtedly, the congressional agenda would be different with more women and ethnic minorities serving in the House and Senate. As noted earlier, greater descriptive representation in Congress would probably lead to more emphasis on human resource issues, such as education, and would probably augment the liberal wings of both political parties. On the other hand, increased partisan congruence in the South between legislators and voters would add conservative Republicans to the Congress who would counterbalance some of the liberalizing tendencies inherent in greater descriptive representation.

Equally important, newcomers to the House and Senate would in all likelihood be drawn from the upper socioeconomic stratum of society, whatever their sex or ethnicity, and political elites would still have powerful incentives to direct their resources toward the encouragement of sympathetic candidates. Furthermore, once female and ethnic legislators are drawn from a broader range of constituencies, they might very well turn out to be individuals who do not share the political beliefs of the women, African-Americans, and Latinos currently in Congress. This would be particularly true if ethnic lawmakers were to begin representing less homogeneous communities.[19] Finally, an influx of Republicans from the Sun Belt, possibly including some Latino lawmakers, would probably offset many of the liber-

---

19. Swain (1993) demonstrates that African-American legislators from heterogeneous districts tend to be less liberal than other African-American members of Congress.

alizing tendencies introduced by increased numbers of women and African-Americans. Thus, the effects of a more representative Congress might be relatively modest in the aggregate, even though they might be significant at the district level.

The ethnic and social backgrounds of candidates may also hold strategic implications for electoral competition, although these variables have never been studied for their relevance to electoral politics.[20] In the 1992 election, for example, conventional wisdom held that women would have an advantage because they were perceived as outsiders. To an electorate fed up with business as usual, many female candidates argued that they represented a departure from the professionalized politics in Congress voters wanted to change. Political commentators echoed these claims, as did some political scientists, even though there was little empirical evidence to justify them. Similarly, race was an important factor in the 1990 North Carolina Senate contest in which commercials aired by the incumbent, Jesse Helms, played on white fears of economic competition from African-Americans. Helms's African-American challenger, David Gantt, lost, albeit by the same margin as Helms's previous white opponent. As these examples illustrate, if voters use gender and race as criteria for choosing their representatives, then political scientists ought to pay attention to how such factors determine winners and losers, how they influence campaign tactics, and how they figure in the nominating process.

A case can be made, however, that more subtle consequences would flow from a Congress with a decidely different makeup. Representation in American politics is a matter of access, not simply policy agreement, and it does not occur uniformly throughout the constituency. In Hero's (1992) view, a lack of identification and contact between legislators and disadvantaged groups is a powerful barrier to their articulating demands on government. Yet there is very little hard evidence about how variables such as race and sex affect contacts between members of Congress and voters. We know that legislators differentiate among their constituents out of both political necessity and personal preference (Fenno 1978), but the considerable literature cited in chapter 4 regarding members' use of personal contact and casework is aimed solely at explaining the incumbency effect. What

---

20. In his review of the literature on the social bases of recruitment, Canon (Forthcoming) reiterates the conventional view that such research has yielded little understanding of legislative behavior, but he does suggest that scholars should pay some attention to the electoral relevance of background variables, particularly as they relate to differences between winners and losers.

has been overlooked are broader questions concerning representation. Do female lawmakers, for example, have distinctively different home styles compared to males? Do African-American or Latino legislators pay more attention to citizens with similar backgrounds? Do constituents feel more inclined to communicate with or request assistance from a representative who is like them? Swain's (1993) work on the home styles of some African-American members of Congress indicates that such considerations are not overly relevant to roll call voting, but they can be important factors influencing members' personal connections with the district. Since these issues presumably are relevant to the degree of trust that citizens feel toward their own representatives and to their perception that the institution arrives at decisions fairly, they are worth exploring further.

More than access may be involved with descriptive representation, however; it may also contribute to a greater sense of empowerment among historically disadvantaged groups. In a study comparing white citizens' political and social participation in the community with that of African-American citizens, Bobo and Gilliam (1990) found that the lower rates of involvement among African-Americans were not simply a function of lower socioeconomic status. Rather, the presence of visible African-American mayors in the respondents' community had a positive, independent effect on a wide range of participatory variables, and it further contributed to a level of political engagement, knowledge and efficacy among African-American citizens that exceeded the level among comparable whites. The authors concluded that civic participation, far from being determined by individual attributes, is sensitive to the cues and symbols conveyed by elective officials. If they are correct, then the highly unrepresentative character of the Congress may be one factor in the widespread disaffection that some citizens express toward the institution.

Few scholars, I think, would dispute the relevance of gender and ethnicity to the concept of representation and the governance of the nation, yet judging from the work of mainstream congressional scholars, such factors are barely acknowledged. A survey of the major texts on Congress reveals the obligatory tables on the gender and ethnicity of incumbent lawmakers, along with data on professional status, religion, and other social background characteristics, but the authors do not take them any more seriously today than they did a decade ago, when Matthews (1983) was reviewing the literature. Similarly, Jacobson's (1992b) excellent synthesis of the research on congressional elections does not contain a single reference to women,

African-Americans, or Hispanics in the index, although "ethnicity" gets a brief nod on page 23.

I do not believe these omissions are a deliberate slight or even an unconscious oversight but instead are an accurate reflection of what congressional scholars have been writing. Textbook writers have a responsiblity to convey the state of the literature and to instruct students on what is fact and proven theory. Having done that faithfully, they cannot be faulted for neglecting topics about which there is so much ambiguity. But the gaps in the literature speak to the tendency in the discipline noted by Barber (1990) to "ghetto-ize" research on the politics of race, sex, and ethnicity. And in surveying past and present research on congressional recruitment, I have been struck by how far congressional scholars have lagged behind colleagues who study state and local politics in examining the effect of social and economic trends on the politics of representation.

Yet we have seen that inattention to candidates extends beyond disadvantaged groups into the realm of partisan realignment, particularly in the South. Both the liberalization of the southern Democratic congressional delegation and the continued inability of the GOP to field successful competitors in many districts are now well-documented trends, but it is impossible to tell what causal role candidates have played in these processes. What accounts for the seemingly different rates of adaptability inside the two parties? How much did political entrepreneurship by individual candidates accelerate change inside the Democratic coalition? To what extent have candidates acted as opportunists in exploiting new issue cleavages among the electorate, and to what extent did they accentuate them? As scholars move to answer these questions, their efforts will further a much broader research agenda developing in the field of American politics on the dynamics of institutional adaptation and development (cf. Swift and Brady 1992).

CHAPTER 6

Candidates and Organizational Change

Much of the strength and efficiency of any government in procuring and securing happiness to the people, depends on opinion, on the general opinion of the goodness of the Government, as well as of the wisdom and integrity of its Governors.
—Benjamin Franklin, at the close of the Constitutional Convention

One of the enduring features of the U.S. Congress is its capacity to adapt internally to new political trends while retaining substantial continuity with the past. A dynamic institution, Congress is constantly in a state of flux, even though at any given time it may seem firmly wedded to the status quo.[1] This mix of rejuvenation and reaction has intrigued several generations of scholars and has sparked competing explanations about the nature of organizational change inside the nation's legislature. One school traces change to periodic electoral shocks that flood the institution with large numbers of freshmen members. The other school sees change as an ongoing process inside Congress in response to external pressures from a variety of political actors. Neither side has been able to establish whether institutional change is caused primarily by the transformation of the membership or by disturbances in the political environment, a scholarly stalemate that cannot be resolved, in my view, without considerably more understanding about how congressional candidates operate in the American system.

Candidacy is most important, of course, to the turnover interpretation of organizational change. According to this hypothesis, when voters remove a sizeable percentage of incumbents from office, they intentionally send representatives to Washington who have very different expectations than their predecessors. The newcomers bring this rejection of the status quo into the party caucuses and committee rooms and through sheer force of numbers compel the institution to adapt to their presence. By initiating the causal sequence that leads to

---

1. This theme was struck by Ralph K. Huitt (1969) in an essay celebrating the continuity and change in Congress.

organizational restructuring, the new-style legislators become the instruments of reform. Their motivations in running for Congress and their objectives once in office become key variables in the analysis of change. Therefore, scholars who pursue this line of explanation typically devote a good deal of time to demonstrating how and why the new lawmakers constitute a distinctive group.

The environmental school of congressional adaptation posits a different set of motivations behind institutional reform. In this view, it is not the members and their goals that change but their ability to realize their ambitions. Because structural alterations are costly, individual lawmakers need powerful personal incentives to overturn the status quo; in effect, they accept prevailing institutional arrangements as long as they can satisfy their objectives of reelection, influence, and public policy. What upsets the institutional equilibrium is pressure from citizens, interest groups, or the executive branch rather than electoral upheaval. The escalation of outside demands on the institution, the argument goes, makes it increasingly difficult for members to satisfy their goals. Legislators eventually find maintaining the status quo more costly than overcoming institutional inertia, and they develop new methods of doing business to meet these external challenges.

From this perspective on reform, the scholars' task is to demonstrate where the outside pressures come from and how the resulting reforms address them. Candidates are not critical here, except in their role as potential replacements for incumbents who retire or fail to see the necessity of institutional change. But scholars operating in this mode of analysis make assumptions about what members of Congress want from their service inside the institution, and they have framed member goals in terms of lengthy political careers. In this respect, the environmental explanation of change depends on members having an investment in Congress that they want to protect, even though the origin and maintenance of such professional instincts are seldom considered.

What had been an abstract discussion among scholars about the nature of causality in legislative institutions suddenly became a nationwide, partisan debate when term limitations erupted as an issue. Proponents claimed that term limits would inject a steady stream of new members into the nation's legislatures and that these new members would keep the institution vital and responsive to evolving public needs. They further argued that term limits would undermine careerism among lawmakers, so that elected representatives would be more concerned with important issues and less preoccupied with protecting their seats and their positions. Opponents, on the other hand, feared that high turnover would breed confusion rather than innovation inside the legislature and would undermine the institution's capacity to foster expertise and leadership. They also contended that the loss of professionalism under term limits would make lawmakers more rather than less susceptible to the influence of interest groups, staff members, and the executive branch. With term limits in place in three states, proposals under consideration in thirty-seven others, and their application to Congress a possibility (Kurtz 1992), the fight over term limits has become a battle between competing views about the long-term implications of legislative careers. The passage in 1992 of term limits in thirteen states now makes this debate much more than an academic exercise.

For scholars, the imposition of term limits raises two important empirical questions. First, what expectations and agendas will successive elections of numerous freshmen lawmakers introduce to the legislature? Second, how will the interruption of the twentieth century pattern of careerism affect member goals in Congress, and what consequences will this change have for the power and effectiveness of the House and Senate? Each of these questions tests the relevance of current research in our discipline about organizational adaptations inside Congress: the former by asking what repeated doses of high turnover will do to the institution and the latter by inquiring what happens to institutional structures when careerism is no longer the dominant motivation of senators and representatives. Thus, they challenge the congressional community to examine its prevailing wisdom about the causes and effects of reform.

Recent trends inside Congress have heightened the saliency of the debate over institutional change. The unprecedented number of open seats in the House created by retirement and redistricting were augmented by a record number of primary defeats.[2] Even if every remaining incumbent had won his or her reelection bid—an unlikely event in what was billed as the year of the antipolitician—a historic number of freshmen were expected in the 103d Congress, exceeding even the 1974 Watergate class. Some projections put the figure at 125 new members and others estimated an extraordinary 150 newcomers to the House. The final tally of 110, while not as great as predicted, nevertheless represented the largest freshman class since 1948. In the Senate, the changes were less dramatic, but even that venerable institution had twelve newcomers, five of whom defeated incumbents.

2. Redistricting and retirement created seventy-seven open seats, and primary defeats created nineteen open seats.

Thus, even without the threat of term limits looming over Congress, the debate over institutional change and the role new members play in bringing it about is unavoidable.

In this chapter, I outline the arguments behind the major theories of institutional change in Congress and then show how they are relevant to the debate over the consequences of term limitations. I conclude that scholars are in a weak position to evaluate the claims of the proponents and opponents of term limits because they lack sufficient understanding of where candidates come from and what motivates them to seek congressional office.

Turnover and Institutional Change

The turnover theory of institutional change is most clearly articulated in the literature that examines the reforms introduced in the House of Representatives during the 1970s. Through a variety of new rules, members engineered an extensive transfer of power from an oligarchy of senior, southern committee chairs to a younger and more representative group of legislators. Some of the reforms were statutory, such as those included in the Legislative Reorganization Act of 1970, but most were adopted through the Democratic Party caucus, such as Hansen I in 1971, Hansen II in 1973, and Hansen III in 1974. Their collective effect was to weaken the committee chairs' influence by modifying the committee assignment process and the seniority rule, by subjecting committee deliberations and floor amendments to public scrutiny, by strengthening the status of subcommittees and their chairpersons, and by making staff resources available to junior members and to the minority party. Within the space of a few years, the predictable, tightly controlled system of decision making that had operated in the House for several generations gave way to a decentralized structure that permitted an unprecedented level of entrepreneurship and autonomy among the members.

Scholars who witnessed this burst of reform energy traced it to the candidate-centered elections that became prevalent by the mid-1960s. Any number of observers on Capitol Hill remarked on the arrival of a new breed of legislator who was more attentive to the constituency, less deferential to established norms, and less amenable to party discipline.[3] These antiestablishment newcomers were a prod-

---

3. Many scholars have written about the emergence of the "New Congress" in the 1970s. In the interest of brevity, I have summarized the general trends and refer the reader for summaries and citations to such authors as Smith and Deering (1984), Loomis (1988), Sinclair (1983 and 1989). The most important writings in depicting the flavor of the new

uct of the tumultuous 1960s—the revolution in social mores and civil rights, the activism against the Vietnam War, and the environmental movement. But the most significant development in their emergence probably was the erosion of party loyalties and organizations that began during that decade. Historically, mavericks have tended to be most prevalent when the national parties are in disarray (Collie 1988). Furthermore, among the challengers surveyed by Fishel (1973, 157–58) in 1964, not only were the self-starting candidates more ambitious than those who were party-sponsored or group-sponsored candidates, but also they were advocates of reform once elected to the House.

However strongly the younger representatives of the 1960s might desire change, the story goes, they apparently could not break the hold of the committee barons. They needed a surge of new members, and they got the allies they were looking for in the Watergate Class of 1974. Not only were the Watergate freshmen numerous and over-whelmingly Democratic, but also they were distinctive in their political attitudes (Loomis 1988). Just as substantial membership turnover turned out to be key in implementing party realignments (Brady 1988), so it appeared to be a necessary condition for institutional reform. Equally important were the unusually high retirement rates in the late 1970s (Cooper and West 1981), which created additional electoral openings for more rampant individualists to descend on Washington.

The new style lawmakers supposedly accentuated the constituency service aspect of the representative's job in an effort to strengthen their personal electoral coalitions. As noted in chapter 4, cohort effects showed up in the trend toward electoral safety as junior members did disproportionately better than their predecessors at the polls. Furthermore, their increased contact with the constituency seemed to pay off in greater electoral security (Parker 1986; Cover 1982; Bond, Covington, and Fleisher 1985). These trends led Parker (1986, 88) to conclude that because newer members entered Congress earlier and were more ambitious, they developed a long-term reelection strategy that diverted their constituents' attention from political issues.

The new legislative breed was not only eager for electoral security but apparently craved influence as well. This generation of lawmakers chafed at the norms of apprenticeship and seniority and was disinclined to defer to committee experts. They sought access to the

---

Congress as it evolved are *Congress in Change,* edited by Norman J. Ornstein (1975), and the *Congress Reconsidered* series, edited by Dodd and Oppenheimer (1977, 1981, 1985, and 1989).

news media to command the attention of their peers (Cook 1989), and they introduced amendments and sponsored bills outside their own legislative domains (Smith 1989). In their pursuit of electoral safety and policy independence, these lawmakers were very difficult to lead. In Sundquist's words, "Junior members accept leadership only on their own terms [and] on a case by case basis" (1981, 391). Thus, case studies of legislative leadership in the 1970s and early 1980s stressed the limited capacity of party leaders to do more than "keep peace in the family" and facilitate the members' own preferences and agendas (cf. Sinclair 1983; Loomis 1984).

The drive for autonomy appeared to carry over into congressional relationships with the executive branch. The growing separation of the presidential and congressional vote has already been noted in a preceding chapter as a sign that congressional candidates were less likely to serve as links between national agendas and local concerns. This trend not only denied the nation's chief executive partisan majorities in one or both houses, it also ensured the independence of those who shared his party label, prompting many scholars to write about the dangers of divided government (Sundquist 1981; Burnham 1982). Fiorina put it most succinctly: "No longer expecting to gain much from the president's success or suffer much from his failures, they have little incentive to bear any risk on his behalf (1984, 218).

In sum, what evolved in the literature of the period was a loose theory of institutional change based on three causal factors deriving from the transformation of candidate recruitment: (1) the declining influence of parties in the nomination and selection of candidates, (2) the changing career aspirations of new members, and (3) the departure of senior members through electoral shocks and retirement. The problem with this scenario, however, is that it neither fitted the facts quite as neatly as the above narrative suggests nor explained more recent institutional changes in the Congress. The declining influence of parties in congressional elections is not in dispute, although some scholars, as we shall see in the next section, would argue that it has been exaggerated. But what is open to question is the appearance of a new breed of legislator on Capitol Hill and the coincidence of institutional reform with periods of high turnover.

The hallmarks of the new breed were their intense pursuit of reelection and their policy entrepreneurship. Certainly the "sophomore surge" and the disappearance of many marginal freshmen who had previously had a high incidence of defeat are facts beyond dispute. At issue is whether these trends were attributable to a new type of candidate running for Congress or were simply another manifestation of the power of incumbency. While junior lawmakers were becoming more electorally secure, senior lawmakers were also experiencing an upward trend in their margins.[4] A few at the very top of the seniority ladder seemed more vulnerable, as noted in chapter 4, but by and large incumbents of all sorts did better for reasons that we have seen are very much in dispute.

Furthermore, it is not clear whether the greater attentiveness among junior members to constituency concerns was a generational phenomenon or a life cycle effect. Fenno (1978) analyzed the frequency of trips home and the allocation of district staff and found weak differences by seniority. But a careful reading of Fenno's classification of legislative home styles indicated that emphasis on casework and pork barrel projects was dictated by the members' personal political philosophy and by the district's expectations, it did not appear to be generational.[5] Parker (1986) found cohort differences in overall district attentiveness, although he reported no seniority effects over the course of members' careers in terms of the number of days spent in the district.

In analyzing home styles, however, Fenno (1978) observed pronounced life cycle effects. House members who were in their early years pursued an *expansionist* style, whereas members who had accumulated service tended toward a *protectionist* style. The former were more likely to cultivate the district and to seek contacts with potential new supporters (Price 1989), while the latter were busy chairing committees in Washington and were more inclined to maintain their existing coalitions. Given the high rates of turnover in 1964 and 1966 and again in 1972 through 1980, which resulted from a combination of electoral defeat and voluntary retirement, the House had a relatively high percentage of newcomers when scholars were writing about the

---

4. However, Hibbing (1991b) indicates that much of the apparent increase in electoral safety among incumbents of all seniority levels is the failure among scholars to take account of what he terms mortality effects. Every cohort loses members, he argues, to defeat or retirement, leaving those in office who are "Olympians," that is to say, members who are extremely interested in and adept at securing reelection.

5. For example, the most adept practitioner of constituency service was Congressman A, a very senior Southerner who did not get home much, whereas the members in Fenno's sample who most epitomized the independence of the new breed, Congressman B, Congressman C, and Congressman E, tended to be issue oriented and not particularly interested in casework. Similarly, the legislators who emphasized casework and personal contact, Congressman A and Congressman F, did so because their constituents demanded it. Only Fenno's Congressmen E, stuck in a heterogeneous district, fit the new breed mold of using district attentiveness to bolster his electoral margins and foster his political independence.

"new breed." These individuals would naturally be actively engaged in expanding their electoral coalitions, and because of their numbers, they could have created the impression of a trend.

Hibbing (1991a) confirmed the presence of the career cycle Fenno observed in a longitudinal study of members' behavior while in office. In his analysis of the period 1946–84, he discovered that lawmakers' attentiveness to home did vary over the cycle of their careers, with more home activity in their early years than later in their tenure. There were generational differences in this cyclical pattern, as well, especially for lawmakers elected in the 1960s and mid-1970s, but they were not necessarily compatible with scholarly expectations about the "new breed." Members elected in these years were likely to become less attentive to their constituents over the course of their service in the House than members elected more recently. Furthermore, members of the class of 1971 went home less in the early stages of their tenure than either the classes of 1965 or 1977, and their rate of travel over their first five terms was lower than the rate for members of the class of 1959 at the end of its seventh term (Hibbing 1991a, 138). Hibbing lacked the data to compare these cohorts with earlier ones, but he suggested that the period effects in the data may be the result of changes over time in the level of appropriations for members' travel rather than changes in member goals.[6]

Further doubts about the uniqueness of the new generation of legislators were raised in other aspects of Hibbing's (1991a) research on congressional careers. Hibbing contended that scholarly interpretations of legislative reform have been skewed by the presence of a few large and highly visible cohorts, such as the Watergate Class of 1974. These lawmakers, he cautioned, were not typical of the average member of Congress, and when he examined the pattern of legislative careers over the past three decades, he found less evidence for a new breed of legislator in Congress than many previous observers. First, he reported that the strategies for pursuing reelection had become so universalized that the relationship between election margins and tenure in the House, which had been curvilinear in past generations, had become nearly flat by the mid-1980s. Second, he discovered that the

---

6. Hibbing (1991a, 136), in his usual careful way, noted that the travel budget measure underestimates trips home, because it leaves out unreimbursed trips that members who live close to Washington or who have families back in the district regularly undertake. He further remarked that travel home rose significantly as long as it was a line item in the members' office budget—that is to say, members could either use it or lose it, but once lawmakers began receiving a general administration budget that they could allocate to staff, travel, and so forth, they reduced the amount they spent going home and put the money into staff support .

reforms of the 1970s had in fact redistributed influence to junior members, but only to a point. After a succession of terms, chairpersonships and party leadership posts bore little relationship to seniority. But Hibbing's most telling finding against the presence of a new breed on Capitol Hill was his questioning of the spirit of policy entrepreneurship that supposedly was the defining feature of this generation of politician. Junior legislators, he found, did not become more active relative to senior ones. Hibbing developed three different measures of the frequency of legislative activity—speeches on the floor, amendments offered on the floor, and the sponsorship of bills—and two measures of what might be termed legislative style—the degree of specialization within committee jurisdictions and the percentage of sponsored bills that were reported from committee and passed on the floor. On each of the frequency measures, he found life-cycle effects in which junior members had low legislative activity, followed by a quick rise, then subsequent leveling off, and eventually another sharp jump after the seventh or eighth term (1991a, 119). To be sure, the class of 1971 was the most active cohort across the board at all levels of tenure, but the classes on either side of it in 1969 and 1973 were significantly less active (1991a, 118).

Hibbing's data also contained a curious finding with respect to the notorious Watergate class. In comparing levels of activity between first-term members and eighth-term members, Hibbing found that the gap noticeably narrowed for the classes of 1971 and 1973 (the 91st and 92d Congresses). But it began to widen again with the class of 1973, and in 1975 it was roughly what it had been in 1967. More important, by the 95th Congress the discrepancy had become extremely pronounced and remained that way through the mid-1980s. In short, the Watergate freshmen were not as active relative to their senior colleagues as their immediate predecessors had been, and all classes subsequent to this supposedly bellwether group of lawmakers have been consistently low in relative activity. Significantly, Hibbing arrived at similar judgments when he examined the trends in his measures of lawmakers' specialization within their own committee jurisdictions and their success in getting bills to the floor and passed by the House.

Hibbing drew two conclusions from these patterns: First, that it is risky to generalize about institutional behavior on the basis of cross-sectional data and an unrepresentative group of legislators as the advocates of the "new breed" school of institutional change had done. Second, the aggregate career patterns of lawmakers inside the House did not show the generational effects attributed to them but have been quite stable over time. He concluded, "if there has been a shift at all, the discrepancy between new- and old-member activity levels has grown" (1991a, 118).

One last piece of evidence calls into question the commonly accepted truths about the origin and consequence of the 1970 reforms. Although it is typical to give the Watergate class credit for pushing the reform agenda, in fact the restructuring of influence in the House went back to the frustrated liberals of the 1950s who formed the Democratic Study Group (DSG) in 1959. Theirs was an ideological rather than a generational struggle, and as Rohde (1991, chap. 2) demonstrated, their reform agenda was intended to strengthen the capacity of the majority within the Democratic party to enact policy and to enhance the accountability of the leaders to the rank and file. Even while decentralizing power through the subcommittee system, they were also strengthening the hand of the speaker in a variety of ways, a feature of the 1970 reforms that political observers intent on analyzing the new breed often slighted. Although the Watergate freshmen were instrumental in the highly publicized removal of three prominent committee chairs and in approving Democratic Caucus ratification of the various subcommittee chairs of the Appropriations Committtee, the more significant changes in terms of the decentralization of power had already been put in place before their arrival.[7] In addition, when the Watergate freshmen confronted the Bolling Commission's recommendations to radically change the jurisdictions of the committee system, their presence did not advance the cause of reform.

Cohort differences did emerge in the House for members elected in the 1970s, although they were connected to the progressive ambition of those who ran for the Senate (Herrick and Moore 1990). Among these upwardly mobile legislators, higher levels of floor activity and constituency attentiveness did occur. What is significant about their activity in terms of explaining institutional change is that it was driven by their goals for higher office rather than their desire for more influence inside the House. Thus, a reform agenda seems to have been incidental to their more fundamental purpose, and the truly interesting question about their impact on Congress is why so many more House members elected in the 1970s developed aspirations for the Senate than in preceding generations.

In sum, it is not clear that the constituency-oriented behavior of

---

7. Credit for this observation goes to one of the anonymous reviewers of my original draft.

lawmakers elected in the 1960s and later was particularly distinctive or that it derived from new members' idiosyncratic conceptions of the job of representation. Nor is it certain that the newcomers to the House were uniquely oriented toward policy innovation and reform. What is most at odds with the turnover theory of institutional change, however, is the emergence of what scholars have labeled the "post-reform Congress" during a period of remarkable membership stability and without any fanfare about a new breed of lawmaker on Capitol Hill. The Congresses of this era are as different from their predecessors of the 1970s and early 1980s as those Congresses were from earlier ones.

The House and Senate of the 1980s are marked by increased visibility of party leaders, the expansion of a variety of institutional arrangements fostering party voting, and increased party unity on the floor. Astonishing as it may seem, scholars have used terms such as "oligarchy" and "hierarchy" when they write about the Congress of the late 1980s and early 1990s (cf. Dodd and Oppenheimer 1989; Davidson 1989 and 1992). But their use of these phrases does not imply a return to the good old days of the committee barons. Rather, Congress appears to have been gradually and rather informally adapting to alterations in its decision-making environment brought about by continuous divided government and intensified interest group pressures.

Environmental Disturbances and Member Goals

Following a decade of decentralizing reform, legislators in both chambers began to vest greater responsibility in party leaders and senior committee chairs during the mid-1980s. Despite the continuation of widespread opportunities for exercising personal power and strong electoral incentives for retaining individual autonomy, members recently have shown a willingness to delegate considerable discretion to their leaders and a decided propensity for party voting. Such behavior is clearly at odds with the dominant view in the literature that the drive for independence to ensure reelection is the alpha and omega of legislative life. Yet scholars have begun to postulate a more complex set of member objectives as determinants of institutional structure and behavior and to look beyond lawmakers for external stimuli that lead to new forms of decision making. In their view, institutional change does not depend on the transformation of the membership but is a response to an altered political environment.

After a steady downhill slide throughout the 1970s, the incidence of party voting turned sharply upward in 1983 in the House and 1985 in the Senate and continued throughout the decade at levels not seen in Congress since the 1950s (Ornstein, Mann, and Malbin 1990, 198). On more than half the recorded roll calls, a majority of Democrats opposed a majority of Republicans. Furthermore, the average party unity score achieved historic postwar highs for Democrats in both the House and Senate in the late 1980s and surpassed its 1970s level throughout the past decade (Ornstein, Mann, and Malbin 1990, 199). As Roger Davidson (1989 and 1991) has noted, the postreform Congress is a highly partisan place.

Equally important has been the enhanced role of party leaders in both chambers in crafting the omnibus budget resolutions and broad legislative packages that have become the hallmark of recent Congresses. In the House, the decisive role of the party leaders has arisen from the increased salience of the budget and the conflicting priorities of a Republican administration and a Democratic legislature (Palazzolo 1992). The leaders have based their influence on several reforms enacted in the previous decade, such as control of the Rules Committee, which has facilitated the adoption of more restrictive rules to govern floor activity. But they have also developed a complex whip system and special task forces to assist in the business of creating coalitions on the floor (Sinclair 1990a and 1990b; Smith 1989). In the Senate, party leaders have continued to operate in an unstructured environment but have enjoyed a climate of more supportive norms for their efforts (Sinclair 1990a; Smith 1989). Both the majority and minority leaders have become highly visible spokesmen for their parties and have governed the chamber through an informal arrangement of unanimous consent agreements and, like their counterparts in the House, through the creation of task forces and expanded whip organizations (Smith 1992).

Some political observers attribute the trend toward greater party cohesion in Congress to the revitalization of the two national parties as campaign organizations. Parties have reasserted themselves in the recruitment of competitive congressional candidates, they argue, and have become important sources of campaign revenue and expert support (Reichley 1985; Herrnson 1990). Some observers believe that the rise in party contributions and coordinated party expenditures was directly responsible for the extraordinary cohesiveness of the Republicans during much of the Reagan era (Kayden and Mahe 1985, 194).[8]

---

8. The thirty-four Republican Senate contestants running in 1986, for instance, split a $10 million party war chest among themselves.

In addition, several studies have depicted parties as playing a far more active role in candidate decision making than many previous observers had acknowledged (Herrnson 1986, 1988, and 1991; Gibson et al. 1983 and 1985; Haeberle 1985; Kunkel 1988; Sabato 1988; Frendreis, Gibson, and Vertz 1990; Kazee and Thornberry 1990). In other words, the old characterization of the relationship between congressional candidates and American parties as "separate organizations pursuing separate tasks" no longer holds (Crotty 1984, 203).

Although the resurrection of the parties in the congressional literature is a welcome trend, it is doubtful that increased party efforts to recruit candidates and fund elections are responsible for the increased partisanship inside Congress. Counteracting the centripetal pull of parties in congressional elections is, after all, the equally strong centrifugal force of PACs, which not only permit members of Congress freedom from party control but often expect them to act independently. In 1988, for example, PACs provided one-third of all funds raised by House and Senate candidates, which represented about 50 percent of House Democrats' spending and 40 percent of House Republicans' spending (Ornstein, Mann, and Malbin 1990, 91). For the Senate the figures were 29 and 26 percent for Democrats and Republicans, respectively (Ornstein, Mann, and Malbin 1990, 92). Parties, in contrast, have increased total revenues supplied to congressional candidates, but their relative share of campaign expenditures has remained relatively flat at roughly 6 to 8 percent (Ornstein, Mann, and Malbin 1990, 91–92). Moreover, far more funds have come from outside the constituency than in the past (Grenzke 1988; Eismeier and Pollock 1988), thus pulling candidates away from local party activists. These realities may account for the relatively weak relationship between party contributions to House members and party unity on the floor (Leyden and Borelli 1990).

Equally important in counteracting the efforts of parties to emphasize unity inside Congress, the electoral conditions that fostered entrepreneurial candidacies in the mid-1960s and 1970s have not appreciably changed in the 1980s. Despite the increase in Republican identifiers during the Reagan years, the electorate still contains the same high proportion of independents that characterized it in the preceding decades. Similarly, voters' propensities for ticket splitting at all levels of elections have persisted throughout the 1980s (cf. Fiorina 1991; Jacobson 1991). If anything, constituency pressures appear to encourage members to maintain a cautious distance from their parties inside Congress.

Far more persuasive explanations of institutional change in the

1980s are found in the writings of Sinclair (1989) and Rohde (1991). Both authors emphasize the importance of environmental constraints in fostering organizational development, although they advance somewhat different arguments.

Sinclair's (1989) comprehensive treatment of the transformation of the Senate begins with the conventional wisdom about new members and the different expectations they inject into the institution. Stressing the election of liberal, northern Democrats in 1958, she credited these senators with the abandonment of the Senate apprenticeship norm in the mid-1960s. Sinclair argued that legislators in the class of 1958 had challenged the party establisment in their home states and therefore pushed hard for changes in the status quo once they arrived in Washington. But she also pointed out that their electoral vulnerability created intense pressures to accomplish their policy goals quickly and acquire the extra visibility at home afforded by a more activist stance.

Yet Sinclair adopted a very different point of view toward the far more significant developments of the 1970s and the 1980s, both of which she saw as a response to external political stimuli. The mobilization of interest groups and the appearance of new issues on the congressional agenda in the 1970s, she argued, created demands on lawmakers that they could not satisfy under the old rules, and the costs of supporting the old regime became unacceptably high.[9] Senior members, subjected to the same political pressures as their junior colleagues, joined in dispersing influence and creating a climate of floor activism and nonspecialization.

In this view of institutional change, far-reaching modifications in Senate norms and procedures arose not from new members bringing new objectives into the chamber but from the incapacity of many members to realize existing goals. Sinclair's view of institutional change assumed multiple goals among members of Congress—not only the desire for reelection but also the achievement of influence and the making of good public policy. Therefore, failure to satisfy any one of these goals for a sufficient number of members could lead to reform.

In subsequent papers, Sinclair applied a similar line of reasoning to the trend toward stronger party leadership in the House (1990b) and to similar but more recent changes in the Senate (1990a). But in these later papers, pressures from the executive branch because of divided

---

9. Davidson (1989) and Smith (1989) also see the transformation of the congressional agenda as the prime influence behind changing patterns of decision making.

government have been added to the demands of interest groups as forces of change. More important, Sinclair contended that the individualism of the earlier Congresses had become dysfunctional, thus causing senators to vest more discretion on an informal basis in the hands of their party leaders. They were not merely acquiescing to leadership from the party but demanding it. Parenthetically, other scholars, such as Arnold (1990) and Segura (1990), have developed compelling explanations of congressional structures by assuming that lawmakers are motivated by far more complex calculations than the maximization of reelection. Arnold, especially, makes a strong case for members' sacrifice of autonomy to obtain desired policy outcomes.

By couching the problem of institutional change in terms of the personal costs of compliance, Sinclair seemed to discount the importance of turnover as a necessary condition for the transformation of the Congress. Yet her insistence on viewing goal-oriented behavior as a multidimensional phenomenon did not altogether eliminate new members as a factor in explaining modifications and innovations in legislative structure. Instead, it raised questions about how incoming legislators developed a particular mix of objectives and what contextual factors led to one goal being dominant among a sizeable number of members.

In this respect, David Rohde's (1991) work on partisanship inside the House provides a nice complement to Sinclair's views on the sources of institutional change. Rohde, too, assumed that members have multiple goals, and he also argued that the individualism and fragmentation of Congress in the 1970s flourished because the political environment encouraged it and because party leaders of that era were disinclined to use the full powers of their offices. Rohde (1991, 35–37) further suggested that the relative weakness of the parties during that decade was overstated at the time by scholars who were used to thinking about party leadership in terms of a system of bossism.

But Rohde's most significant contribution to the understanding of institutional change in the House came from his analysis of the ideological divisions within the Democratic coalition. Despite the adoption of reforms in the House to strengthen party structures, he contended, the members could not be disciplined along party lines as long as the split between southern conservatives and northern liberals divided the majority. With the gradual shrinkage of this gap over civil rights, domestic welfare and national defense that occurred between 1972 and 1986, not only could Democrats be led, but they wanted the party to set an agenda and pass a program. The transformation occured because both senior lawmakers and newcomers from the South became more liberal, largely in response to the mobilization of African-American voters in the region. The Democrats' greater cohesiveness, in turn, sparked heightened partisanship among the Republicans, who became increasingly aggrieved and alienated during the Reagan and Bush years over their treatment at the hands of a resurgent majority.

Ultimately, Rohde (1991) identified the chief cause of reform as electoral. Procedural changes enacted in the 1970s to strengthen the majority party failed to meet the ideological objectives of liberal reformers because the internal divisions within the Democratic coalition prevented them from taking effect and in fact permitted the flowering of behavior quite different from what the DSG liberals and their allies had intended. But if the homogeneity of the membership in Congress was a necessary condition for the more centralized body envisioned by reformers, it could not take place overnight. Gradual transformation of southern representatives through conversion and generational replacement required several electoral cycles rather than sudden shocks to the system.

In this sense, Rohde saw the emergence of the postreform House as the culmination of the 1970 reforms rather than as a departure from the established course—an end result made possible because of electoral changes in the South. Yet, at the same time, Rohde's treatment of party leadership remained close to Sinclair's in asserting that external constraints, such as presidential action and interest group activity, were critical in creating the incentives for members to see party cooperation rather than individual entrepreneurship as the principal means for satisfying their political objectives.

In the Congress today these pressures seem to be pushing the members even closer to a model of party goverment inside Congress. Racked by intense public criticism, high retirements, and mounting antagonism between Republicans and Democrats, the House and Senate have begun to examine procedural reform as a means of improving institutional performance. A bipartisan, bicameral commission was formed in the summer of 1992 to consider a broad range of modifications to the existing rules, and the House Democratic Caucus recently adopted a reform package that contained several provisions designed to make the operation of the House more responsive to the majority. Members have been frustrated by the inability to frame and act on a national agenda, by the acrimony between the parties and between the Congress and the president, and by the inefficiency of the committee system. In short, the prolonged period of divided government and budgetary crisis has stymied members on both sides of the aisle from achieving policy objectives and political influence. A few left in disgust,[10] but those who stayed were primed for serious changes to improve the deliberative and decision-making capacities of the institution, and they intended to be ready with a package of reforms when the class of 1992 arrived in Washington.

How, then, should we evaluate the constantly evolving organizational patterns inside Congress? From the perspective of the 1970s, institutional change seemed to depend on membership turnover, both in terms of the numbers and types of politicians seeking congressional careers and their means of attaining office. With the benefit of hindsight, however, the transformation of the House and Senate membership seems to have been exaggerated as the prime mover of reform, and the absence of stable political coalitions appears to have had as much to do with the fragmentation of authority that characterized the institution as personal desires. More recently, the close association between trends in organizational arrangements and changes in the external environment seems to emphasize the costs of adhering to an old institutional order when outside pressures demand a new one. Yet even the current view of organizational development depends on electoral change to promote the cohesive parties inside Congress necessary to implement change while it assumes the continuation of careerist goals among the members. In the 103d Congress, it appears that both turnover and environmental pressures will come to bear on the business of reform as members seek a remedy for their frustrations over divided government by harnessing the energies of the giant freshman class elected in 1992. Thus, the two seemingly rival explanations of institutional reform share some common ground in their perception of the importance of electoral politics and their emphasis on member goals.

Despite these similarities, the theories are irreconcilable because of differences in their approach to political ambition. The turnover theory of institutional change assumed that new members brought new aspirations to Congress and that their desire for electoral safety and personal power led directly to institutional change. The environmental theory, however, held that members adapted their behavior to maintain their existing goals and reacted to events not of their making. It is

---

10. Moore and Hibbing (1992) contend that press accounts of the discontent among retiring members in 1992 exaggerated the level of disaffection. Most retirements followed the same pattern as earlier years, that is to say, redistricting was the biggest factor, followed by age and the availability of large amounts of convertible funds left over from past election campaigns.

here in the realm of politicians' motivations that the now-familiar ambiguity about recruitment in American politics appears. Once again, we see legislators both as instigators of political trends and as mirrors of broader disturbances in the political system.

The duality in the way scholars interpret institutional change has significant implications for how we understand the debate over term limits. If we view candidates as an engine of change in the American system, then the most direct way to bring about a new congressional order is to change the incentives attached to the pursuit of public office. This is why term limit advocates are so confident that their reform will bring a new style of legislator into Congress who will in turn conduct the public's business along very different lines. But if we view candidacy as the reflection of a whole complex of institutional and environmental arrangements, then it hardly seems likely that changing a single facet of the relationship will produce the intended result. In my view, we know too little about ambition and the early stages of candidate recruitment to speak with much authority about the claims of either side.

Candidacy and Term Limitations

In the popular view, the contemporary Congress is comprised of self-serving individuals who are out of touch with their constituents and incapable of acting collectively for the good of the nation. The combination of reduced electoral competition and entrenched membership has sparked a public outcry against incumbent representatives and senators and the insular "Beltway" mentality they have come to personify. Disturbed by lopsided contests that deny voters a real choice at the polls and frustrated by the seeming imperviousness of Congress to social and political changes in the electorate, reformers on both the left and the right have begun advocating the adoption of legislation that would restrict federal lawmakers to a fixed number of terms. A similar backlash against state legislators before the 1992 election had already resulted in the adoption of term limitations in California, Colorado and Oklahoma and the narrow defeat of restrictions in Washington that would have applied to both state legislators and members of the House. As of this writing, thirteen states, including Washington, have enacted similar restraints on the length of legislative careers.

It is rare in American politics for procedural issues to strike a popular chord or for grass roots movements to form around an idea as abstract as term limitations. Nevertheless, the proposal has widespread appeal because it conforms to public prejudices against career politicians and the clientele-based politics legislators have adopted to maintain themselves in office. More important, the personalized electoral coalitions so prevalent today practically guarantee that dissatisfaction with the performance of governmental institutions will quickly fasten onto the men and women who serve in public office. By changing the rules of the game, reformers hope to bring different personnel into the legislature and therefore produce different policy outcomes.

Typically, the reforms entail restrictions of four or five two-year terms for House members and two six-year terms for senators.[11] The proposals vary in how the limitations would be implemented. For example, some provide for a grandfather clause that would protect the tenure of those already in the House; some allow for phased implementation geared to the level of prior service; and others require retirement at the end of the current term for all legislators over the legal limit of service. Yet the intended limits are quite close to the average tenure of legislators serving in Congress over the past decade—a mean of 5.8 terms for representatives and 1.6 terms of senators (Ornstein, Mann, and Malbin 1992, 18–19). Their immediate effect would therefore be the elimination—either gradually or suddenly—of legislators with higher than average periods of service.

This group of senior lawmakers represented about 40 percent of the House and 30 percent of the Senate in the 102d Congress, although the high turnover in 1992 has rendered them a proportionately smaller group in the 103d Congress. Still, their departure would be immediately felt inside Congress because they have held all the top party and committee leadership posts and posted the most active legislative records (Hibbing 1991a, 177–80).

Many supporters of the reform contend that the American political tradition has deep roots in theories of governance by ordinary citizens. Petracca (1992), for example, has argued that mandatory rotation in office is deeply imbedded in classic democratic theory because it prevented any one group from monopolizing governmental power and compelled citizens to exercise their responsibilities to the polity. He pointed to the prevalence of limits for state legislators, governors, and even for members of the Continental Congress as indicators of the general acceptance of this view.[12] Indeed, Petracca's

---

11. Some proposals allow for reelection after a waiting period of varying length, while others impose an absolute limit on the number of years served.
12. This restriction was quietly dropped after several years.

position sounds similar to arguments the Anti-Federalists advanced during the debate over ratification 200 years ago.

But the impetus for reform is more than philosophical. Term limit advocates contend that shortening tenure would have the practical effect of improving electoral competition by eliminating some of the advantages of incumbency. Parties and PACs, they argue, would have fewer incentives to invest in long-term relationships with senior lawmakers and would therefore contribute a greater proportion of their campaign resources to challengers and open-seat contests. The reformers further argue that if incumbents knew they could only serve a fixed number of terms, they would be less concerned with reelection and more inclined to make choices that were unpopular with special interests. Finally, proponents of term limits claim that more quality candidates would be likely to run for Congress if they did not have to confront entrenched incumbents.

With the power of incumbency diminished, some political analysts predict the restoration of congressional elections as national referenda. Voters would have weaker attachments to particular legislators and would therefore be more inclined to return to partisanship as a voting cue. Popular presidential candidates would have their coattails restored and would therefore have greater prospects for working majorities in the House and Senate. These conditions would enable citizens once again to use off-year elections to punish the party of the president for failed performance.

Similarly, reformers believe fewer incumbents running in any given election year would provide women and ethnic minorities with improved opportunities to gain seats. In this respect, the pace of expanded representation in Congress would be accelerated.

The goal of improved competition is only part of the reformers' agenda, however. At bottom, they reject the rise of what they see as a political class in the American democracy, and they abhor the notion that representation requires a particular temperament or specialized skills. With term limits they hope to inaugurate a Congress dominated by citizen legislators whose occupation in private life and interest in the public welfare would lead to more responsive and responsible policies. These public-minded citizens would presumably tend to look for the common good instead of seeking support from special interests and would be more likely to consider the long-range implications of programs without personal career considerations warping their judgment.

Opponents counter that whatever the merits of term limits for state legislatures, similar restrictions on Congress are unconstitutional.[13] At issue is whether or not states can add prior officeholding experience to the list of qualifications for members of Congress beyond those already mentioned in Article I. The framers did debate the possibility of giving state legislatures the authority to set property requirements or other eligibility criteria for House members, to nominate candidates, and even to select the actual representatives, but in the end they agreed with Madison's view that "the qualifications of electors and elected were fundamental articles in a Republican Government and ought to be fixed by the Constitution. If the legislature could regulate those of either, it [could] by degrees subvert the Constitution" (Madison 1987, 427).

Beyond the legality of term limitations, however, opponents of term limitations contend that citizens should not be denied the right to choose an incumbent who has done a good job. They point to the high approval ratings most representatives receive from their constituents as evidence that the electorate is satisfied with the representation it is receiving, even though it gives the Congress low marks as an institution. Reform is a plot, they surmise, by Republicans who cannot recruit strong candidates to unseat such popular legislators in a straight contest.

Finally, the foes of term limits question the legitimacy and effectiveness of a legislature comprised of political amateurs. They are quick to point out that the Anti-Federalist conception of the citizen lawmaker was rejected at the constitutional convention in favor of the views of Hamilton and Madison. Both men had argued strongly that members of Congress needed time to learn about the country's problems and to develop expertise in finding solutions—a process that required effort and commitment to the art of governing. Brief tenure in Congress, Hamilton argued, would provide little incentive for talented men to make such an investment. Moreover, as noted in chapter 2, Madison feared the volatility of a legislature filled with newcomers and urged the necessity of leadership from those senior members whom he described as "masters of the public business" (*The Federalist* No. 53). Incidentally, similar thinking lay behind the reform efforts of the 1950s and 1960s to improve the performance of state legislatures by professionalizing them.

---

13. In a court case testing the legality of the California law, the state's Supreme Court sided with the advocates of term limits. It ruled that "restrictions on the succession of incumbents serves a rational public policy. . . . although [they] may deny qualified men an opportunity to serve" . . . "as a general rule the overall health of the body politic is enhanced by limitations on continuous tenure" (*New York Times,* October 11, 1991, A1, A19).

In assessing the claims and counterclaims swirling around the term limits controversy, it is easy to get mired in historical analogies with the nineteenth century or to get side-tracked by institutional comparisons between the legislative and executive branches.[14] It also is tempting to construct scenarios of unintended consequences in an effort to assess the relative merits of the term limits proposal.[15] In my view, however, the fundamental question for both sides of the term limits debate is how much congressional candidacy and institutional patterns of decision making depend on a particular set of political career incentives. Both proponents and opponents must come to a judgment about the importance of individual ambition as a determinant of institutional performance. In effect, they must weigh the merits of the two explanations of organizational change—turnover versus environmental pressures—in predicting the likely consequences of term limits in Congress.

If membership turnover is to yield new institutional behaviors, then certain conditions pertaining to the supply of candidates have to be met. First, candidates have to be numerous enough to crop up in a large number of districts when the political winds shift, and they have to be sufficiently different from the old guard to deliver the fresh style of representation demanded by the times. Second, these antiestablishment politicians have to be able to survive the winnowing process and obtain party nominations by co-opting existing political elites or by mobilizing a new source of campaign funds and volunteers. Third, they must have the capacity to exploit existing institutional rules inside Congress to deliver whatever mix of services and policies the new era demands. In the case of term limits, then, what reformers hope to see in the 1990s is the emergence of antipoliticians seeking seats in Congress—another new breed of legislators—who would be willing to interrupt productive careers in the private sector for public service,

---

14. Proponents, for example, suggest that the prevalence of rotation in the nineteenth century is a lost ideal to which we should return, whereas opponents counter that the high turnover of that era resulted in corruption and incompetence. Similarly, advocates of term limits draw parallels with their widespread application to the office of governor, while foes claim that restrictions on state executives were intended to weaken them politically vis-à-vis the legislature and that Congress is already at such a disadvantage with respect to the presidency that it cannot take any further constraints on its political influence.

15. Here, the advantage is with the opposition, which asserts a variety of perverse outcomes: that competition will actually decrease because the most qualified candidates will wait for incumbents' compulsory retirement rather than take them on at the polls; that the influence of lobbyists will increase because inexperienced lawmakers will not have the expertise to evaluate their claims; and that legislative outcomes will be less responsive to the popular will because lawmakers will be at the mercy of professional staff and federal bureaucrats for information.

who would run for office without the benefit of support from interest groups or parties, and who would find the means to reconfigure the modern welfare state through a combination of cost-cutting measures and programmatic innovations.

If all this seems a bit farfetched, it is no more strained an argument than the scenario for the new breed of the 1970s and its capture of the entire federal government, which enjoyed such widespread currency in our discipline for over a decade (Fiorina 1977). Yet the very implausibility of the causal chain the term limit reformers would set in motion forces us to ask some basic questions: Where would these new legislators come from? How would they get around the existing political establishment? What incentives would move them toward a new mix of policy outcomes on Capitol Hill? These questions need to be addressed if we are going to make intelligent assessments about the likely impact of term limits.

Unfortunately, congressional scholars are not in a position to cast much light on such issues. We did not ask about the origin and pursuit of political ambition in the earlier eras of institutional change, and we seem poorly positioned to do better today. We have no information on the pool of prospective candidates, other than the case studies conducted by Kazee in 1983 and by Fowler and McClure in 1989 and the pilot projects conducted by Kazee (1993) and his colleagues. Consequently, we lack time-series analyses of how the candidate pool changes over time or systematic investigations of how structural and contextual variables affect its composition in different places and in different political eras.

Nor do we have survey data on declared candidates, other than polls done by Fishel (1973) in 1964, Maisel (1982) in 1978, and Herrnson (1988) in 1984 because studies of candidate recruitment went out of fashion at about the time they were most needed (Canon forthcoming). Moreover, the studies that are available, including the new survey by Norris and Darcy (1992), concentrated primarily on the strategic aspects of candidacy, so that they contained few items on the respondents' motives in running, their views on representation if elected, or their understanding of how Congress should operate as an institution. Not surprisingly, then, we are not in a position to speak to the motivations that drive politicians' congressional careers.

Similarly, we lack basic data about the nature of party activists below the presidential election level and possess only the most rudimentary understanding about the behavior of individual campaign contributors and volunteers. Our view of interest groups is focused almost entirely on lobbying in Washington rather than on activism in the constituency. Although we know how much money PACs raise and whom they support, we have a limited picture of why they allocate their resources in a particular fashion. This problem is especially noticeable at the level of primary elections, in the decision to back the occasional challenger, and in the distribution of funds to open-seat candidates. As a result, we cannot explain how nominees are winnowed from the pack of prospective candidates and what systematic biases the selection process introduces into the legislative process.

Finally, because we have these gaps in our ability to explain candidates' emergence, we cannot fully appreciate the incentives that shape their behavior. This lack, in turn, limits our capacity to weigh the influence of legislators' personal and political goals once in office against the expectations of the electorate. Accordingly, we are in a poor position to decide whether citizens have the kind of Congress they desire, as scholars such as Jacobson (1991) argue, or whether voters have been victimized by selfish and self-serving professional politicians, as many reformers claim.

In short, we cannot say what impact term limits would have on the men and women who would run for Congress and how they would go about getting elected. Most important, we cannot predict whether voters would continue to reward the style of representation they have supported up to now or whether, if given the choice imposed through term limits, they would in fact elect a new breed of legislator.

From the perspective of the environmental disturbance theory of institutional change, the issue of term limits looks somewhat different. In applying this model, the problem is not the emergence of a sufficient supply of candidates to implement the goals of reformers but rather the exercise of individual and institutional will to move Congress in a positive direction. The scholars who have written in this vein tell us two things are important. First, the members of Congress have to care enough about the Congress and their careers within its chambers to invest in changing its manner of doing business. Second, they need to have sufficient organizational autonomy so that whatever changes they adopt will move the institution in the intended direction.

Students of mature organizations understand that members find informal ways to accomplish their goals when formal procedures get in the way. They recognize that if enough individuals are trying to accomplish the same ends, they will eventually create norms and rules that will institutionalize their ability to pursue particular objectives. At the same time, they acknowledge that existing rules are far from neutral and tilt organizational decisions in particular directions. In addition, organizational theorists speak convincingly about the difficulties of mobilizing members of voluntary organizations to provide collective goods.

Each of these constraints on organizational change are pertinent to the reform of Congress, and that is why scholars such as Sinclair and Rohde placed such a premium on member goals in their writings. They grasped the importance of incentives for members to bear the costs of formalizing new ways of doing things, of overcoming whatever tactical advantage existing rules confer on supporters of the status quo, and of pursuing cooperative strategies in providing for the collective good of organizational competence. But they were writing about a Congress in which the desire for long service was an established fact and career-minded legislators had well-defined goals that induced them to invest in the institution.

Under term limits, however, it is not clear what goals the members will be pursuing or whether they will feel obliged to make a commitment to their institution. Perhaps Congress will be rejuvenated by a new wave of citizen lawmakers, as the reformers hope. Perhaps it will simply be a way station for politicians running through a string of public offices as it was in the nineteenth century (Swenson 1982). Perhaps it will be a place for personal aggrandizement as lawmakers swap votes for favors with lobbyists and administration officials. Or perhaps it will become a soapbox for people with any number of causes. We have no basis as scholars for predicting which mix of objectives will predominate in a Congress of limited tenure, but at least one school of thought pertaining to institutional change tells us we ought to worry about such things.

Equally important, however, is the role that external actors and long-term electoral patterns play in bringing about reform. If change in legislative structures occurs because senators and representatives need to adapt their chambers to outside pressures, it follows, I think, that new modes of decision making will not be forthcoming in the absence of those pressures. Similarly, if the implementation of reform requires stable coalitions inside Congress, not only to agree on a new set of rules but to see that they are carried out, then creating the electoral underpinnings for those coalitions is critical to any reform effort. Thus, large numbers of new members bringing new political concerns to the legislature may be a necessary but not sufficient condition for institutional change.

Such considerations are particularly important when considering how term limits will affect the performance of the legislative branch, because term limits, though intended to have repercussions throughout the political system, have not been proposed as part of an overall plan for improving governmental decision making. They do not restrict the behavior of other actors—lobbyists, bureaucrats, executive officials, or constituents—or compel them to adopt a particular mode of doing business with lawmakers. Nor do they address the alienation of voters toward the political parties or their need for better information in electoral campaigns.

Scholars have no basis for predicting how all these players will respond to changes in the legislature wrought by term limits, so we can only assume that they will be governed by the same institutional and personal imperatives that motivate them under the present system. But common sense tells us that term limits without comparable reforms in the areas of campaign finance, lobbying, administrative procedure, executive discretion, and party organization, to name a few, will probably have unintended consequences. Without a clearer understanding of how external actors affect members' attitudes toward the internal workings of Congress, however, we can do no more than speculate about what these consequences might be.[16]

In the end, the debate over term limits compels us to examine our understanding of institutional change and reminds us once more of the salience of candidate recruitment to broad concerns in American politics. Yet in exploring the literature in this area, as in so many others, we are left with a perplexing question: do congressional candidates create political events and patterns, or do they simply reflect them?

---

16. Benjamin and Malbin 1992 offer plenty of food for thought along these lines.

CHAPTER 7

Conclusion

. . . among democratic nations, ambition is ardent and continual, but
its aim is not habitually lofty; and life is generally spent in eagerly
coveting small objects that are within reach.
—Alexis de Tocqueville, *Democracy in America*

Candidates are responsible for much of the continuity and dynamism
in American politics. They energize electoral competition and articu-
late policy conflicts. They reflect dominant cleavages in the society
and give voice to newly emergent partisan alignments and social
groups. They mediate demands on institutions from the external political environment and create their own pressures for organizational
adaptation. Yet scholars and citizens seldom acknowledge this perva-
sive influence over the day-to-day operation of representative government and its responsiveness to change.

Candidates typically command only episodic attention. Like
other campaign phenomena—sound bites and bumper stickers—they
briefly claim center stage during the months before an election and
then quickly recede into obscurity. We take for granted that ambitious
individuals will want to run for office without questioning where they
come from. We tally up the winners and losers without considering
how the election might have turned out with different choices on the
ballot. In short, we rarely think about candidates outside the immediate context of a campaign.

This narrow focus has obscured the broad functions of candidacy in promoting political change in the United States. Partisan
realignments within the electorate, for example, cannot take place
without candidates to help them along. The representation of newly
mobilized constituencies, such as women and ethnic minorities, can
falter if group members cannot obtain nominations. Organizational
adaptation can stall if politicians' career orientations and external
pressures on legislative institutions fail to mesh. Not only do such
trends take a good deal of time to manifest themselves, but they are
difficult to disentangle from the numerous short-term influences of
any particular election. In this respect, the stimulative effect of can-

didacy, as it moves voters in one direction or another during the campaign, often masks its long-term implications.

Even within the limited sphere of election campaigns, however, the role of candidates in promoting competition is unclear. The cumulative research effort of dozens of congressional scholars confirms that the strength and quality of candidates matter significantly to the vote choice. Hard-fought races generate more information, which then enables voters to evaluate the candidates. Low-key races, on the other hand, rarely create sufficient recognition of the candidates to overcome inertial forces favoring a particular party or incumbent. But having convincingly established that candidates' organizational skills and political appeals matter a great deal over the course of an election cycle, scholars have yet to explain what mix of incumbency, local contexts and national events brings strong competitors into the electoral arena and what combination of factors inhibits their emergence.

Several different aspects of the scholarly enterprise associated with recruitment and candidates account for this state of affairs. First, the theory of recruitment separated candidates from their social and institutional milieu quite early in the game. The recruitment theorists tended to see candidacy as the product of social and psychological conditioning imposed by the environment. In contrast, the ambition theorists concentrated on individual goals and regarded candidacy largely as a strategic exercise concerned with winning and losing. Their perspective has dominated the literature since the mid-1960s. Only in the past several years have a few scholars taken the first tentative steps toward reconciling the cost-benefit calculus of would-be candidates with the structures that enhance or inhibit their ambitions.

Second, the empirical investigation of candidacy has focused almost entirely on the careers of incumbent politicians. Although progressive ambition is an undeniably important factor promoting individual candidacy, it is only part of the story. A focus on incumbent officeholders obviously leaves out amateurs—a significant proportion of whom actually end up in the House and Senate. It relegates long-shot candidacies to the realm of political irrationality, it fails to account for the entry of new types of politicians, and it assumes a good deal more regularity in career ladders across communities than probably exists. The net effect of so much emphasis on incumbents, then, is an inability to explain the onset of ambition and its development over time.

Third, the theoretical and empirical stress on strategic choice among career politicians has led to neglect of the contextual and structural features that determine the candidate pool. Scholars have been more interested in the end product of candidacy—electoral victory—than on the self-selection and process of elimination that produce a small list of eligibles from the broader ranks of political activists. As a result, variation across states and districts in the numbers and qualifications of likely candidates has been largely ignored. Moreover, because scholars have spent so little time identifying the types of individuals likely to develop congressional ambition, they have had few bases for analyzing how various elites, such as interest groups, PACs, individual contributors, and party organizations, decide whom to support or eliminate.

Consequently, the status of candidates in American politics remains quite ambiguous despite several generations of scholarship on recruitment and congressional elections. In some studies, candidates emerge as prime movers in causal sequences governing outcomes as diverse as election victory or institutional change. In other studies, would-be candidates are controlled by elites and events that they may only dimly recognize. In some studies, the impact of candidates is more implied than explicit. In still others, their influence is ill-defined because the causal arrows seem to run simultaneously in different directions. Taken as a whole, this vast literature seems to raise as many questions as it answers.

What are the prospects for coming to a richer and more complete understanding of candidacy in American politics? They are not very good if political scientists simply do more of what we have done in the past. To be sure, some of the questions raised in this book will greatly benefit from theoretical innovations, new candidate surveys, better measures, and more sophisticated methodologies. I have identified many such possibilities throughout this book.

But over the long run, I think the present ambiguities about candidacy reflect several limitations in the way legislative scholars generally approach the study of American politics. Most important, I believe, is our neglect of the intermediary role of political elites. We tend to focus on either elective officials or the mass public and neglect the layer of activists in the middle. But I also believe that we have been too inclined to focus on the short-term aspects of candidacy for the very good reason that longitudinal studies are exceedingly costly and labor intensive. Finally, I would argue that we need to pay serious attention to the nature of political ambition, in particular how it is affected over time by public policy.

Political Elites and Political Change

Candidacy originates and flourishes in a realm of political elites where few political scientists conduct research. The vast majority of specialists in American politics concentrates on the mass public. A substantial minority of scholars examines the conduct of elective officials in office. Only a relative handful examines the activists who occupy the middle ground between these two polar extremes of political behavior. Their domain includes interest groups, party activists and delegates, campaign contributors and volunteers, and local and state party leaders. That candidacy arises in this nether world of political science accounts for many of the ambiguities and unanswered questions I have raised throughout this book.

Political elites exercise enormous influence in American politics because institutional power is fragmented and party organizations are decentralized. The public and its government in Washington are remote from each other and have few institutionalized mechanisms of communication, other than the noisy and imperfect system of periodic elections. Ordinary citizens are too inattentive and disorganized to deal directly with elective officials; elective officials too often have a skewed vision of what the public wants. When voters desire something new, therefore, or elective officials want to move the country in a different direction, they both require channels through which they can signal their intentions. Political elites fill these gaps by acting as intermediaries between the two sets of actors. Consequently, they are indispensible agents of political change.

The influence of political elites is not always apparent, however, because they occupy a niche that has vague boundaries and a shifting cast of characters. These participants enjoy special status based on their high levels of political sophistication and activism, but they also invite suspicion because they are not representative of the mass public nor constrained by the rules and procedures that regulate elective officials. They operate around the edges of governmental institutions, not just in their own communities but across local and state boundaries. Through myriad acts of political entrepreneurship, they define their varying levels of influence. Political elites generally lack the legitimacy of numbers and the power of institutionalized authority; nevertheless, they are critical participants in the American democracy.

The fluid, self-defining character of political elites makes them a tough subject for political analysts, however. Students of mass behavior depend on national samples and aggregate statistics, which are relatively precise and accessible. Researchers investigating elective officials rely on participant observations and public records, which vary in quality but are at least manageable in scope. But those who examine political elites have neither established sources of data nor specific sample populations from which to draw inferences. The target group is too small and variable to be captured through nationwide surveys and indicators, it is too large for systematic interviewing, and it is too amorphous to inspire public record keeping. Instead, scholars improvise, using a mix of qualitative data, case studies, ad hoc measures, and narrowly targeted sample surveys.

Under such constraints, researchers working in this middle realm can seldom do justice to the widespread influence of activists in American politics. They typically are unable to examine the interconnections among various segments of the elite population on any comprehensive or sustained basis. They cannot produce the longitudinal analyses of elite behavior that would illuminate activists' contribution to political change. Thus, when social and structural evolutions eventually find their way into the political arena, scholars are often oblivious to their occurrence until a crisis or defining event announces their presence.

Given the general difficulties associated with analyzing political elites, it is understandable that researchers working in the field of recruitment were attracted to the cost-benefit model of decision making and its presumption of individual autonomy. This attraction inevitably led to a concentration on declared candidates and incumbent careers and the avoidance of prospective office seekers. Scholars could not simply slice cross-sectionally into the network of elites and uncover the deliberations of potential candidates. They had little knowledge about the layers of relationships that loosely link the various elite participants who influence candidate decisions. They could not systematically control for the many institutional contexts that constrain political activists under a variety of circumstances. Lacking such information, it was probably wiser not to speculate about the nature and size of the candidate pool. It certainly was impractical to sort out the processes by which a few nominees were winnowed from among the many eligible candidates.

In light of these realities, then, it does not seem very likely that scholars will develop better explanations of candidacy unless considerably more research is conducted on the broad spectrum of elite behavior. Scholars who seek explanations for the emergence of congressional candidates will need help mapping the political terrain that lies between the mass public and elective officials.

The Dynamics of Candidacy

Much of what political scientists know about congressional candidates lacks historical perspective because of the dominance of cross-sectional analyses in the literature. Some multiyear comparisons exist, particularly in the realm of campaign finance, and some time-series research has been done with aggregate electoral results, economic data, and turnover. But for the most part, candidates as we portray them today are disconnected from candidates of the past.

There are two types of historical frames of reference that would enhance an appreciation of candidacy in American politics. The first entails changes in the characteristics and experiences of contemporary candidates in comparison to those of other eras. The second concerns the nature of candidate influence on partisan realignments within the electorate. Both types of analysis would provide information about how candidacy figures in long-term patterns of representation in the American democracy. Yet both require a shift away from the current concentration on predicting election outcomes.

Enough change has taken place in the postwar years among people who have run for Congress to justify a longer backward glance into the realm of candidacy. First, the quantity and officeholding experience of House candidates dropped significantly over the past two decades, leading to a rise in uncontested seats and noncompetitive races. Second, the manifest offices for launching congressional careers have significantly altered over the same period. Substantially more state legislators sought seats in the House, although the number of lawmakers from small states actually declined. Modest increases occurred in the frequency of party officials and legislative staffers who entered the House. An upsurge in the number of House members pursuing Senate careers also took place. Third, the social diversity of the Congress broadened through the gradual expansion in the numbers of women and ethnic minorities serving in the House (and to a very modest extent in the Senate).

In looking at these various changes in membership over a generation, it is obvious that scholars have few benchmarks from the past to evaluate them. We have no way of knowing, for example, whether the contemporary decline in the number and quality of House candidates is a recent phenomenon or whether such aberrations have taken place in the past. Similarly, we have few indicators of the types of manifest, or stepping-stone, offices members have used as entries to Congress in past eras and what circumstances foster change in typical career ladders. Nineteenth-century lawmakers usually had prior political experience, although its nature and extent is unknown. Furthermore, although Congress has absorbed representatives from successive waves of immigrant groups during its history, we have little information about the rate of inclusion or the conditions in the constituency and the country as a whole that foster such political assimilation. Consequently, we do not have much basis for determining whether or not the current rates of progress for women, African-Americans, Hispanics, and newer generations of immigrants are typical.

Historical analyses of members of Congress have focused largely on careerism and a few social characteristics. A number of scholars have given extensive attention to patterns of turnover, length of service, and leadership apprenticeship inside the House and Senate. Others have mapped certain social attributes of the members, such as occupation, age, or religious affiliation, seniority, and turnover. But broad questions about how changes in the experiences and characteristics of prospective candidates come about still require answers.

Complementing research on the historical patterns of candidates' emergence would be an investigation of their role in partisan realignments. We have seen that several different interpretations of realignment theory implicated candidates as agents of electoral change. In Brady's (1988) analysis, for example, a necessary condition for realignment was a large supply of competitive candidates in marginal districts who generated substantial seat swings with relatively small shifts in the total vote. Canon (1990b) arrived at a similar view of candidates in accounting for the slow progress of the secular realignment underway in the South. Carmines and Stimson (1984) emphasized candidates' issue positions rather than their numbers as instrumental in realignments because they reinforced voters' budding predilections for one party. Shafer (1991), in contrast, concluded that party elites prevented the long-awaited realignment of the contemporary era from taking place because they supported candidates who represented cross-cutting cleavages in each party. In this way, neither party could command a majority coalition to control both branches of government and enact its policies.

These hypothetical relationships between candidacy and realignment are quite provocative. Not only do they speak directly to the ambiguous causal status of candidacy in American politics, but also they highlight the transformative potential of political elites. An examination of the historical conditions that affect candidate emergence during periods of realignment should therefore illuminate many of the broad issues raised in this volume.

Such inquiries into the recruitment of past generations of legislators will depend on more detailed information about former members and the politicians who ran against them. They will also need systematic data about constituency and institutional contexts. Information of this sort is not available at present, although an effort organized by Elaine Swift, David Canon, and others and funded by the National Science Foundation has laid some of the groundwork to support such research in the future. But a good deal more information needs to be collected and made accessible. Until then, scholars will be hampered in assessing contempory congressional candidates in the context of the past.

Ambition and Public Policy

Ambition is the dirty little secret of American politics. As much as we despise politicians who openly display ambition we could not do without them and their intense desire for political power. The nation has no constitutional provisions to cultivate public servants, and it has dismantled the capacity of political parties to groom office seekers. Instead of institutions for recruiting and training elective officials, the United States relies on personal ambition. This is entirely appropriate to our individualistic culture and our antipathy to the idea of a political class, but it places the responsibility for many of the basic features of democratic government—electoral competition, representation, and instititonal competence—in the hands of self-motivated individuals.

Given the importance of ambition in American politics, citizens and scholars ought to be concerned about incentives. Do they generate an adequate supply of prospective candidates in the right places? Do they prompt competent and public-minded individuals to seek elective office? Do they encourage adequate expression of the diverse interests and values in the society?

Americans have not historically paid much attention to questions of this sort, and our negligence has often proven costly, as Lord Bryce noted a century ago. We have tended to take our candidates as we find them and assume that there will always be others to replace them. During some periods, we have legislated new incentive structures for candidates without necessarily being aware of the potential consequences. Progressive-era reformers, for example, inadvertantly encouraged careerism in Congress because of their attacks on the parties' control of nominations. In effect, they paved the way for professional legislators to replace professional politicians: hardly the kind of democratization of public office they had in mind.

Similarly, reformers in the 1990s seem bent on a wide range of institutional changes that in one way or another will alter the calculations of prospective congressional candidates. In the case of term limits, altering the incentives for office seeking is quite deliberate. Both proponents and opponents agree that future congressional candidates will behave quite differently under the new rules, even though they make contradictory predictions about the benefits and costs of the proposal.

But other reforms, such as campaign finance regulations, are also aimed at introducing new incentives for candidates. Public financing of House and Senate elections, if it is undertaken at realistically high levels, is intended to increase the supply of competitive challengers. Whether the money will actually encourage strong candidates to compete for Congress or end up wasted in the hands the same weak opponents that run today is an open question. A similar objective lies behind proposals to restrict PAC contributions to incumbents. Limits on total campaign spending, however, while designed to limit the overall influence of money in electoral politics, will undoubtedly make it harder for some challengers to defeat incumbents.

Similarly, redistricting reforms implemented by the courts to promote increased representation of African-Americans and Hispanics have affected the incentives for office seeking among both prospective white and prospective ethnic candidates. In the short run, these changes have resulted in the election of more African-American and Hispanic lawmakers to Congress, particularly in 1992. In the long run, however, the districting rules may end up concentrating prospective minority candidates in a relatively few areas. Or they may end up limiting the number of districts in which a solid minority base of 20 to 30 percent encourages the emergence of African-American and white candidates who can appeal across ethnic lines.

The point is not whether the various reforms being proposed or already implemented are good or bad for Congress. The issue for scholars, rather, is what the potential effect of all these different proposals will have on political ambition. Are some changes more promising than others? Are some actually perverse? Are some combinations of reform synergistic or counterproductive? The simple truth is that we do not have credible answers to such questions. Nor is it likely, as this book has stressed over and over, that we will produce better responses quickly or easily.

But I think we have to take responsibility for the fact that our inattention to candidacy in its broadest sense and our neglect of the earliest phases of individual recruitment have fostered a particular mentality among the public. For too long, we have taken ambition as a given in American politics and encouraged citizens to do likewise. It is time to recognize that candidates are a precious resource that our democracy cannot afford to take for granted or squander.

References

Aberbach, Joel D., Robert D. Putnam, and Bert A. Rockman. 1981. *Bureaucrats and Politicians in Western Democracies.* Cambridge, Mass.: Harvard University Press.

Abramowitz, Alan I. 1975. "Name Familiarity, Reputation, and the Incumbency Effect in a Congressional Election." *Western Political Quarterly* 28:668–84.

———. 1983. "Partisan Redistricting and the 1982 Congressional Elections." *Journal of Politics* 45:767–70.

———. 1984. "National Issues, Strategic Politicians, and Voting Behavior in the 1980 and 1982 Congressional Elections." *American Journal of Political Science* 28:710–21.

———. 1988. "Explaining Senate Election Outcomes." *American Political Science Review* 82:385–403.

———. 1991. "Incumbency, Campaign Spending, and the Decline of Competition in U.S. House Elections." *Journal of Politics* 53:34–56.

Abramowitz, Alan I., and Jeffrey A. Segal. 1986. "Determinants of the Outcomes of U.S. Senate Elections." *Journal of Politics* 48:433–39.

Abramson, Paul R., John H. Aldrich, and David W. Rohde. 1987. "Progressive Ambition among United States Senators: 1972–1988." *Journal of Politics* 49:3–35.

Achen, Christopher H. 1977. "Measuring Representation: The Perils of the Correlation Coefficient." *American Journal of Political Science* 21:805–15.

———. 1978. "Measuring Representation." *American Journal of Political Science* 22:475–510.

Alford, John R., and John R. Hibbing. 1981. "Increased Incumbency Advantage in the House." *Journal of Politics* 43:1042–61.

Almond, Gabriel A. 1960. "A Functional Approach to Comparative Politics." In *The Politics of the Developing Areas,* ed. Gabriel A. Almond and James S. Coleman. Princeton, N.J.: Princeton University Press.

Andersen, Kristi. 1979. *The Creation of a Democratic Majority, 1928–1936.* Chicago: University of Chicago Press.

Andersen, Kristi, and Stuart S. Thorson. 1984. "Congressional Turnover and the Election of Women." *Western Political Quarterly* 37:143–56.

Ansolabehere, Stephen, David Brady, and Morris Fiorina. 1988. "The Marginals Never Vanished?" Working Paper P-88-1. Hoover Institution, Stanford University.

Arnold, R. Douglas. 1982. "Overtilled and Undertilled Fields in American Politics." *Political Science Quarterly* 97:91–103.

———. 1990. *The Logic of Congressional Action.* New Haven, Conn.: Yale University Press.

Auden, W. H., and Louis Kronenberger. [1962] 1981. *The Viking Book of Aphorisms: A Personal Selection.* New York: The Viking Press.

Baird, Frank L. 1977. "The Search for a Constituency: Political Validation of Mexican-American Candidates in the Texas Great Plains." In *Mexican-Americans: Political Power, Influence, or Resource,* ed. Frank L. Baird. Lubbock, Tex.: Texas Tech Press.

Baker, John, and Linda Bennett. 1991. "The Quest for a Congressional Seat: Nonincumbent Candidates in the 1990 U.S. House Primary Elections." Paper presented at the annual meeting of the American Political Science Association, Washington, D.C., September.

Banks, Jeffrey S., and D. Roderick Kiewiet. 1989. "Explaining Patterns of Candidate Competition in Congressional Elections." *American Journal of Political Science* 33:997–1015.

Barber, Benjamin. 1990. "The Nature of Contemporary Political Science: A Roundtable Discussion." *PS: Political Science and Politics* 23 (March): 40.

Barber, James David. 1965. *The Lawmakers: Recruitment and Adaptation to Legislative Life.* New Haven, Conn.: Yale University Press.

Barker, Lucius J., and Jesse J. McCorry, Jr. 1980. *Black Americans and the Political System.* Cambridge, Mass.: Winthrop.

Barone, Michael, and Grant Ujifusa. 1985. *The Almanac of American Politics— 1986.* Washington, D.C.: National Journal.

———. 1987. *The Almanac of American Politics—1988.* Washington, D.C.: National Journal.

———. 1989. *The Almanac of American Politics—1990.* Washington, D.C.: National Journal.

———. 1991. *The Almanac of American Politics—1992.* Washington, D.C.: National Journal.

Bauer, Monica, and John R. Hibbing. 1989. "Which Incumbents Lose in House Elections: A Response to Jacobson's 'The Marginals Never Vanished.'" *American Journal of Political Science* 33:262–71.

Beck, Paul Allen. 1984. "The Dealignment Era in America." In *Electoral Change in Advanced Industrial Democracies,* ed. Russell J. Dalton, Scott C. Flanagan, and Paul Allen Beck. Princeton, N.J.: Princeton University Press.

———. 1989. "Incomplete Realignment: The Reagan Legacy for Parties and Elections." In *The Reagan Legacy,* ed. Charles O. Jones. Chatham, N.J.: Chatham House.

Benjamin, Gerald, and Michael J. Malbin. 1992. *Limiting Legislative Terms.* Washington, D.C.: CQ Press.

Berelson, Bernard R., Paul Lazersfeld, and William N. McPhee. 1954. *Voting.* Chicago: University of Chicago Press.

Berkman, Michael. 1990. "The Changing Composition of Congress: The Rise of Former State Legislators." Paper presented at the Carl Albert Center's Conference, "Back to the Future: Congress into the Twenty-First Century," University of Oklahoma, April 11–13.

Bernstein, Robert A. 1986. "Why Are There So Few Women in the House?" *Western Political Quarterly* 39:155–64.

———. 1989. *Elections, Representation, and Congressional Voting Behavior.* Englewood Cliffs, N.J.: Prentice Hall.

Bianco, William T. 1984. "Strategic Decisions on Candidacy in U.S. Congressional Districts." *Legislative Studies Quarterly* 9:351–64.

Bibby, John F., ed. 1983. *Congress off the Record: The Candid Analysis of Seven Members.* Washington, D.C.: American Enterprise Institute.

Black, Earl, and Merle Black. 1987. *Politics and Society in the South.* Cambridge, Mass.: Harvard University Press.

Black, Gordon S. 1972. "A Theory of Political Ambition: Career Choices and the Role of Structural Incentives." *American Political Science Review* 66:144–59.

Bledsoe, Timothy, and Mary Herring. 1990. "Victims of Circumstances: Women in Pursuit of Political Office." *American Political Science Review* 84:213–23.

Bobo, Lawrence, and Franklin D. Gilliam, Jr. 1990. "Race, Sociopolitical Participation, and Black Empowerment." *American Political Science Review* 84:377–94.

Bogue, Allan G., Jerome M. Clubb, Carroll R. McKibbin, and Santa A. Traugott. 1976. "Members of the House of Representatives and the Process of Modernization: 1789–1960." *Journal of American History* 63:275–302.

Bond, Jon R., Cary Covington, and Richard Fleisher. 1985. "Explaining Challenger Quality in Congressional Elections." *Journal of Politics* 47:510–29.

Born, Richard. 1979. "Generational Replacement and the Growth of Incumbent Reelection Margins in the U.S. House." *American Political Science Review* 73:811–17.

———. 1985. "Partisan Intentions and Election Day Realities in the Congressional Redistricting Process." *American Political Science Review* 79:305–19.

———. 1986. "Strategic Politicians and Unresponsive Voters." *American Political Science Review* 80:599–612.

———. 1990. "Surge and Decline, Negative Voting, and the Midterm Loss Phenomenon: A Simultaneous Choice Analysis." *American Journal of Political Science* 34:615–45.

Bositis, David A. 1991. "Political Parties, Black Elites and Recruitment." Paper presented at the annual meeting of the Midwest Political Science Association, Chicago, April 18–20.

Brace, Paul. 1984. "Progressive Ambition in the House: A Probabilistic Approach." *Journal of Politics* 46:556–71.

Brady, David W. 1973. *Congressional Voting in a Partisan Era.* Lawrence: University of Kansas Press.

———. 1988. *Critical Elections and Congressional Policy Making.* Stanford, Calif.: Stanford University Press.

Brady, David, and Bernard Grofman, 1991. "Sectional Differences in Partisan Bias and Electoral Responsiveness in U.S. House Elections, 1850–1980." *American Journal of Political Science* 21:247–56.

Browning, Rufus P. 1968. "The Interaction of Personality and Political System in Decisions to Run for Office: Some Data and a Simulation Technique." *Journal of Social Issues* 24:93–109.

Browning, Rufus P., and Herbert Jacob. 1964. "Power Motivation and the Political Personality." *Public Opinion Quarterly* 28:75–90.

Bryce, James. [1916] 1961. *Reflections on American Institutions, Selections from The American Commonwealth.* Reprint. New York: Fawcett Publications, Inc.

Bullock, Charles S., III. 1972. "House Careerists: Changing Patterns of Longevity and Attrition." *American Political Science Review* 66:1295–1305.

———. 1988. "Regional Realignment from an Officeholding Perspective." *Journal of Politics* 50:553–74.

Bullock, Charles S., III, and Bruce A. Campbell. 1984. "Racist or Racial Voting in the 1981 Atlanta Municipal Elections." *Urban Affairs Quarterly* 20:149–64.

Bullock, Charles S., III, and Patricia Heys." 1972. "Recruitment of Women for Congress: A Research Note." *Western Political Quarterly* 25:416–23.

Bullock, Charles S., III, and Susan MacManus. 1991. "Municipal Electoral Structure and the Election of Councilwomen." *Journal of Politics* 53:75–89.

Burnham, Walter Dean. 1970. *Critical Elections and the Mainsprings of American Politics.* New York: W. W. Norton and Company.

———. 1982. *The Current Crisis in American Politics.* New York: Oxford University Press.

Burrell, Barbara. 1985. "Women's and Men's Campaigns for the U.S. House of Representatives, 1972–1982: A Finance Gap?" *American Politics Quarterly* 13:251–72.

———. 1991. "Women's Candidacies and the Role of Gender in Open Seat Primaries for the U.S. House of Representatives, 1968–1990." Paper presented at the annual meeting of the Midwest Political Science Association, Chicago, April 17–19.

———. 1992. "Party Politics and Gender in the United States." Paper presented at the annual meeting of the American Political Science Association, Chicago, September 3–6.

Butler, David, and Bruce Cain. 1992. *Congressional Redistricting: Comparative and Theoretical Perspectives.* New York: Macmillan Publishing Company.

Cain, Bruce, and Janet C. Campagna. 1987. "Predicting Partisan Congressional Redistricting Plans: The 'Jupiter' Effect." *Legislative Studies Quarterly* 12:265–74.

Cain, Bruce. 1985. "Assessing the Partisan Effects of Redistricting." *American Political Science Review* 79:320–33.

Cain, Bruce, Morris P. Fiorina and John Ferejohn. 1987. *The Personal Vote.* Cambridge, Mass.: Harvard University Press.

Campbell, Angus. 1967. "Surge and Decline: A Study of Electoral Change," In *Elections and the Political Order,* by Angus Campbell, Philip E. Converse, Warren E. Miller, and Donald E. Stokes. 40–62. New York: John Wiley.

Campbell, James E. 1990. "The Presidential Pulse of Congressional Elections: National Evidence from 1868–1988." Paper presented at the Conference, "Back to the Future: The U.S. Congress at the Bicentennial," The Carl Albert Congressional Research and Studies Center, University of Oklahoma, Norman, April 12–14.

———. 1991. "Divided Government, Partisan Bias, and Turnout in Congressional Elections: Do Democrats Sit in the 'Cheap Seats'?" Paper presented at the annual meeting of the American Political Science Association, Washington, D.C., September.

Campbell, James E., John R. Alford, and Keith Henry. 1984. "Television Markets and Congressional Elections." *Legislative Studies Quarterly* 9:665–78.

Canon, David T. 1989a. "Contesting Primaries in Congressional Elections." Presented to the annual meeting of the Midwest Political Science Association, Chicago, April 13–15.

———. 1989b. "Political Amateurism in the United States Congress," In *Congress Reconsidered*, 4th ed., ed. Lawrence C. Dodd and Bruce I. Oppenheimer, 65–90. Washington, D.C.: CQ Press.

———. 1990a. *Actors, Athletes, and Astronauts: Political Amateurs in the United States Congress.* Chicago: University of Chicago Press.

———. 1990b. "Political Ambition, Political Opportunity, and the Emergence of the Republican Party in the South, 1964–1988." Paper presented at the Conference, "Back to the Future": The U.S. Congress in the Twenty-first Century, The Carl Albert Center, University of Oklahoma, Norman, April 11–13.

———. 1992. "The Emergence of the Republican Party in the South, 1964–1988." In *The Atomistic Congress: An Interpretation of Congressional Change*, ed. Allen D. Hertzke and Ronald M. Peters, Jr., 73–105. Armonk, N.Y.: M. E. Sharpe.

———. Forthcoming. "The Social Bases of Legislative Recruitment." In *Encyclopedia of the American Legislative System,* ed. Joel Silbey. New York: Charles Scribner's Sons.

Canon, David T., Matthew Schousen, and Patrick Sellers. 1992. "A Formula for Uncertainty: Creating a Black Majority District in North Carolina." Paper presented at the annual meeting of the Midwestern Political Science Association, Chicago, April 9–11.

Canon, David T., and David J. Sousa. 1992. "Party System Change and Political Career Structures in the U.S. Congress." *Legislative Studies Quarterly* 17:347–63.

Carmines, Edward G., and James A. Stimson. 1984. "The Dynamics of Issue Evolution: The United States." In *Electoral Change in Advanced Industrial Democracies: Realignment or Dealignment?* ed. Russell J. Dalton, et al., 134–58. Princeton: Princeton University Press.

———. 1989. *Issue Evolution: Race and the Transformation of American Politics.* Princeton, N.J.: Princeton University Press.

Carroll, Susan J. 1985. *Women as Candidates in American Politics.* Bloomington: Indiana University Press.

———. 1989a. "The Career Paths of Elected Women Politicians: A Review of the Literature and Research Agenda." Paper presented at the Conference on Elective Politicians, Institute of Politics, John F. Kennedy School of Government, Cambridge, Mass., December 7–8.

———. 1989b. "The Personal is Political: The Intersection of Private Lives and Public Roles among Women and Men in Elective Office." *Women and Politics* 9:51–67.

Cassie, William E., Joel A. Thompson, and Malcolm E. Jewell. 1992. "The Pattern of PAC Contributions in Legislative Elections: An Eleven State

Analysis." Paper presented at the annual meeting of the American Political Science Association, Chicago, September 3–6.

Center for the American Woman and Politics. 1988. "Fact Sheet: Women in State Legislatures." Eagleton Institute, Rutgers University, New Brunswick, N.J.

Clapp, Charles. 1963. *The Congressman: His Works as He Sees It.* Washington, D.C.: Brookings Institution.

Clubb, Jerome M., William H. Flanigan, Nancy H. Zingale. 1980. *Partisan Realignment: Voters, Parties, and Government in American History.* Beverly Hills, Calif.: Sage Publications.

Collie, Melissa P. 1981. "Incumbency, Electoral Safety, and Turnover in the House of Representatives, 1952–1976." *American Political Science Review* 75:119–31.

———. 1988. "Electoral Patterns and Voting Alignments in the U.S. House of Representatives, 1886–1986." Presented at the American Political Science Association, Washington, D.C., September.

Cook, Timothy E. 1989. *Making Laws and Making News: Media Strategies in the U.S. House of Representatives.* Washington, D.C.: Brookings Institution.

Cooper, Joseph, and David W. Brady. 1981. "Toward a Diachronic Analysis of Congress." *American Political Science Review* 75:988–1006.

Cooper, Joseph, and William West. 1981. "The Congressional Career in the 1970s," In *Congress Reconsidered,* 2d ed., ed. Lawrence C. Dodd and Bruce I. Oppenheimer. Washington, D.C.: CQ Press.

Copeland, Gary W. 1989. "Choosing to Run: Why House Members Seek Election to the Senate." *Legislative Studies Quarterly* 14:549–65.

Costantini, Edmond. 1990. "Political Women and Political Ambition: Closing the Gender Gap." *American Journal of Political Science* 34:741–70.

Cotter, Cornelius P., James L. Gibson, John F. Bibby, and Robert J. Huckshorn. 1984. *Party Organizations in American Politics.* New York: Praeger.

Cover, Albert D. 1977. "One Good Term Deserves Another: The Advantage of Incumbency in Congressional Elections." *American Journal of Political Science* 21:523–41.

Cover, Albert D., and Bruce S. Brumberg. 1982. "Baby Books and Ballots: The Impact of Congressional Mail on Constituent Opinion." *American Political Science Review* 76:347–59.

Cox, Gary W., and Samuel Kernell, eds. 1991. The Politics of Divided Government. Boulder, Colo.: Westview Press.

Crotty, William. 1984. *American Parties in Decline,* 2d. ed. Boston: Little, Brown.

Czudnowski, Moshe M. 1975. "Political Recruitment." In *Handbook of Political Science,* vol. 2., ed. Fred I. Greenstein and Nelson W. Polsby. Reading, Mass.: Addison-Wesley Publishing Co.

———. 1982. "Introduction: A Statement of the Issues." In *Does Who Governs Matter? Elite Circulation in Contemporary Societies,* ed. Moshe M. Czudnowski. DeKalb: Northern Illinois University Press.

Dahl, Robert A. 1956. *A Preface to Democratic Theory.* Chicago: University of Chicago Press.

Darcy, Robert, and Charles D. Hadley. 1988. "Black Women in Politics: The Puzzle of Success." *Social Science Quarterly* 69:629–45.

Darcy, Robert, and Sarah Slavin Schramm. 1977. "When Women Run against Men." *Public Opinion Quarterly* 41:1–12.

Darcy, Robert, and Susan Welch, and Janet Clark. 1987. *Women, Elections, and Representation.* New York: Longman Inc.

Davidson, Roger H. 1969. *The Role of the Congressman.* New York: Pegasus.

———. 1989. "The Impact of Agenda on the Post-Reform Congress." Paper presented at the annual meeting of the American Political Science Association, Atlanta, September.

———. 1992. "The Emergence of the Post-Reform Congress," In *The Post-Reform Congress,* ed. Roger Davidson, 3–24. New York: St. Martin's Press.

Deber, Raisa B. 1982. "'The Fault, Dear Brutus': Women as Congressional Candidates in Pennsylvania." *Journal of Politics* 44:463–79.

Deering, Christopher S., and Steven S. Smith. 1985. "Subcommittees in Congress." In *Congress Reconsidered,* 3d ed., ed. Lawrence C. Dodd and Bruce I. Oppenheimer, 189–210. Washington, D. C.: CQ Press.

DiRenzo, Gordon J. 1967a. *Personality, Power and Politics: A Social Psychological Analysis of the Italian Deputy and His Parliamentary System.* Notre Dame, Ind.: University of Notre Dame Press.

———. 1967b. "Professional Politicians and Personality Structures." *American Journal of Sociology* 73:217–25.

Dodd, Lawrence C. 1985. "Congress and the Quest for Power." In *Studies of Congress,* ed. Glenn R. Parker. Washington, D.C.: CQ Press.

———. 1986. "The Cycles of Legislative Change: Building a Dynamic Theory," In *Political Science: The Science of Politics,* ed. Herbert F. Weisberg, 82–104. New York: Agathon Press.

Dodd, Lawrence C., and Bruce I. Oppenheimer. 1989a. "Consolidating Power in the House: The Rise of a New Oligarchy." In *Congress Reconsidered,* 4th ed., ed. Lawrence C. Dodd and Bruce I. Oppenheimer, 39–64. Washington, D.C.: CQ Press, Inc.

———, eds. 1977. *Congress Reconsidered.* New York: Praeger.

———. 1981. *Congress Reconsidered,* 2d ed. Washington, D.C.: CQ Press.

———. 1985. *Congress Reconsidered,* 3d ed. Washington, D.C.: CQ Press.

———. 1989b. *Congress Reconsidered,* 4th ed. Washington, D.C.: CQ Press.

Dodd, Lawrence C., and Richard Schott. 1979. *Congress and the Administrative State.* New York: John Wiley and Sons.

Ehrenhalt, Alan. 1991. *The United States of Ambition: Politicians, Power and the Pursuit of Office.* New York: Random House.

Eismeier, Theodore, and Philip H. Pollock, III. 1988. "The Political Geography of Political Action Committees: National Cash and the Local Connection in Congressional Elections." Presented at the annual meeting of the American Political Science Association, Washington, D.C.

Eldersveld, Samuel J. 1989. *Political Elites in Modern Societies.* Ann Arbor: University of Michigan Press.

Epstein, Leon D. 1986. *Political Parties in the American Mold.* Madison: University of Wisconsin Press.

Erikson, Robert S. 1971. "The Advantage of Incumbency in Congressional Elections." *Polity* 3:395–405.

———. 1972. "Malapportionment, Gerrymandering, and Party Fortunes in Congressional Elections." *American Political Science Review* 66:1234–55.

————. 1978. "Constituency Opinion and Congressional Behavior: A Reexamination of the Miller-Stokes Representation Study." *American Journal of Political Science* 22:511–35.

————. 1990a. "Economic Conditions and the Congressional Vote: A Review of the Macrolevel Evidence." *American Journal of Political Science* 34:373–99.

————. 1990b. "Roll Calls, Reputations and Representation in the U.S. Senate." *Legislative Studies Quarterly* 15:623–42.

Eubank, Robert B. 1985. "Incumbent Effects on Individual-Level Voting Behavior in Congressional Elections: A Decade of Exaggeration." *Journal of Politics* 47:958–67.

Eubank, Robert B., and David John Gow. 1983. "The Pro-Incumbent Bias in the 1978 and 1980 National Election Studies." *American Journal of Political Science* 27:122–39.

Eulau, Heinz. 1976. "Elite Analysis and Democratic Theory: The Contribution of Harold Lasswell." In *Elite Recruitment in Democratic Politics: Comparative Studies Across Nations,* ed. Heinz Eulau and Moshe M. Czudnowski, 7–28. New York: Sage Publications, Inc.

Eulau, Heinz, and Paul D. Karps. 1977. "The Puzzle of Representation: Specifying Components of Responsiveness." *Legislative Studies Quarterly* 2:233–54.

Eulau, Heinz, and John D. Sprague. 1964. *Lawyers in Politics: A Study in Professional Convergence.* Indianapolis: Bobbs-Merrill.

The Federalist. Ed. James Madison, Alexander Hamilton, and John Jay. New York: Modern Library.

Fenno, Richard F., Jr. 1973. *Congressmen in Committees.* Boston: Little, Brown.

————. 1978. *Home Style: House Members in Their Districts.* Boston: Little, Brown.

————. 1986. "Observation, Context, and Sequence in the Study of Politics." *American Political Science Review* 80:3–15.

Ferejohn, John A. 1977. "On the Decline in Competition in Congressional Elections." *American Political Science Review* 71:166–76.

Fiorina, Morris P. 1977. *Congress: Keystone of the Washington Establishment.* New Haven, Conn.: Yale University Press.

————. 1981a. *Retrospective Voting in American National Elections.* New Haven, Conn.: Yale University Press.

————. 1981b. "Some Problems in Studying the Effects of Resource Allocation in Congressional Elections." *American Political Science Review* 75:543–67.

————. 1984. "The Presidency and the Contemporary Electoral System," In *The Presidency and the Political System,* ed. Michael Nelson. Washington, D.C.: CQ Press.

————. 1991. *Divided Government.* New York: Macmillan Publishing Company.

Fiorina, Morris P., and Roger G. Noll. 1979. "Majority Rule Models and Legislative Elections." *Journal of Politics* 42:1081–1104.

Fiorina, Morris P., David W. Rohde, and Peter Wissel. 1975. "Historical Change in House Turnover." In *Congress in Change,* ed. Norman J. Ornstein, 24–57. New York: Praeger.

Fishel, Jeff. 1973. *Party and Opposition.* New York: David McKay, Inc.

Fleisher, Richard, and Jon R. Bond. 1992. "Strategic Politicians and Competition for Open House Seats, 1976–1988." Paper presented at the annual meeting of the Midwest Political Science Association, Chicago, April 9–11.

Fowler, Linda L. 1979. "The Electoral Lottery: Decisions to Run for Congress." *Public Choice* 34:399–418.

———. 1980. "Candidate Perceptions of Electoral Coalitions." *American Politics Quarterly* 8:483–94.

———. 1989. "Local Influences on Congressional Recruitment." Presented to the annual meeting of the Midwest Political Science Association, Chicago, April 13–15.

———. 1991. "The Partisan Context of Congressional Recruitment," In *Political Parties and Elections in the United States: An Encyclopedia,* ed. L. Sandy Maisel. New York: Garland Publishing.

Fowler, Linda L., Ruth S. Jones, L. Sandy Maisel, and Walter J. Stone. 1988. "Collaborative Research on Congressional Candidate Emergence. Manuscript.

Fowler, Linda L., and L. Sandy Maisel. 1991. "The Changing Supply of Competitive Candidates in House Election, 1982–1988." Revised version of a paper presented at the 1989 annual meeting of the American Political Science Association, Atlanta, August 31–September 3.

Fowler, Linda L., and Robert D. McClure. 1989. *Political Ambition: Who Decides to Run for Congress.* New Haven, Conn.: Yale University Press.

Fowler, Linda L., Mark Rupprecht, and Nina Tamrowski. 1987. "A Few Good Women: Gender Differences in Fundraising for Open Seat Primaries." Paper presented at the Southern Political Science Association, Charlotte, N.C., November.

Francis, Wayne L. 1991. "Testing a Theory of Legislative Goal Seeking and Progressive Ambition." Manuscript. University of Florida, Gainesville.

Franklin, Charles. 1991a. "Candidate Strategy and Voter Response in the 1990 Senate Elections." Paper presented at the annual meeting of the American Political Science Association, Washington, D.C., September.

———. 1991b. "Eschewing Obfuscation? Campaigns and the Perception of U.S. Senate Incumbents." *American Political Science Review* 85:1193–214.

Freeman, Jo. 1986. "The Political Culture of the Democratic and Republican Parties." *Political Science Quarterly* 101:327–56.

Frendreis, John P., James L. Gibson, and Laura L. Vertz. 1990. "The Electoral Relevance of Local Party Organizations." *American Political Science Review* 84:225–36.

Frendreis, John P. and L. Marvin Overby. 1992. "Reversal of Fortune: The Rise and Fall of the Southern Republican Senate Class of 1980." Paper presented at the annual meeting of the Midwestern Political Science Association, Chicago, April 9–11.

George, Alexander L., and Juliette George. 1956. *Woodrow Wilson and Colonel House: A Personality Study.* New York: S. Day Co.

Gertzog, Irwin W. 1979. "Changing Patterns of Female Recruitment to the U.S. House of Representatives." *Legislative Studies Quarterly* 4:429–45.

———. 1984. *Congressional Women: Their Recruitment, Treatment and Behavior.* New York: Praeger.

Gibson, James L., Cornelius P. Cotter, John F. Bibby, and Robert J. Huckshorn.

1983. "Assessing Party Organizational Strength." *American Journal of Political Science* 27:193–222.

――――. 1985. "Whither the Local Parties?: A Cross-Sectional and Longitudinal Analysis of the Strength of Party Organizations." *American Journal of Political Science* 29:139–60.

Gilmour, John, and Paul Rothstein. 1991. "Early Republican Retirement: A Cause of Democratic Dominance in the House of Representatives." Paper presented at the annual meeting of the American Political Science Association, Washington, D.C., September.

Glad, Betty. 1986. *Key Pittman: The Tragedy of a Senate Insider.* New York: Columbia University Press.

Goldenberg, Edie, and Michael Traugott. 1984. *Campaigning for Congress.* Washington, D.C.: CQ Press.

Goldenberg, Edie N., Michael W. Traugott, and Frank R. Baumgartner. 1986. "Preemptive and Reactive Spending in U.S. House Races." *Political Behavior* 8:3–20.

Gopoian, J. David, and Darrell M. West. 1984. "Trading Security for Seats: Strategic Considerations in the Redistricting Process." *Journal of Politics* 46:1080–96.

Gow, David John, and Robert B. Eubank. 1984. "The Pro-Incumbent Bias in the 1982 National Election Study." *American Journal of Political Science* 28:224–30.

Green, Donald Philip, and Jonathan S. Krasno. 1988. "Salvation for the Spendthrift Incumbent: Reestimating the Effects of Campaign Spending in House Elections." *American Journal of Political Science* 32:884–907.

――――. 1990. "Rebuttal to Jacobson's 'New Evidence for Old Arguments.'" *American Journal of Political Science* 34:363–72.

Green, Donald, James Robins, and Jonathan Krasno. 1991. "Using Polls to Estimate the Effects of Campaign Spending by U.S. House Incumbents." Paper presented at the annual meeting of the American Political Science Association, Washington, D.C., September.

Greene, Kevin. 1991. "The Best Kept Secret in America: The Congressional Black Caucus and Its Alternative Quality of Life Budget." Unpublished Honors Thesis, Syracuse University.

Greenstein, Fred I. 1975. "Personality and Politics." In *Handbook of Political Science: Micro Explanations,* vol, 2, ed. Nelson Polsby and Fred I. Greenstein, 1–92. Reading, Mass.: Addison Wesley, Inc.

Grenzke, Janet M. 1988. "Comparing Contributions to U.S. House Members from Outside their Districts." *Legislative Studies Quarterly* 13:83–103.

――――. 1989. "PACs and the Congressional Supermarket: The Currency Is Complex." *American Journal of Political Science* 33:1–24.

Grofman, Bernard, Robert Griffin, and Amihai Glazer. 1992. "The Effect of Black Population on Electing Democrats and Liberals to the House of Representatives." *Legislative Studies Quarterly* 17:365–80.

Grofman, Bernard, and Lisa Handley. 1989. "Black Representation: Making Sense of Electoral Geography at Different Levels of Government." *Legislative Studies Quarterly* 14:265–79.

Gronke, Paul. 1992. "Overreporting the Vote in the 1988 Senate Election Study: A Response to Wright." *Legislative Studies Quarterly* 17:113–29.

Guerra, Fernando J. 1989. "The Career Paths of Minority Elected Politicians: Resemblances and Differences." Paper presented at the Conference on Elective Politicians, Institute of Politics, John F. Kennedy School of Government, Cambridge, Mass., December 7.

Haeberle, Steven H. 1985. "Closed Primaries and Party Support in Congress." *American Politics Quarterly* 13:341–52.

Hermann, Margaret G. 1986. "Prologue: What is Political Psychology?" In *Political Psychology,* ed. Margaret S. Hermann, 1–10. San Francisco: Jossey-Bass Publishers.

Hero, Rodney E. 1992. "Two-Tiered Pluralism: An Interpretation of the Place of Latinos and Other Minority Groups in U.S. Politics." Paper presented at the conference on the Dynamics of American Politics: Approaches and Interpretations, University of Colorado, Boulder, February 20–22.

Herrick, Rebekah, and Michael K. Moore. 1991. "Ambition's Influence on Behavior: An Analysis of Congressional Careers." Paper presented at the annual meeting of the Midwest Political Science Association, Chicago, April 18–20.

Herrnson, Paul S. 1986. "Do Parties Make a Difference?: The Role of Party Organizations in Congressional Elections." *Journal of Politics* 48:589–615.

———. 1988. *Party Campaigning in the 1980s.* Cambridge, Mass.: Harvard University Press.

———. 1989. "Campaign Professionalism and Fundraising in Congressional Elections." Manuscript.

———. 1990. "Reemergent National Party Organizations." *The Parties Respond: Changes in the American Party System,* ed. In L. Sandy Maisel, 41–60. Boulder, Colo.: Westview Press.

———. 1991. "Congressional Staff as Congressional Candidates: Some Preliminary Findings." Paper presented at the annual meeting of the Midwest Political Science Association, Chicago, April 18–20.

Hibbing, John R. 1989. "The Career Paths of Members of Congress." Paper presented at the Conference on Elective Politicians, Institute of Politics, John F. Kennedy School of Government, Harvard University, Cambridge, Mass., December 7–8.

———. 1991a. *Congressional Careers: Contours of Life in the U.S. House of Representatives.* Chapel Hill: University of North Carolina Press.

———. 1991b. "Contours of the Modern Congressional Career." *American Political Science Review* 85:405–28.

———. Forthcoming. "The 1992 House Elections and Congressional Careers. In *Extension of Remarks,* ed. Lawrence C. Dodd, special issue of *Legislative Studies Section Newsletter.*

Hinckley, Barbara. 1980. "House Re-elections and Senate Defeats: The Role of the Challenger." *British Journal of Political Science* 10:441–60.

Hodgson, Richard C., Daniel J. Levinson and Abraham Zaleznik. 1965. *The Executive Role Constellation.* Boston: Harvard University Graduate School of Business Adminstration, Division of Research.

Huckshorn, Robert J. and Robert C. Spencer. 1971. *The Politics of Defeat: Campaigning for Congress.* Amherst: University of Massachusetts Press.

Huitt, Ralph K. 1969. "Congress: The Durable Partner." In *Congress: Two De-*

cades of Analysis, ed. Ralph K. Huitt and Robert L. Peabody. New York: Harper and Row.

Jacobson, Gary C. 1980. *Money in Congressional Elections.* New Haven, Conn.: Yale University Press.

————. 1987a. "The Marginals Never Vanished: Incumbency and Competition in Elections to the U.S. House of Representatives." *American Journal of Political Science* 31:126–41.

————. 1987b. *The Politics of Congressional Elections.* 2d ed. Boston: Little, Brown.

————. 1989. "Strategic Politicians and the Dynamics of U.S. House Elections, 1946–1986." *American Political Science Review* 83:773–93.

————. 1990a. "The Effects of Campaign Spending in House Elections: New Evidence for Old Arguments." *American Journal of Political Science* 34:334–62.

————. 1990b. *The Electoral Origins of Divided Government.* Boulder, Colo.: Westview Press.

————. 1991. "The Persistence of Democratic House Majorities," In *The Politics of Divided Government,* ed. Gary W. Cox and Samuell Kernell, 57–86. Boulder, Colo.: Westview Press.

————. 1992a. "Deficit Politics and the 1990 Elections." Paper presented at the annual meeting of the American Political Science Association, Chicago, September 3–6.

————. 1992b. *The Politics of Congressional Elections.* 3d ed. New York: Harper Collins.

————. 1992c. "When Opportunity Knocks, No One's Home: The Misallocation of Resources in House Campaigns." Paper presented at the Midwest Political Science Association, Chicago, April 9–11.

Jacobson, Gary C., and Samuel Kernell. 1981. *Strategy and Choice in Congressional Elections.* New Haven, Conn.: Yale University Press.

————. 1990. "National Forces in the 1986 U.S. House Elections." *Legislative Studies Quarterly* 15:65–87.

Jacobson, Gary C., and Raymond E. Wolfinger. 1989. "Information and Voting in California Senate Elections." *Legislative Studies Quarterly* 14:509–29.

Jennings, M. Kent. 1990. "Women in Party Politics." In *Women, Politics and Change,* ed. Louise Tilly and Patricia Gurin. New York: Russell Sage Foundation.

Jewell, Malcom E. 1970. "Attitudinal Determinants of Legislative Behavior: The Utility of Role Analysis," In *Legislatures in Developmental Perspective,* ed. Allan Kornberg and Lloyd Musolf. Durham, N.C.: Duke University Press.

Johannes, John R., and John C. McAdams. 1981. "The Congressional Incumbency Effect: Is It Casework, Policy Compatibility, or Something Else?" *American Journal of Political Science* 25:512–42.

Johnson, Loch K. 1977. "Operational Codes and the Prediction of Leadership Behavior: Senator Frank Church at Mid-Career," In *A Psychological Examination of Political Leaders,* ed. Margaret G. Hermann, 82–119. New York: Free Press.

Jones, Charles O. 1981. "New Directions in U.S. Congressional Research: A Review Article." *Legislative Studies Quarterly* 6:455–68.

Kahn, Kim, and Edie Goldenberg. 1991. "Women Candidates in the News: An Examination of Gender Differences in U.S. Senate Campaign Coverage." *Public Opinion Quarterly* 55 (Summer): 180–99.

Kawato, Sadafumi. 1987. "Nationalization and Partisan Realignment in Congressional Elections." *American Political Science Review* 81:1235–50.

Kayden, Xandra, and Eddie Mahe, Jr. 1985. *The Party Goes On: The Persistence of the Two-Party System in the United States.* New York: Basic Books.

Kazee, Thomas A. 1980. "The Decision to Run for the U.S. Congress." *Legislative Studies Quarterly* 5:79–100.

———. 1983. "The Deterrent Effect of Incumbency on Recruiting Challengers in U.S. House Elections." *Legislative Studies Quarterly* 8:469–80.

———, ed. Forthcoming. *Deciding Not to Run: Strategic Ambition and Candidate Emergence.* Manuscript.

Kazee, Thomas A., and Susan Roberts. 1992. "Challenging a 'Safe' Incumbent: Latent Competition in North Carolina's Ninth District." Paper presented at the annual meeting of the Midwestern Political Science Association, Chicago, April 9–11.

Kazee, Thomas A., and Mary C. Thornberry. 1990. "Where's the Party? Congressional Candidate Recruitment and American Party Organizations." *Western Political Quarterly* 43:61–80.

Kearns (Goodwin), Doris. 1976. *Lyndon Johnson and the American Dream.* New York: Harper & Row.

Keith, Bruce E., et al. 1992. *The Myth of the Independent Voter.* Berkeley: University of California Press.

Keller, Suzanne Infeld. 1963. *Beyond the Ruling Class: Strategic Elites in Modern Society.* New York: Random House.

Kenny, Christopher. 1992. "A Dynamic Model of the Effect of Campaign Spending on Congressional Vote Choice." *American Journal of Political Science* 36:923–37.

Kernell, Samuel. 1977. "Toward Understanding 19th Century Congressional Careers: Ambition, Competition and Rotation." *American Journal of Political Science* 11:669–93.

Key, V. O. 1949. *Southern Politics in State and Nation.* New York: Alfred A. Knopf.

———. 1955. "A Theory of Critical Elections." *Journal of Politics* 17:3–18.

———. 1956. *American State Political Parties.* New York: Alfred Knopf.

———. 1958. *Politics, Parties and Pressure Groups.* 4th ed. New York: Thomas Y. Crowell.

———. 1959. "Secular Realignment and the Party System." *Journal of Politics* 21:198–210.

Kiewiet, D. Roderick. 1983. *Microeconomics and Macropolitics: The Electoral Effects of Economic Issues.* Chicago: University of Chicago Press.

King, Gary. 1991. "Constituency Service and Incumbency Advantage." *British Journal of Political Science* 21:119–28.

King, Gary, and Andrew Gelman. 1991. "Systemic Consequences of Incumbency Advantage in U.S. House Elections." *American Journal of Political Science* 35:110–38.

Kingdon, John W. 1968. *Candidates for Office: Beliefs and Strategies.* New York: Random House.

Kramer, Gerald H. 1971. "Short-Term Fluctuations in U.S. Voting Behavior, 1896–1964." *American Political Science Review* 65:131–43.

Krasno, Jonathan S., and Donald Philip Green. 1988. "Preempting Quality Challengers in House Elections." *Journal of Politics* 50:920–36.

Krehbiel, Keith, and John R. Wright. 1983. "The Incumbency Effect in Congressional Elections: A Test of Two Explanations." *American Journal of Political Science* 27:140–57.

Kuklinski, James H., and Darrell M. West. 1981. "Economic Expectations and Voting Behavior in United States House and Senate Elections." *American Political Science Review* 74:436–47.

Kunkel, Joseph A., III. 1988. "Party Endorsement and Incumbency in Minnesota Legislative Nominations." *Legislative Studies Quarterly* 13:211–23.

Kurtz, Karl T. 1992. "Limiting Terms: What's in Store?" *State Legislatures* 18:32–34.

Ladd, Everett Carll. 1991. "Like Waiting for Godot: The Uselessness of 'Realignment' for Understanding Change in Contemporary American Politics." In *The End of Realignment? Interpreting American Electoral Eras,* ed. Byron E. Shafer. Madison: University of Wisconsin Press.

Lascher, Edward L., Jr. 1989. "Do You Have to Be Crazy to Do this Job?: Recruitment, Job Satisfaction, and Turnover Among Local Legislators." Paper presented at the Conference on Elective Politicians, Institute of Politics, John F. Kennedy School of Government, Cambridge, Mass., December.

Lasswell, Harold D. [1930] 1960. *Psychopathology and Politics.* Chicago: University of Chicago Press. Reprinted. New York: Free Press.

———. 1948. *Power and Personality.* New York: Norton.

———. 1951. *Politics: Who Gets What, When, How, in The Writings of Harold D. Lasswell.* New York: Free Press.

Lasswell, Harold D., and Abraham Kaplan. 1950. *Power and Society: A Framework for Political Inquiry.* New Haven, Conn.: Yale University Press.

Leuthold, David A. 1968. *Electioneering in a Democracy: Campaigns for Congress.* New York: Wiley.

Levine, Martin D., and Mark S. Hyde. 1977. "Incumbency and the Theory of Political Ambition: A Rational Choice Model." *Journal of Politics* 39:959–83.

Lewis-Beck, Michael S., and Tom W. Rice. 1986. "Are Senate Election Outcomes Predictable?" *PS: Political Science and Politics* 18:746–54.

Leyden, Kevin M., and Stephen A. Borelli. 1990. "Party Contribution and Party Unity: Can Loyalty Be Bought?" *Western Political Quarterly* 43:343–65.

Lipset, Seymour Martin. 1983. "The Congressional Candidate." *Journal of Contemporary Studies* 6:87–105.

Loomis, Burdett A. 1984. "Congressional Careers and Party Leadership in the Contemporary House of Representatives." *American Journal of Political Science* 28:180–202.

———. 1988. *The New American Politician.* New York: Basic Books.

McClain, Paula, and Albert K. Karnig. 1990. "Black and Hispanic Socioeconomic Political Competition." *American Political Science Review* 84 (June): 535–45.

McClosky, Herbert. 1964. "Consensus and Ideology in American Politics." *American Political Science Review* 54:361–82.

McConaughy, John B. 1950. "Certain Personality Factors of State Legislators in South Carolina." *American Political Science Review* 44:897–903.

Mack, W. R. 1992. "Repeat Challengers: Are They the Best Challengers Around?" Paper presented at the annual meeting of the Midwest Political Science Association, Chicago, April 9–11.

Madison, James. 1987. *Notes of Debates in the Federal Convention of 1787.* Bicentennial ed. New York: W. W. Norton & Co.

Magleby, David B., and Candice J. Nelson. 1990. *The Money Chase.* Washington, D.C.: Brookings Institution.

Maisel, L. Sandy. 1982. *From Obscurity to Oblivion: Running in the Congressional Primary.* Knoxville: University of Tennessee Press.

———. 1987. "Candidates and Non-Candidates in the 1986 Congressional Elections. " Paper presented to the annual meeting of the Midwest Political Science Association, Chicago, April 9–11.

———. 1991. "You Can't Beat Somebody With Nobody: Divided Politics in 1992 and Beyond." Paper presented at the Annual Meeting of the Japanese Political Science Association, Tokyo, October.

Maisel, L. Sandy, and Joseph Cooper. 1981. *Congressional Elections.* Beverly Hills, Calif.: Sage Publications.

Maisel, L. Sandy, Linda L. Fowler, Ruth S. Jones, and Walter J. Stone. 1990. "The Naming of Candidates: Recruitment or Emergence?" In *The Parties Respond: Changes in the American Party System,* ed. L. Sandy Maisel, 137–59. Boulder, Colo.: Westview Press.

Mandel, Ruth B. 1981. *In the Running: The New Woman Candidate.* New Haven, Conn.: Ticknor & Fields.

Mann, Thomas E. 1978. *Unsafe at Any Margin.* Washington, D.C.: American Enterprise Institute.

Mann, Thomas E., and Raymond E. Wolfinger. 1980. "Candidates and Parties in Congressional Elections." *American Political Science Review* 74:617–32

Manski, Charles F., and Daniel McFadden. 1981. *Structural Analysis of Discrete Data with Econometric Applications.* Cambridge, Mass.: MIT Press.

Marra, Robin F., and Charles W. Ostrom, Jr. 1989. "Explaining Seat Change in the U.S. House of Representatives, 1950–1986." *American Journal of Political Science* 33:541–69.

Marvick, Dwaine. 1976. "Continuities in Recruitment Theory and Research: Toward a New Model." In *Elite Recruitment in Democratic Politics: Comparative Studies across Nations,* ed. Heinz Eulau and Moshe M. Czudnowski. New York: Sage Publications.

Matthews, Donald R. 1954. *The Social Background of Political Decision-Makers.* Garden City, N.Y.: Doubleday.

———. 1960. *U.S. Senators and Their World.* Chapel Hill: University of North Carolina Press.

———. 1983. "Legislative Recruitment and Legislative Careers." In *Handbook of Legislative Research,* ed. Gerhard Loewenberg, Samuel C. Patterson, and Malcolm E. Jewell. Cambridge, Mass.: Harvard University Press.

Mayhew, David. R. 1974a. *Congress: The Electoral Connection.* New Haven, Conn.: Yale University Press.

———. 1974b. "Congressional Elections: The Case of the Vanishing Marginals." *Polity.* 6:295–317.

———. 1986. *Placing the Parties in American Politics.* Princeton, N.J.: Princeton University Press.

———. 1991. *Divided We Govern: Party Control, Lawmaking, and Investigations, 1946–1990.* New Haven, Conn.: Yale University Press.

Mezey, Michael L. 1970. "Ambition Theory and the Office of Congressmen." *Journal of Politics* 32:563.

Michels, Roberto. 1962. *Political Parties: A Sociological Study of the Oligarchical Tendencies of Modern Democracy.* New York: Free Press. Published in German in 1911 and in Italian in 1912.

Miller, Arthur H. 1990. "Public Judgments of Senate and House Candidates." *Legislative Studies Quarterly* 15:525–42.

Mongard, Thomas M. 1974. "Personality and Decision-Making: JFK in Four Crisis Decisions." In *Personality and Politics,* ed. Gordon J. DiRenzo, 334–72. Garden City, NY.: Anchor Books.

Moore, Michael K., and John R. Hibbing. 1992. "Is Serving in Congress Fun Again? Voluntary Retirements from the House since the 1970s." *American Journal of Political Science* 36:824–28.

Mosca, Gaetano. 1939. *The Ruling Class.* New York: McGraw-Hill Book Co.

National Women's Political Caucus. 1992. Press Release on Women Candiates for Federal and Statewide Offices as of October 5. Washington, D.C.

Nechemias, Carol. 1987. "Changes in the Election of Women to U.S. State Legislative Seats." *Legislative Studies Quarterly* 12:125–42.

Nelson, Candice. 1978–79. "The Effect of Incumbency on Voting in Congressional Elections." *Political Science Quarterly* 93:665–78.

Niemi, Richard G., and Simon Jackman. 1991. "Bias and Responsiveness in State Legislative Districting." *Legislative Studies Quarterly* 16:183–202.

Niemi, Richard G., Lynda W. Powell, and Patricia L. Bicknell. 1986. "The Effects of Congruity Between Community and District on Salience of U.S. House Candidates." *Legislative Studies Quarterly* 11:187–201.

Niemi, Richard G., and Stephen G. Wright. 1990. "Majority Win Percentages: An Approach to the Votes-Seats Relationship in Light of *Davis* v. *Bandemer.*" In *Toward Fair and Effective Representation: Political Gerrymandering and the Courts,* ed. Bernard Grofman. New York: Agathon.

Norris, Pippa, and Joni Lovenduski. 1992. "'If Only More Candidates Came Forward . . . : Supply-Side Explanations of Political Representation in Britain." Paper presented at the annual meeting of the American Political Science Association, Chicago, September 3–6.

Norris, Pippa, and Robert Darcy. 1992. "The American Candidate Study, 1992." Manuscript.

Oppenheimer, Bruce I., James A. Stimson, and Richard W. Waterman. 1986. "Interpreting U.S. Congressional Elections: The Exposure Thesis." *Legislative Studies Quarterly* 11:227–47.

Ornstein, Norman J. 1975. *Congress in Charge: Evolution and Reform.* New York: Praeger Publishers.

Ornstein, Norman J., Thomas E. Mann, and Michael J. Malbin. 1990. *Vital Statistics on Congress, 1989–1990* (Washington, D.C.: American Enterprise Institute.

———. 1992. *Vital Statistics on Congress 1991–1992.* Washington, D.C.: American Enterprise Institute.

Owens, John R., and Edward C. Olson. 1980. "Economic Fluctuations and Congressional Elections." *American Journal of Political Science* 24:469–93.

Palazzolo, Daniel J. 1992. "From Decentralization to Centralization: Members' Changing Expectations for House Leaders." In *The Postreform Congress,* Roger H. Davidson, 112–28. Washington, D.C.: St. Martin's Press.

Pareto, Vilfredo. 1935. *The Mind and Society.* New York: Harcourt, Brace & Co.

Parker, Frank L. 1991. *Black Votes Count: Political Empowerment in Mississippi after 1965.* Chapel Hill: University of North Carolina Press.

Parker, Glenn R. 1981. "Incumbent Popularity and Electoral Success." In *Congressional Elections,* ed. Joseph Cooper and L. Sandy Maisel, 249–79. Beverly Hills: Sage Publications.

———. 1986. *Homeward Bound: Explaining Changes in Congressional Behavior.* Pittsburgh: University of Pittsburgh Press.

Payne, James L., et al. 1984. *The Motivation of Politicians.* Chicago: Nelson-Hall Publishers.

Petracca, Mark P. 1992. "Rotation in Office: The History of an Idea." In *Limiting Legislative Terms,* ed. Gerald Benjamin and Michael J. Malbin, 19–52. Washington, D. C.: CQ Press.

Petrocik, John R. 1987. "Realignmnet: New Party Coalitions and the Nationalization of the South." *Journal of Politics* 49:347–75.

———. 1991. "Divided Government: Is It All in the Campaigns?" In *The Politics of Divided Government,* ed. Gary W. Cox and Samuel Kernell, 13–38. Boulder, CO.: Westview Press.

Pitkin, Hannah. 1967. The Concept of Representation. Berkeley: University of California Press.

Polinard, Jerry, and Robert Wrunkle. 1991. "The Impact of District Elections on the Mexican-American Community: The Electoral Perspective." *Social Science Quarterly* 72 (September): 608–14.

Polsby, Nelson W. 1968. "The Institutionalization of the U.S. House of Representatives." *American Political Science Review* 62:144–68.

———. 1981. "Coalition and Faction in American Politics: An Institutional View." In *Party Coalitions in the 1980s,* ed. S. M. Lipset, 153–7. San Francisco: Institute for Contemporary Studies.

———. 1990. "Limiting Terms Won't Curb Special Interests, Improve the Legislature, or Enhance Democracy." *Public Affairs Report,* Institute of Governmental Studies, University of California at Berkeley, November, 9.

Polsby, Nelson W., Miriam Gallaher, and Barry Spencer Rundquist. 1969. "The Growth of the Seniority System in the U.S. House of Representatives." *American Political Science Review* 63:787–807.

Poole, Keith T., and L. Harmon Ziegler. 1985. *Women, Public Opinion, and Politics: Changing Political Attitudes of American Women.* New York: Longman, Inc.

Prestage, Jewel L. 1977. "Black Women in State Legislatures: A Profile." In *A Portrait of Marginality,* ed. Marianne Githens and Jewel Prestage, 401–18. New York: McKay.

———. 1980. "Political Behavior of the American Black Woman: An Overview." In *The Black Woman,* ed. La Frances Ridgers-Rose. Beverly Hills: Sage.

Prewitt, Kenneth. 1970. *The Recruitment of Political Leaders: A Study of Citizen Politicians.* Indianapolis: Bobbs-Merrill Co.

———. 1974. "Political Ambition, Volunteerism and Electoral Accountability." In *Public Opinion and Political Attitudes,* ed. Allen Wilcox. New York: John Wiley.

Prewitt, Kenneth, and Heinz Eulau. 1971. "Social Bias in Leadership Selection, Political Recruitment, and Electoral Context." *Journal of Politics* 33 (May): 293–315.

Price, David. 1989. "From Outsider to Insider." In *Congress Reconsidered,* 4th ed., ed. Lawrence C. Dodd and Bruce I. Oppenheimer, 413–32. Washington, D.C.: CQ Press.

Price, H. Douglas. 1971. "The Congressional Career: Then and Now." In *Congressional Behavior,* ed. Nelson A. Polsby, 14–27. New York: Random House.

———. 1975. "Congress and the Evolution of Legislative 'Professionalism.'" In *Congress in Change,* ed. Norman Ornstein, 2–23. New York: Praeger.

Prinz, Timothy S. 1989. "The Career Paths of Elected Politicians: A Review and Prospectus." Paper presented at the Conference on Elective Politicians, Institute of Politics, John F. Kennedy School of Government, Harvard University, December 7–8.

Radcliff, Benjamin. 1988. "Solving a Puzzle: Aggregate Analysis and Economic Voting Revisited." *Journal of Politics* 50:440–45.

Ragsdale, Lyn. 1981. "Incumbent Popularity, Challenger Invisibility, and Congressional Voters." *Legislative Studies Quarterly* 6:201–18.

Ragsdale, Lyn, and Timothy E. Cook. 1987. "Representatives' Actions and Challengers' Reactions: Limits to Candidate Connections in the House." *American Journal of Political Science* 31:45–81.

Reichley, A. James. 1985. "The Rise of National Parties." In *The New Direction in American Politics,* ed. John E. Chubb and Paul E. Peterson, 175–202. Washington, D.C.: Brookings Institution.

Rivers, Douglas, and Morris P. Fiorina. 1989. "Constituency Service, Reputation, and the Incumbency Advantage." In *Home Style and Washington Work,* ed. Morris P. Fiorina and David W. Rohde. Ann Arbor: University of Michigan Press.

Robek, Bruce. 1982. "State Legislator Candidacies for the U.S. House: Prospects for Success." *Legislative Studies Quarterly* 7:507–14.

Robinson, Michael J. 1975. "A Twentieth-Century Medium in a Nineteenth-Century Legislature: The Effects of Television on the American Congress." In *Congress in Change,* ed. Norman J. Ornstein,240–61. New York: Praeger.

Rohde, David W. 1979. "Risk-Bearing and Progressive Ambition: The Case of Members of the United States House of Representatives." *American Journal of Political Science* 23:1–26.

———. 1989a. "Democratic Party Leadership, Agenda Control, and the Resurgence of Partisanship in the House." Paper presented at the annual meeting of the American Political Science Association, Atlanta, September.

————. 1989b. "Something's Happening Here; What it Is Ain't Exactly Clear: Southern Democrats in the House of Representatives." In *Home Style and Washington Work: Studies of Congressional Politics*, ed. Morris P. Fiorina and David Rohde, 137–64. Ann Arbor: University of Michigan Press.

————. 1991. *Parties and Leaders in the Postreform House.* Chicago: University of Chicago Press.

————. 1992. "Electoral Forces, Political Agendas, and Partisanship in the House and Senate." In *The Postreform Congress,* ed. Roger H. Davidson, 27–47. New York: St. Martin's Press.

Sabato, Larry J. 1988. *The Party's Just Begun: Shaping Political Parties for America's Future.* Boston: Little, Brown.

Sapiro, Virginia. 1981–82. "If U.S. Senator Baker Were a Woman: An Experimental Study of Candidate Images." *Political Psychology* 3:61–83.

————. 1982. "Private Costs of Public Commitments or Public Costs of Private Commitments? Family Roles versus Political Ambition." *American Journal of Political Science* 26:265–79.

Schlesinger, Joseph A. 1966. *Ambition and Politics: Political Careers in the United States.* Chicago: Rand McNally and Co.

————. 1985. "The New American Political Party." *American Political Science Review* 79:1152–69.

Schumpeter, Joseph A. 1942. *Capitalism, Socialism and Democracy.* New York: Harper & Brothers.

Segura, Gary M. 1990. "If David Mayhew is Right, Why Do Members of Congress Act as They Do?" Paper presented at the annual meeting of the American Political Science Association, San Francisco, September.

Segura, Gary M., and Stephen P. Nicholson. 1992. "Split-Party United States Senate Delegations: A Riddle Wrapped in an Enigma." Paper presented at the annual meeting of the American Political Science Association, Chicago, September 3–6.

Seligman, Lester G. 1961. "Political Recruitment and Party Structure: A Case Study." *American Political Science Review* 55:77–86.

————. 1971. *Recruiting Political Elites.* New York: General Learning Press.

Seligman, Lester G., Michael King, Chong Lim Kim, and Roland Smith. 1974. *Patterns of Recruitment: A State Chooses Its Lawmakers.* Chicago: Rand McNally.

Serra, George, and Albert D. Cover. 1992. "The Electoral Consequences of Perquisite Use: The Casework Case." *Legislative Studies Quarterly* 17:233–46.

Shafer, Byron E. 1991. "The Notion of an Electoral Order: The Structure of Electoral Politics at the Accession of George Bush." In *The End of Realignment? Interpreting American Electoral Eras,* ed. Byron E. Shafer. Madison: University of Wisconsin Press.

Shils, Edward. 1950–51. "The Legislator and His Environment." *University of Chicago Law Review* 18:571–84.

————. 1982. "The Political Class in the Age of Mass Society: Collectivistic Liberalism and Social Democracy." In *Does Who Governs Matter? Elite Circulation in Contemporary Societies,* ed. Moshe M. Czudnowski, 13–32. Dekalb: Northern Illinois University Press.

Sigelman, Lee, and Susan Welch. 1984. "Race, Gender and Opinion toward Black and Female Presidential Candidates." *Public Opinion Quarterly* 48:467–75.

Silbey, Joel H. 1991. "Beyond Realignment and Realignment Theory: American Political Eras." In *The End of Realignment?: Interpreting American Electoral Eras,* ed. Byron E. Shafer, 3–23. Madison: University of Wisconsin Press.

Simon, Dennis M., Charles W. Ostrom, Jr., and Robin F. Marra. 1991. "The President, Referendum Voting and Subnational Elections in the United States." *American Political Science Review* 85:1127–92.

Sinclair, Barbara. 1983. *Majority Party Leadership in the U.S. House.* Baltimore: Johns Hopkins University Press.

———. 1989. *The Transformation of the U.S. Senate.* Baltimore: Johns Hopkins University Press.

———. 1990a. "Institutional Persistence and Institutional Change: House and Senate from the 1950s through the 1980s." Paper presented at the conference in honor of William H. Riker, University of Rochester, Rochester, N.Y., October 11–13.

———. 1990b. "Strong Party Leadership in a Weak Party Era—The Evolution of Party Leadership in the Modern House." Paper presented at the conference, "Back to the Future: The United States Congress in the Twenty-first Century," Carl Albert Center, University of Oklahoma, Norman, April 11–13.

Smith, Robert C. 1988. "Financing Black Politics: A Study of Congressional Elections." *The Review of Black Political Economy,* 5–30.

Smith, Steven S. 1989. *Call to Order: Floor Politics in the House and Senate.* Washington, D.C.: Brookings Institution.

———. 1992. "Forces of Change in Senate Party Leadership and Organization." In *Congress Reconsidered,* 5th ed., ed. Lawrence O. Dodd and Bruce I. Oppenheimer. Washington, D.C.: CQ Press.

Smith, Steven S., and Christopher J. Deering. 1984. *Committees in Congress.* Washington, D.C.: CQ Press.

Snowiss, Leo M. 1966. "Congressional Recruitment and Representation." *American Political Science Review* 60:627–39.

Sorauf, Frank J. 1963. *Party and Representation: Legislative Politics in Pennsylvania.* New York: Atherton Press.

Squire, Peverill. 1989a. "Challengers in U.S. Senate Elections." *Legislative Studies Quarterly* 14:531–47.

———. 1989b. "Competition and Uncontested Seats in U.S. House Elections." *Legislative Studies Quarterly* 14:281–95.

———. 1991. "Preemptive Fundraising and Challenger Profile in Senate Elections." *Journal of Politics* 53:1150–64.

———. 1992a. "Challenger Quality and Voting Behavior in U.S. Senate Elections." *Legislative Studies Quarterly* 17:247–63.

———. 1992b. "Legislative Professionalism and Membership Diversity in State Legislatures." *Legislative Studies Quarterly* 17:69–79.

Squire, Peverill, and Eric R. A. N. Smith. 1984. "Repeat Challengers in Congressional Elections." American Politics Quarterly 12:51–70.

Squire, Peverill, and John R. Wright. 1990. "Fundraising by Nonincumbent

Candidates for the U.S. House of Representatives." *Legislative Studies Quarterly* 15:89–98.

Stanley, Harold W. 1988. "Southern Partisan Change: Dealignment, Realignment, or Both?" Journal of Politics 50:64–88.

Stewart, Charles, III. 1989. "A Sequential Model of U.S. Senate Elections." *Legislative Studies Quarterly* 14:567–601.

Stewart, Charles, III, and Mark Reynolds. 1990. "Television Markets and U.S. Senate Elections." *Legislative Studies Quarterly* 15:495–523.

Stokes, Donald E., and Warren E. Miller. 1967. "Party Government and the Saliency of Congress." In *Elections and the Political Order,* ed. Angus Campbell, Philip E. Converse, Warren E. Miller, and Donald E. Stokes, 194–211. New York: John Wiley and Sons, Inc.

Studler, Donley, and Susan Welch. 1991. "Does the District Magnitude Matter? Women Candidates in London Local Elections." *Western Political Quarterly* 44 (June): 457–66.

Sullivan, John L., and Robert E. O'Connor. 1972. "Electoral Choice and Popular Control of Public Policy: The Case of the 1966 House Elections." *American Political Science Review* 57:1256–1268.

Sundquist, James L. 1981. *The Decline and Resurgence of Congress.* Washington, D.C.: Brookings Institution.

Swain, Carol M. 1991. "Black Representation of Majority White Districts: The Cases of Alan Wheat, Katie Hall, and Ronald Dellums." Paper presented at the annual meeting of the American Political Science Association, Chicago, August 29–September 1.

———. 1993. *Black Faces, Black Interests: The Representation of African American Interests in Congress.* Cambridge, Mass.: Harvard University Press.

Swenson, Peter. 1982. "The Influence of Recruitment on the Structure of Power in the U.S. House, 1870–1940." *Legislative Studies Quarterly* 7:7–36.

Swift, Elaine K. 1989. *Reconstitutive Change in the United States Congress: The Transformation of the Senate, 1789–1841.* Phd. dissertation, Harvard University.

Swift, Elaine K., and David Brady. 1992. "The Contributions of History to Statist, Organizational, and Rational Choice Theories of American National Political Institutions." Paper presented at the conference on the Dynamics of American Politics: Approaches and Interpretations, University of Colorado, Boulder, February 20–22.

Thomas, Scott J. 1989. "Do Incumbent Campaign Expenditures Matter?" *Journal of Politics* 51:965–76.

Thomas, Sue. 1991. "The Impact of Women on State Legislative Policies." *Journal of Politics* 53 (November): 958–76.

Thompson, Margaret S. 1985. *The Spider Wed: Congress and Lobbying in the Age of Grant.* Ithaca, N.Y.: Cornell University Press.

Tobin, Richard J., and Edward Keynes. 1975. "Institutional Differences in the Recruitment Process: A Four State Study." *American Journal of Political Science* 19:667–81.

Tocqueville, Alexis de. 1945. *Democracy in America,* Vols. 1 and 2. New York: Vintage Books.

Tufte, Edward R. 1973. "The Relationship between Seats and Votes in Two-Party Systems." *American Political Science Review* 67:540–54.

———. 1975. "Determinants of Outcomes of Midterm Congressional Elections." *American Political Science Review* 69:812–26.

Uhlaner, Carole Jean, and Kay Lehman Schlozman. 1986. "Candidate Gender and Congressional Campaign Receipts." *Journal of Politics* 48:30–50.

U.S. Bureau of the Census. 1989. *Population Reports: Voting and Registration in the Election of November 1988.* Washington, D.C.: Government Printing Office, October.

U.S. House of Representatives Congressional Hispanic Caucus. 1993. "Hispanic Members of Congress." Typescript.

Uslaner, Eric M., and M. Margaret Conway. 1985. "The Responsible Congressional Electorate: Watergate, the Economy and Vote Choice in 1974." *American Political Science Review* 79:788–803.

Vertz, Laura L., John P. Frendreis, and James L. Gibson. 1987. "Nationalization of the Electorate in the United States." *American Political Science Review* 81:961–72.

Wahlke, John C., and Heinz Eulau. 1959. *Legislative Behavior: A Reader in Theory and Research.* Glencoe, Ill.: The Free Press.

Wahlke, John C., Heinz Eulau, William Buchanan, and LeRoy C. Ferguson. 1962. *The Legislative System: Explorations in Legislative Behavior.* New York: Wiley.

Waterman, Richard W. 1990. "Comparing Senate and House Electoral Outcomes: The Exposure Thesis." *Legislative Studies Quarterly* 15:99–114.

Wattenberg, Martin P. 1991a. "The Republican Presidential Advantage in the Age of Party Disunity." In *The Politics of Divided Government,* ed. Gary W. Cox and Samuel Kernell, 39–56. Boulder, CO.: Westview Press.

———. 1991b. *The Rise of Candidate-Centered Politics: Presidential Elections of the 1980s.* Cambridge, Mass.: Harvard University Press.

Weber, Max. 1965. "Politics as Vocation." In *The Political Vocation,* ed. Paul Tillet, 15–61. New York: Basic Books.

Welch, Susan. 1985. "Are Women More Liberal than Men in the U.S. Congress?" *Legislative Studies Quarterly* 10:125–34.

Welch, Susan, and John R. Hibbing. 1984. "Hispanic Representation in Congress." *Social Science Quarterly* 65 (June): 328–5.

Welch, Susan, and Donley Studlar. 1990. "Multi-Member Districts and the Representation of Women: Evidence from Britain and the United States." *Journal of Politics* 52:391–412.

Westlye, Mark C. 1983. "Competitiveness of Senate Seats and Voting Behavior in Senate Elections." *American Journal of Political Science* 27:253–83.

———. 1992. *Senate Elections and Campaign Intensity.* Baltimore: Johns Hopkins University Press.

Whitby, Kenny, and Franklin Gilliam, Jr. 1991. "A Longitudinal Analysis of Competing Explanations for the Transformation of Southern Congressional Politics." *Journal of Politics* 53 (May): 504–18.

Wilcox, Clyde. 1987. "The Timing of Strategic Decisions: Candidacy Decisions in 1982 and 1984." *Legislative Studies Quarterly* 12:565–72.

Wilcox, Clyde, and Bob Biersack. 1990. "Research Update: The Timing of

Candidacy Decisions in the U.S. House, 1982–1988." *Legislative Studies Quarterly* 15:115–26.

Wilhite, Allen, and John Theilman. 1986. "Women, Blacks, and PAC Discrimination." *Social Science Quarterly* 67:283–98.

Williams, Eddie N. 1982. "Introductory Essay: Black Women in Politics and Government." In *Contributions of Black Women to America,* vol 2, ed. Marianna W. Davis. Columbia, S.C.: Kenday.

Witmer, T. Richard. 1964. "The Aging of the House." *Political Science Quarterly* 79:526–41.

Wright, Gerald C. 1990. "Misreports of Vote Choice in the 1988 NES Senate Election Study." *Legislative Studies Quarterly* 15:543–63.

———. 1992. "Reported versus Actual Vote: There Is a Difference and It Matters." *Legislative Studies Quarterly* 17:131–42.

Wright, Gerald C., Jr., and Michael B. Berkman. 1986. "Candidates and Policy in United States Senate Elections." *American Political Science Review* 80:567–90.

Wright, John R. 1989. "Contributions, Lobbying and Committee Voting in the U.S. House of Representatives." Manuscript.

Wyckoff, Mikel L., and Ellen M. Dran. 1992. "Voter Decisionmaking in the 1990 Senate Elections: Candidate and Issue Factors in the Simon-Martin Race." Paper presented at the annual meeting of the American Political Science Association, Chicago, September 3–6.

Yiannakis, Diana Evans. 1981. "The Grateful Electorate: Casework and Congressional Elections." *American Journal of Political Science* 25:568–80.

Young, James S. 1966. *The Washington Community.* New York: Columbia University Press.

Ziller, Robert C., William F. Stone, Robert M. Jackson, and Natalie J. Terbovic. 1977. "Self-Other Orientations and Political Behavior." In *A Psychological Examination of Political Leaders,* ed. Margaret G. Hermann and Thomas W. Milburn, 174–204. New York: Free Press.

Index